The Transmission of Knowledge

How do we transmit or distribute knowledge, as distinct from generating or producing it? In this book, John Greco examines the interpersonal relations and social structures that enable and inhibit the sharing of knowledge within and across epistemic communities. Drawing on resources from moral theory, the philosophy of language, action theory, and the cognitive sciences, he considers the role of interpersonal trust in transmitting knowledge, and argues that sharing knowledge involves a kind of shared agency similar to giving a gift or passing a ball. He also explains why transmitting knowledge is easy in some social contexts, such as those involving friendship or caregiving, but impossible in contexts characterized by suspicion and competition rather than by trust and cooperation. His book explores phenomena that have been undertheorized by traditional epistemology, and throws new light on existing problems in social epistemology and the epistemology of testimony.

JOHN GRECO holds the Robert L. McDevitt, K.S.G., K.C.H.S. and Catherine H. McDevitt L.C.H.S Chair in the Department of Philosophy at Georgetown University. His publications include *Putting Skeptics in Their Place: The Nature of Skeptical Arguments and Their Role in Philosophical Inquiry* (Cambridge, 2000) and *Achieving Knowledge: A Virtue-Theoretic Account of Epistemic Normativity* (Cambridge, 2010). He is co-editor (with Christoph Kelp) of *Virtue-Theoretic Epistemology: New Methods and Approaches* (Cambridge, 2020).

T0370888

The Transmission of Knowledge

JOHN GRECO
Georgetown University, Washington, DC

CAMBRIDGE
UNIVERSITY PRESS

University Printing House, Cambridge CB2 8BS, United Kingdom

One Liberty Plaza, 20th Floor, New York, NY 10006, USA

477 Williamstown Road, Port Melbourne, VIC 3207, Australia

314-321, 3rd Floor, Plot 3, Splendor Forum, Jasola District Centre, New Delhi - 110025, India

103 Penang Road, #05-06/07, Visioncrest Commercial, Singapore 238467

Cambridge University Press is part of the University of Cambridge.

It furthers the University's mission by disseminating knowledge in the pursuit of
education, learning and research at the highest international levels of excellence.

www.cambridge.org
Information on this title: www.cambridge.org/9781108460057
DOI: 10.1017/9781108560818

First published 2021
First paperback edition 2022

A catalogue record for this publication is available from the British Library

Library of Congress Cataloging in Publication data
Names: Greco, John, author.
Title: The transmission of knowledge / John Greco, Georgetown University,
Washington DC.
Description: New York : Cambridge University Press, 2020. | Includes
bibliographical references and index.
Identifiers: LCCN 2020019436 (print) | LCCN 2020019437 (ebook) |
ISBN 9781108472623 (hardback) | ISBN 9781108560818 (epub)
Subjects: LCSH: Knowledge, Theory of.
Classification: LCC BD161 .G727 2020 (print) | LCC BD161 (ebook) |
DDC 121–dc23
LC record available at https://lccn.loc.gov/2020019436
LC ebook record available at https://lccn.loc.gov/2020019437

ISBN 978-1-108-47262-3 Hardback
ISBN 978-1-108-46005-7 Paperback

Contents

Preface

I first began thinking about the epistemology of testimony in the context of an objection to virtue epistemology. Jennifer Lackey, and then others, had put forward a persistent objection to that approach, arguing that it could not adequately account for testimonial knowledge. Moreover, Lackey had formulated the objection so as to target my own version of virtue epistemology specifically. In what sense, she asked, was it appropriate to think of testimonial knowledge as true belief attributable to the virtuous cognitive agency of the hearer rather than that of the speaker? Put in different terms, in what sense could testimonial knowledge be considered an achievement of the hearer rather than the speaker? I recognized that this was an important line of objection, so I turned to the newly burgeoning epistemology of testimony literature to get up to speed. Once I encountered that literature, however, I became interested in the range of issues that it raised in their own right.

At the same time, I had the persistent impression that the contemporary literature on testimony was not cutting matters at the joints. On the contrary, it seemed to me that, at least often, the ways in which the literature framed those issues were distorting, and even preventing progress. This would be understandable enough, given that these discussions were in such early stages. Work by Welbourne, Hardwig, Coady, Fricker, Hinchman, Moran, Faulkner, Lackey, and others was truly groundbreaking, articulating issues and defending positions that had been largely neglected, or not even recognized, by traditional epistemology. Nevertheless, I thought that we could do better – that some of the most important issues that these authors had uncovered, or started to uncover, could be better framed and then better addressed.

One such issue concerned whether testimonial knowledge could be reduced to some other kind of knowledge. This issue was stated clearly enough by Coady, but then quickly clouded by others, who wedded any number of inessential theses to both the reductionist and anti-reductionist positions. Another intriguing issue was whether, in some interesting and important sense, testimony has the distinctive function of transmitting knowledge rather than generating it. Welbourne seemed to be on to the question in early formulations, but then, once again, subsequent discussion by others seemed to distort the issue, and even to obscure it from view.

Also important in the early literature on testimony, and overlapping with discussions about reduction and transmission, were questions about the nature of the relationship between the speaker and hearer in a testimonial exchange Focus on this relationship gave rise to a host of further, interesting issues, including the nature and extent of epistemic dependence, the importance of an epistemic division of labor, and the role of trust in testimonial justification and knowledge.

In the background of all of these discussions, and sometimes in the foreground, were questions about the discipline of epistemology itself. Namely, was traditional epistemology adequate to the task of theorizing such issues, or was epistemology as traditionally conceived hopelessly impoverished in this regard. Put differently, was epistemology itself in need of a revolution in order to adequately theorize such phenomena as social epistemic dependence and the epistemic division of labor – issues that were now being recognized as ubiquitous in the sciences and other cognitive domains?

Again, all these issues seemed to me to be clearly important, and theoretically interesting in their own right. This book is the result of my trying to address them. The way that I have done so is to emphasize the big picture rather than to work through my disagreements with other authors in painstaking detail. This is in fact appropriate to the task at hand, for two reasons. First, I am here arguing for a revision of the literature's categories in favor of a new general framework for thinking about testimonial knowledge in general and the transmission of knowledge in particular. That makes close engagement with extant positions difficult, insofar as those positions are framed in terms that I mean to reject. Second, I am here most interested in defending a *general framework* for thinking through the relevant issues, rather than a position that is worked out in fine detail. The reason for this is that I believe (and argue!) that the framework is largely consistent with any number of substantive approaches in social epistemology and in normative epistemology more broadly. My central task, then, is not to refute other authors, but to defend an approach that better articulates the relevant issues and the possibilities for addressing them. To put things another way, I am here largely concerned to help allies rather than to defeat opponents.

Finally, it has not been lost on me that the theoretical issues treated in this book are of practical importance as well. And in fact, their practical importance has been highlighted by our current social and political situation, characterized as it is by anti-scientism, tribalism, a revolt against expertise, and increasing incivility. In many ways, it seems to me, the current situation can be diagnosed as a disintegration of epistemic communities, attended by increased suspicion and decreasing charity toward any perceived outsider. A salient feature is the ways in which those outside one's own intellectual circles – those with whom one disagrees – are increasingly characterized as morally and/or intellectually flawed. Our only explanation of opinions that diverge from our own is that those who hold them must be either immoral, ignorant, or irrational, or perhaps some combination of these.

And it is precisely here, I believe, that social epistemology can be of practical use. In particular, social epistemology looks to describe the various ways in which the quality of a person's epistemic position depends not just on their individual cognitive resources, but on the good health and proper functioning of a broader epistemic community. Relatedly, social epistemology looks to detail the features of a well-functioning epistemic community, and to thereby understand not only how things go well when they do, but also how things can go wrong. In light of this, a successful social epistemology might be in a better position to diagnose the ills of our current social and political situation, and in a way that sees those who we disagree with through a more complex and more charitable lens. It is my hope that this book makes a contribution to this kind of practical project as well, however indirectly.

Acknowledgments

I am indebted to a number of people for help with this book. First and foremost, I want to acknowledge Lizzie Fricker, Sandy Goldberg, Peter Graham, David Henderson, Jennifer Lackey, and Deb Tollefsen for helping me to think through the range of issues treated here. I also owe a special thanks to Haicheng Zhao, who commented on the entire manuscript and helped me to prepare it for publication, and to Hilary Gaskin at Cambridge University Press, who supported the project from early on.

In addition to these, countless others have helped me as well in conversation and/or correspondence, including Jason Baehr, Heather Battaly, Donald Bungum, Vincent Colapietro, Benjamin Elzinga, Georgi Gardiner, Stephen Grimm, Adam Green, Allan Hazlett, Krista Hyde, Sahar Joakim, Jesper Kallestrup, Christopher Kelp, Kareem Khalifa, Jon Kvanvig, Alexandre Meyer Luz, Luis Pinto de Sa, Roger Pouivet, Duncan Pritchard, Jonathan Reibsamen, Joe Salerno, John Schellenberg, Daniel Smith, Ernest Sosa, Eleonore Stump, Katherine Sweet, Alessandra Tanesini, John Turri, Eric Wiland, Tedla Woldeyohannes, Stephen Wright, Stephen Wykstra, and Brett Yardley. I am sure that I have left people out.

I have also been blessed with the opportunity to present material in the book at various colloquia and conferences, including the *Third Annual Chambers Philosophy Conference: The Point and Purpose of Epistemic Evaluation*, at the University of Nebraska, Lincoln; the *Bled Philosophical Conference*; the *American Catholic Philosophical Association*, New Orleans; *Baylor University Philosophy of Religion Conference*; *First International Conference on Analytic Epistemology*, Federal University of Santa Maria, Brazil; *Humble Minds: The Philosophy of Regulative Intellectual Virtues*, Munich School of Philosophy; *Leuven Epistemology Group*, KU Leuven; *Faith and Humility* conference, Washington University, St. Louis; *The Collective Dimension of Science*, Nancy; *Texas Tech University*

Annual Graduate Student Conference; *Social Epistemology of Religious Belief*, Indiana University; *Tennessee Philosophical Association Annual Meeting*, Vanderbilt University; *The Edinburgh Graduate Epistemology Conference*; *Edinburgh University Philosophy Society*; *Epistemology of Groups* conference, Northwestern University; *Philosophical Dimensions of Trust*, University of Innsbruck; 2011 *Rutgers Epistemology Conference*; *11th Annual Episteme Conference*, Phuket; *Epistemic Angst* conference, University of Paris-Sorbonne; *The Epistemology of Atheism* conference, Université de Lorraine/LHSP-Archives Poincaré; *The Right to Believe: Perspectives in Religious Epistemology*, Bydgoszcz; *Epistemology of Religious Beliefs*, Warsaw; *Epistemic Dependence on People and Instruments*, Autonomous University of Madrid; *VI International Workshop in Epistemology (VI I WiE): The Value of Reflection*, Federal University of Bahia; *Society of Christian Philosophers* conference on *Faith and Humility*, Biola University; *Southeastern Epistemology Conference*, Mobile; and lectures and colloquia at Biola University; British Wittgenstein Society, Edinburgh; the Carleton College and St. Olaf College Annual Philosophical Retreat; Catholic Academy of Bavaria; Edinburgh University; Fordham University; Georgetown University; Illinois State University; McMurry University; Munich School of Philosophy; Oxford University; Rice University; University of Pennsylvania; University of Missouri, Saint Louis; University of Saskatchewan; University of St. Thomas, St. Paul; University of Tennessee, Knoxville; University of Vermont. I would like to thank the participants and audiences at all of these.

I would also like to thank the participants of several graduate seminars at Saint Louis University, as well as participants in the *Philosophy and Theology of Intellectual Humility* grant, hosted at Saint Louis University and co-directed by Eleonore Stump and myself. That grant was funded by the John Templeton Foundation and this book benefited in various ways from it. I thank the Templeton Foundation for its support.

Finally, several chapters draw on material from previous publications. I would like to thank the publishers and editors of these for allowing me to use them here. Parts of Chapter 1 draw on material in "What Is Transmission?", *Episteme* 13, 4 (December 2016): 481–498. Chapter 2 revises material from "Testimonial Knowledge and the Flow of Information," in David Henderson and John Greco, eds., *Epistemic Evaluation* (Oxford: Oxford University Press, 2015). Chapters 3 and 5 draw on material from "The Role of Trust in Testimonial Knowledge," in Katherine Dormandy, ed., *Trust in Epistemology* (New York: Routledge, 2019); "Knowledge, Virtue and Achievement," in Heather Battaly, ed., *The Routledge Handbook of Virtue Epistemology* (New York: Routledge, 2019); and "Achievement, Joint Achievement and the Value of Knowledge," *Journal of Dialectics of Nature* 40, 2 (2018): 1–10. Chapter 6 draws on material from both "Common Knowledge," *The International Journal for the Study of Scepticism* 6 (2016): 309–325; and "Hinge Epistemology and the Prospects for a Unified Theory of Knowledge," *Synthese* (2019). Chapter 7 uses material in "Education and the Transmission of Understanding," *Acta Philosophica II*, 27 (2018): 237–249; and "*Episteme*: Knowledge and Understanding," in Kevin Timpe and Craig Boyd, eds., *Virtues and Their Vices* (Oxford: Oxford University Press, 2013). Chapter 9 uses material from "Knowledge of God," W. Abraham and F. Aquino, eds., *Oxford Handbook of the Epistemology of Theology* (Oxford: Oxford University Press, 2017); "Testimony and the Transmission of Religious Knowledge," translated into Russian and published with replies in *Epistemology and Philosophy of Science* 53, 3 (2017): 19–47; "Die Verborgenheit Gottes und die sozialen Dimensionen religiöser Erkenntnis," (Divine Hiddenness and the Social Dimensions of Religious Knowledge) transl. Liselotte Gierstl, *zur debatte* 3 (2016): 29–32; "No-Fault Atheism," in Adam Green and Eleonore Stump, eds., *Hidden Divinity and Religious Belief: New Perspectives* (Cambridge: Cambridge University Press, 2015); "Religious Belief and Evidence from Testimony," in Dariusz Lukasiewics and Roger Pouivet, eds., *The Right to Believe: Perspectives in Religious Epistemology* (Frankfurt: Ontos Verlag, 2012); "Religious Knowledge in the Context of Conflicting Testimony," *Proceedings of the American Catholic Philosophical Association* 82 (2009): 61–76; and "Friendly Theism," James Kraft, ed., in *Religious Tolerance through Epistemic Humility* (Aldershot: Ashgate, 2008). And finally, the Appendix includes material from "The Transmission of Knowledge and Garbage," *Synthese* (2019); and "Transmitting Faith (and Garbage)," *European Journal for Philosophy of Religion* 10, 3 (2018): 85–104.

1 | *Introduction*

Testimony and the Transmission of Knowledge

The purpose of this book is to identify, and then theorize, a distinctive and important phenomenon that has gone largely unrecognized in epistemology. To get a rough idea of the phenomenon I have in mind, we can invoke an intuitive distinction between the *generation* of knowledge and the *transmission* of knowledge. Very roughly, generation concerns coming to know "for oneself," as when one perceives something, or reasons to a conclusion on the basis of good evidence. Transmission, in contrast, concerns coming to know "from someone else," as when one is told by someone else who knows. Another way to locate the phenomenon of interest is to invoke a distinction between the production of knowledge and its distribution. Knowledge generation is about producing knowledge, in the sense of bringing it into existence. Knowledge transmission is about distributing knowledge that already exists.

I said that the phenomenon of knowledge transmission has gone largely unrecognized in epistemology. The lack of recognition comes in two varieties. First, most of the epistemological tradition has been entirely oblivious to the phenomenon. It is not implausible that traditional epistemology – for example, empiricism, rationalism, Kantian constructivism – has been concerned with the generation of knowledge *rather* than the transmission of knowledge. If we think of an economy of knowledge, composed of the production and distribution of epistemic goods, traditional epistemology has left out half the economy.

A second variety of unrecognition characterizes more recent epistemology. Contemporary authors have indeed shown interest in the transmission of knowledge, but their discussions have been groping, and often distorting. One cause of the distortion is that many authors think that *all* testimonial knowledge involves knowledge transmission. Accordingly, they try to give a general epistemology of testimony, rather than an epistemology of knowledge transmission proper. A second cause of the distortion has been the absence of adequate categories for theorizing the transmission of knowledge. To use a different metaphor, contemporary discussions in the epistemology of testimony are framed by categories that fail to cut at the joints.

Later in this first chapter, I work to address both of these distorting influences. In Section 1.1, I locate our target phenomenon in such a way that some but not all testimony is at the service of knowledge transmission, with the result that some but not all testimonial knowledge counts as transmitted knowledge. In Section 1.2, I redraw some familiar categories in the epistemology of testimony so as to better characterize our target and related phenomena. Completing these tasks will allow us to better frame our questions, and to better see the possible answers.

A central thesis of the book is that knowledge transmission is irreducible to knowledge generation, and for that reason requires its own theoretical treatment. More specifically, I will argue that an adequate account of transmission must go beyond the usual theoretical resources of traditional epistemology – i.e., beyond those resources that the tradition uses to theorize knowledge generation. Accordingly, the overarching project of the book is to properly articulate and adequately defend an anti-reductionist theory of knowledge transmission.

1.1 Locating the Phenomenon

The purpose of this first part of the chapter is to locate our target phenomenon – what I have been calling the transmission of knowledge, understood in such a way as to be distinct from knowledge generation. We may begin by considering what some contemporary philosophers have said about knowledge transmission. As I said above, I believe that theorizing about the phenomenon has had a groping quality to it, sometimes to the point of being distorting. Nevertheless, it will be helpful to consider what some philosophers have claimed about the general idea of transmitting knowledge, and why they have thought it to be an interesting phenomenon.

First, it is common to assign knowledge transmission a special role in the economy of knowledge. Whereas perception, introspection, reasoning, and the like serve to generate or produce knowledge, testimony is often thought to serve a different role. This special role motivates a second theme in the contemporary literature: that a necessary condition for transmitting knowledge that p, is that the speaker knows that p. The idea here is that one cannot transmit what one does not have, and so those who occupy the transmission role must have knowledge to transmit.

A third common theme is that knowledge transmission serves to relieve the hearer of the usual burdens associated with non-testimonial knowledge. Thus, testimony is often thought to transmit knowledge, rather than generate it, in a way that hearers need not "do the usual work" involved in coming to know for oneself.[1] A related idea is that transmission allows for epistemic *dependence* of a distinctive and important sort, and a further related idea is that transmission allows for an epistemic division of labor.[2]

A fourth common theme is that some such phenomenon is necessary to account for the extent of our knowledge. That is, we need something like knowledge transmission, and the epistemic dependence and division of labor that it allows, to account for all the knowledge that we think we have. Indeed, one of the strongest motivations for defending knowledge transmission, in the special sense intended, has been to avoid unwelcome skeptical results.[3]

Next, let's consider some paradigmatic examples of our target phenomenon. In all of these cases, assuming that the speaker knows the thing she is telling, the hearer plausibly comes to know by means of being told. This is not to say, necessarily, that the hearer comes to know *merely* by being told. Thus, one can accept that there is a special phenomenon of knowledge transmission without endorsing the idea that transmission requires no epistemic work at all on the part of the hearer. More importantly, it is plausible that the hearer depends on the speaker for her knowledge in some significant and distinctive way. In some important sense, the speaker manages to "pass on" or "hand down" her knowledge to the hearer, and in a way that relieves the

---

[1] As Alejandro Pérez Carballo comments, not all non-testimonial knowledge involves a lot of work. For example, consider easy perceptual knowledge. Accordingly, talk about "the usual burdens" is more felicitous than talk about "the usual work." Similarly, talk about "not doing the same work" is more felicitous than talk about "doing less work." See Alejandro Pérez Carballo, "On Greco on Transmission," *Episteme* 13, 4 (2016): 499–505.

[2] For example, Michael Welbourne, *The Community of Knowledge* (Aberdeen: Aberdeen University Press, 1986). For an extended discussion of the division of epistemic labor, see Sanford Goldberg, "The Division of Epistemic Labor," *Episteme* 8, 1 (2011): 112–125.

[3] For example, see John Hardwig, "Epistemic Dependence," *Journal of Philosophy* 82, 7 (1985): 335–349; and C.A.J. Coady, *Testimony: A Philosophical Study* (Oxford: Oxford University Press, 1992).

hearer of the usual burdens associated with non-testimonial knowledge. Here are some cases that seem to fit that bill:

Case 1. A mother tells her three-year-old son that there is milk in the refrigerator, and he believes her.[4]

Case 2. A second-grade social studies teacher points to the map and tells his students that the United States is in North America. On that basis, his students come to believe that this is the case.

Case 3. An accountant tells her client that the tax laws for the current year have changed, and that as a result some previous deductions are no longer allowed. The client believes her and acts accordingly.

Case 4. A doctor tells her patient that his lab results have come back negative. He believes her and is relieved.

Case 5. A city clerk tells a resident that plastic bottles can be left at the transfer station for recycling. The resident believes her and heads for the transfer station.

Again, in each of these cases it is natural to think that the hearer comes to know by being told, and in a way that "passes on" knowledge from speaker to hearer. Furthermore, it is plausible to think that, by virtue of the testimonial exchange, the hearer is relieved of at least some of the burden involved in coming to know in non-testimonial ways. Importantly, these features are *not* plausibly present in all testimonial exchanges. For example, consider the following cases:

Case 6. A used car salesman tells a customer that the car has had one previous owner, and has never been in an accident. The customer believes him and happily buys the car on that basis.

Case 7. A personnel director interviewing a job applicant asks her if she has relevant experience, and she assures him that she does. The director believes her and hires her on the spot.

Case 8. A police officer asks a suspect whether he was at the scene of the crime, and the suspect tells him he was not. The officer believes him and goes on to question someone else.

[4] Sanford Goldberg, "Testimonial Knowledge in Early Childhood, Revisited," *Philosophy and Phenomenological Research* 76, 1 (2008): 11.

In these latter cases, even if the speaker is telling the truth, and knows what she tells, it is not natural to think that the speaker is in the same sense "passing on" knowledge to the hearer. Likewise, in these cases it is plausible that the hearer *does* incur burdens similar to those involved in non-testimonial knowledge. For example, in Case 6, the buyer had better have some evidence that the salesman is being honest. In Case 8, the police officer had better have some evidence that corroborates what the suspect says. Accordingly, even theorists who embrace the idea of knowledge transmission should not hold that all testimonial exchanges transmit knowledge – not even in all cases where the speaker knows, and not even in all cases where the hearer comes to know via a knowledgeable speaker's testimony. The better idea is that knowledge transmission is a special phenomenon, even within the category of testimonial knowledge.[5]

By way of summary, I have been trying to better locate a distinctive phenomenon of important epistemological interest – a phenomenon I have labeled the *transmission of knowledge*. By way of doing so, I have looked at some things that are commonly said about knowledge transmission, and I have pointed to some seemingly paradigmatic cases. Specifically, knowledge transmission, in the special sense intended, is something *opposed* to knowledge generation, playing a different role in the economy of knowledge, so to speak. Moreover, in cases of knowledge transmission, the hearer depends on the speaker in a way that allows the hearer to know, but without incurring the usual epistemic burdens associated with other ways of coming to know. In this sense, a division of epistemic labor is achieved, allowing the hearer to know more while doing less. On the other hand, we should recognize that not all testimonial exchanges manage to transmit knowledge. Even in cases in which the speaker has knowledge, the hearer sometimes must do considerable epistemic work to gain knowledge from testimony. That is, in some testimonial exchanges, the hearer incurs the same or similar burdens associated with coming to know in non-testimonial cases.

---

[5] In this respect see John Greco, "Recent Work on Testimonial Knowledge," *American Philosophical Quarterly* 49, 1 (2012): 15–28; and Stephan Wright, "In Defence of Transmission," *Episteme* 12, 1 (2015): 13–28. For similar reasons, Faulkner and others distinguish between "knowledge from testimony" and "testimonial knowledge." See Paul Faulkner, *Knowledge on Trust* (Oxford: Oxford University Press, 2011).

The general picture that I will develop and defend in this book is consistent with these characteristic claims about transmission canvassed above, and explanatory of our paradigmatic cases. First and foremost, that picture endorses the anti-reductionist thesis already articulated above: Knowledge generation and knowledge transmission constitute distinct phenomena, and in such a way that the latter is not reducible to the former.

I said that knowledge transmission, understood this way, has been more or less off the radar screen of traditional epistemology, and under-theorized in the contemporary literature. It is true, as we have seen, that contemporary epistemology does talk about "the transmission of knowledge." But in many cases, what is meant by "transmission" is not a distinctive phenomenon of special interest. For example, many contemporary theorists in effect treat knowledge transmission as back-to-back cases of knowledge generation: First, knowledge is generated in one person by some standard source, for example by perception, and then knowledge is generated in a second person by a different source, in this case testimony. For example, evidentialists often make a distinction between perceptual evidence and testimonial evidence, but then treat both perceptual and testimonial knowledge as true belief grounded in the knower's evidence. Likewise, virtue theorists often make a distinction between testimonial and non-testimonial virtues, but then treat all knowledge as true belief produced by virtues seated in the knower. Put differently, both theories treat testimonial and non-testimonial knowledge as species of a common genus, and both think of the genus in terms of knowledge *generation*. In that sense, there is nothing particularly special, and nothing very interesting, about the transmission of knowledge.

It is important to note that this is the attitude even of many so-called "anti-reductionists" about testimonial knowledge. Thus, to count as an anti-reductionist on the contemporary scene, it is enough to hold that testimonial knowledge has a different *source* than other kinds of knowledge (different evidence, different processes, different virtues). But one can hold that and still think that transmission is constituted by back-to-back cases of generation, that transmission can be "reduced" to generation in that sense. The alternative view, and the one that I will be defending here, is that knowledge transmission is a distinctive phenomenon, irreducible to knowledge generation. Again, the analogy to an economy is helpful: production is one thing, distribution another.

Suppose that this general picture is right – that knowledge generation and knowledge transmission are distinct and important phenomena, neither reducible to the other. One consequence of this is that there really are two ways of "coming to know." That is, there is *coming to know for oneself*, via some generating source of knowledge, and there is *coming to know from someone else*, via knowledge transmission. On the one hand, this is highly intuitive – it can seem like no more than a platitude about our familiar epistemic lives. On the other hand, it means that all of traditional epistemology, and almost all of contemporary epistemology, leave out half the story about "coming to know." It would be as if standard economics textbooks talked only about the production of economic goods, leaving out the entire topic of distribution!

My approach, then, will be to embrace the intuitive distinction from the beginning of the chapter. It will be to treat generation and transmission as distinctive phenomena, and to give knowledge transmission its own theoretical treatment. To that end, it will be necessary to first engage in some further stage setting. In Section 1.2, I do some reorganizing according to my own categories. This reorganization is designed to take seriously the distinction between knowledge generation and knowledge transmission, and to bring the importance of transmission into high relief. Section 1.3 looks at the theoretical options for epistemology, once the distinction between transmission and generation is taken seriously. One important issue here regards whether a "unified" epistemology is still possible. That is, even if we agree that knowledge transmission cannot be reduced to knowledge generation, we can still ask whether both can be understood within a common theoretical framework, such as reliabilism or evidentialism. Section 1.4 outlines the remainder of the book.

1.2 Redrawing Categories in the Epistemology of Testimony

The issue that has perhaps most dominated the epistemology of testimony is the debate between so-called reductionists and anti-reductionists. Very roughly, reductionists think that testimonial knowledge can be subsumed under some other species of knowledge – for example, inductive knowledge. The idea here is that testimonial knowledge is just more inductive knowledge, distinguished only by the epistemically superficial fact that the induction concerns testimony and testifiers. For example, in testimonial knowledge we generalize from previous experience regarding what kinds of testifiers are trustworthy, what kinds of conditions promote true testimony, etc. The anti-reductionist idea is that testimonial knowledge cannot be understood as a species of some other kind of knowledge – that testimonial knowledge is its "own kind of thing" and cannot be reduced to something else.

In fact, there are many different "reductionism–anti-reductionism" debates in the testimony literature, as these terms have been defined in a myriad of ways. For example, some philosophers associate anti-reductionism with a view about default justification, or the idea that testimonial beliefs are "innocent until proven guilty." Other philosophers have framed the debate in terms of whether testimonial beliefs are "foundational," in the sense of not based on reasons or evidence. What is worse, many philosophers have written as if these various positions (and more) cluster together, so that if one is a reductionist (or anti-reductionist) in one sense, one must be a reductionist (or anti-reductionist) in the others. On my view, these various ways of framing the issues have led to confusion and impeded progress.[6] Accordingly, I want to impose some categories that I think better cut at the joints of the phenomena in play. In particular, I want to define two kinds of reductionism – what I will call "source reductionism" and "transmission reductionism." In this system, one can be an "anti-reductionist about testimonial knowledge" either by denying source reductionism or by denying transmission reductionism (or by denying both).

1.2.1 Knowledge Generation and Source Reductionism

"Source reductionism" is best understood as a claim about species of knowledge. Specifically, it claims that the genus *Knowledge* has several species – such as *perceptual* knowledge, *inductive* knowledge, and *introspective* knowledge – according to the different ways that knowledge can be generated. It also claims that testimonial knowledge does *not* constitute an additional species alongside these others.[7] Put

---

[6] See my "Recent Work on Testimonial Knowledge" for further discussion on this point.

[7] By "generative source," I mean simply a source for generating knowledge. It should be noted here that my use of the term "generative source" is different from Lackey's. On her terminology, testimony is a "generative source" just in case it is

differently, source reductionism claims that testimonial knowledge can be understood in terms of these other species of knowledge, perhaps as a sub-species of one of the others, or perhaps as involving some combination of the others. Suppose we were to construct a diagram marking the various species of the genus *Knowledge*. According to source reductionism, you don't need a separate species for testimonial knowledge.

Source reductionism, then, divides the genus *Knowledge* into species according to specific ways that knowledge can be generated, and claims that testimonial knowledge can be understood entirely in terms of non-testimonial generative sources. "Source anti-reductionism" denies this by claiming that testimonial knowledge requires its own generative source. Put differently, it claims that testimonial knowledge cannot be understood entirely in terms of non-testimonial generative sources, and this is because testimony is its own kind of generative source (Figure 1.1).

Source reductionism and source anti-reductionism will look somewhat different on different theories of knowledge, according to how they understand the various species in Figure 1.1. For example, evidentialists will think that perceptual knowledge is grounded in perceptual evidence, inductive knowledge is grounded in inductive evidence,

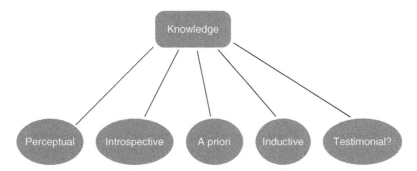

Figure 1.1

possible for a hearer to gain testimonial knowledge from a speaker who does not know. See Jennifer Lackey, "Testimonial Knowledge and Transmission," *Philosophical Quarterly* 49, 197 (1999): 471–490; and *Learning from Words: Testimony as a Source of Knowledge* (Oxford: Oxford University Press, 2008). For further discussion regarding differences in my terminology and Lackey's, see note 9.

a-priori knowledge is grounded in a-priori evidence, etc. The dispute between source reductionists and source anti-reductionists will then be over whether testimonial knowledge requires its own kind of evidence – that is, whether testimonial evidence is reducible to some other species of evidence. Process reliabilists, on the other hand, will think of our species as specifying different kinds of cognitive processes; perceptual knowledge is generated by reliable perceptual processes, inductive knowledge is generated by reliable inductive reasoning processes, etc. The dispute among process reliabilists, then, will be over whether testimonial knowledge requires a distinctive process, irreducible to the processes already accounted for in the other species. Virtue theorists, of course, will frame the dispute in terms of "testimonial virtues." But whatever their more substantive view about knowledge, source reductionists agree that testimony does not constitute an irreducible generative source of knowledge, alongside other generative sources. Source anti-reductionists agree that it does.

1.2.2 *Knowledge Transmission and Transmission Reductionism*

Another set of issues that has dominated the contemporary literature on testimony regards the transmission of knowledge. But to my mind, these discussions tend to skirt around the most interesting and important issues in the neighborhood, and at times even obscure the phenomenon that I have been arguing should be the focus of our attention. One problem here, as with the terminology of "reductionism" and "anti-reductionism," is that the term "transmission" is used in various ways in the literature. At times, it is used to mark our target phenomenon. That is, it is used to mark an important and special function of testimony – to transmit knowledge, *as opposed to* generate knowledge, in a community of knowers. On this use of the term, it is assumed that transmission is something special, and it is decried that the phenomenon has been largely off the radar screen of traditional epistemology.[8] At other times, however, the term is used to mark something that is not necessarily interesting at all – it refers simply to coming to know from

---

[8] For example, see Michael Welbourne, "The Transmission of Knowledge," *Philosophical Quarterly* 29, 114 (1979): 1–9; "The Community of Knowledge," *Philosophical Quarterly* 31, 125 (1981): 302–314; and his *The Community of Knowledge*.

a speaker who knows, without any connotation that this involves anything of particular epistemic interest or importance.[9]

For the purposes of clarity, let's begin with a neutral characterization of knowledge transmission. We can stipulate as follows:

Knowledge that p is transmitted from a speaker S to a hearer H just in case (1) S knows that p, (2) S testifies to H that p, (3) H believes that p on the grounds of S's so testifying, and (4) as a result of conditions 1–3, H comes to know that p.

The characterization is "neutral" in the sense that it leaves condition (4) entirely open; that is, it says nothing about *how* one comes to know as a result of conditions (1)–(3). Notice that on this neutral characterization, no one should deny that transmission is a real phenomenon or that it actually occurs on a daily basis. That is, no one should deny that people often come to know on the basis of testimony given by someone else who already knows. Importantly, both source reductionists and source anti-reductionists can be perfectly happy with this neutral characterization, since it is simply silent on whether testimonial knowledge is reducible to other generative species. For example, the characterization is perfectly consistent with the position that testimonial knowledge is simply a species of inductive knowledge, and that *the way* H comes to know in cases of transmission is via relevant inductive evidence about the speaker and the circumstances of testimony.

If we are working with this neutral characterization of transmission, the question arises whether all testimonial knowledge is transmitted knowledge. More specifically, the question arises whether all testimonial knowledge requires speaker knowledge. Many philosophers have

---

[9] For example, see Jonathan Adler, "Transmitting Knowledge," *Noûs* 30, 1 (1996): 99–111; Jennifer Lackey, "Testimonial Knowledge and Transmission"; Lackey, *Learning from Words: Testimony as a Source of Knowledge*; Peter Graham, "Transferring Knowledge," *Noûs* 34, 1 (2000): 131–152. Likewise, for Lackey, testimony is a "generative source" just in case it is possible for a hearer to gain testimonial knowledge from a speaker who does not know (see note 7). Notice that on Lackey's terminology, one can hold that testimony is a "generative source" (it is possible for a hearer to gain testimonial knowledge from a speaker who does not know) and *also* embrace source reductionism (testimonial knowledge is reducible to some other species of knowledge). All this is to say that the standard terminology (or standard categories) in the epistemology of testimony literature does not serve our purposes here. That is, the standard categories tend to obscure, rather than illuminate, the distinctive phenomenon of knowledge transmission that we are after.

endorsed the natural assumption that all testimonial knowledge does require speaker knowledge, while others have argued that it does not. And indeed, this has been the major issue of concern in discussions about "transmission" in the more recent literature.[10]

Such discussions are interesting, at least to a point.[11] But to my mind, they frame things in a way that obscures what is most interesting and important about the transmission of knowledge. Put differently, they focus on an issue that is not central to the understanding of transmission, and to understanding transmission's central role in an economy of knowledge. For even if not all testimonial knowledge requires speaker knowledge, there might still be a distinctive and epistemologically interesting phenomenon that *does* essentially involve speaker knowledge being transmitted to a hearer. Put differently, it might be that not all testimonial knowledge is "transmitted" knowledge, but that knowledge transmission is nevertheless an important and neglected epistemological phenomenon.

Accordingly, we may ask a second question about transmission that better frames what is at interest in this book: *How does knowledge transmission occur – how is knowledge transmitted from speaker to hearer – when it does occur?* That is, suppose that the neutral characterization above correctly describes conditions for knowledge transmission, although it may not describe conditions for coming to know by testimony in general. If so, then it describes those conditions only in general and uninformative terms. What, more specifically, is required for knowledge transmission to occur?

At this point, we may note a more conservative and a more radical answer to our question. On the conservative view, the transmission of knowledge simply reduces to two instances of generation. First, knowledge is somehow generated in the speaker. Then, on the basis of speaker testimony, knowledge is generated in the hearer. Perhaps the testimonial knowledge generated in the hearer is reducible to some broader species of knowledge, such as inductive knowledge. Or perhaps the

---

[10] For example, see Lackey "Testimonial Knowledge and Transmission" and *Learning from Words*; and Graham "Transferring Knowledge."

[11] For my own part, I was pre-theoretically disposed to think that all testimonial knowledge does require speaker knowledge, but I have since been persuaded by various arguments and examples that it does not. Again, see Lackey "Testimonial Knowledge and Transmission" and *Learning from Words*; and Graham "Transferring Knowledge."

testimonial knowledge generated in the hearer is irreducible to any non-testimonial generative source. Either way, on the conservative view, the transmission of knowledge from speaker to hearer can be reduced to two instances of generation. By denying this conservative view, we get a second kind of anti-reductionism, which we can label "transmission anti-reductionism."

On the more radical view, knowledge transmission is not reducible to two instances of generation, but is rather a distinctive phenomenon. How radical does the more radical view have to be? Some philosophers have argued that an adequate understanding of knowledge transmission requires a fundamental reorientation of epistemology. On this view, traditional epistemology has been off on the wrong track and is now severely impoverished. As a result, it simply lacks the theoretical resources for understanding the full range of epistemic phenomena, including testimonial knowledge and knowledge transmission. This is perhaps the best way to understand at least some "trust" and "assurance" theorists.[12] Other philosophers have disagreed, arguing that both testimonial knowledge and knowledge transmission can be understood using traditional epistemological categories, such as evidence or reliability. Perhaps some tweaking is necessary, but nothing more than that.[13] In the next section I consider some theoretical options in this regard.

So far I have distinguished two kinds of reductionism in the epistemology of testimony. Source reductionism is a claim that can be put in terms of the different species of knowledge generation. It is the claim that testimonial knowledge can be entirely understood in terms of familiar, non-testimonial generative species such as inductive knowledge, perceptual knowledge, introspective knowledge, etc. Transmission reductionism claims that knowledge transmission is reducible to knowledge generation. In particular, knowledge transmission can be understood as back-to-back cases of knowledge generation. Transmission anti-reductionism denies this, claiming that knowledge

---

[12] For example, Edward Hinchman, "Telling as Inviting to Trust," *Philosophy and Phenomenological Research* 70, 3 (2005): 562–587; and Richard Moran, "Getting Told and Being Believed," in Jennifer Lackey and Ernest Sosa, eds., *The Epistemology of Testimony* (Oxford: Oxford University Press, 2006), pp. 272–306. Such "interpersonal views" are discussed by Lackey in chapter 8 of *Learning from Words*.

[13] Reductionists can be understood this way.

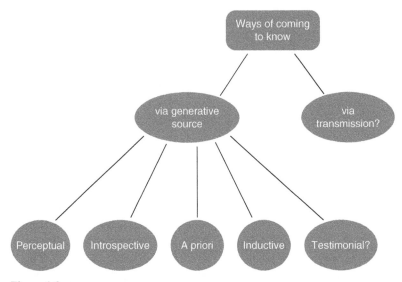

Figure 1.2

transmission is a distinctive phenomenon, irreducible to knowledge generation.

Using these categories, we may now see that there are two ways to be an anti-reductionist about testimonial knowledge (Figure 1.2). Let the most general anti-reductionist thesis be this: *Not all testimonial knowledge can be understood as a species of some other kind of knowledge.* We may now see that there are two ways (actually three) to hold this thesis: One can endorse source anti-reductionism, one can endorse transmission anti-reductionism, or one can endorse both.

Here are some further observations. First, vis-à-vis traditional epistemology, the most conservative option is to be a reductionist on both counts: testimonial knowledge does not require a distinctive source, and neither is there anything special about the transmission of knowledge. Second, it is clear that one can be a source anti-reductionist and a transmission reductionist. That is, one might consistently hold that testimony is an irreducible generative source of knowledge, but still understand transmission in terms of back-to-back generation: First, knowledge is somehow generated in the speaker, then knowledge is generated in the hearer via testimony, considered as an irreducible source. And in fact, this combination of source anti-reductionism and transmission reductionism is plausibly a common position in the field. Thus, a number of philosophers explicitly argue that testimony is an irreducible source of knowledge, but seem happy to think about transmission as consecutive cases of generation. At the very least, this is a consistent position.

Third, one can be a source reductionist and a transmission anti-reductionist. That is, one might endorse the central thesis of this book – that knowledge transmission is irreducible to knowledge generation – but still be a reductionist on the level of generation. This combination is also plausibly a common position in the field. Thus, many philosophers who insist that testimonial knowledge is distinctive seem also to think that testimony is not a generative source of knowledge in our sense; that is, they seem not to think that testimony is a species of generative source, alongside other species.

The take-home point for present purposes is this: Thinking about knowledge generation, there is room for the position that testimony is an irreducible generative source and also room for the position that it is not. But *both* of these positions are consistent with anti-reductionism about transmission. That is, both are consistent with the idea that knowledge transmission is a distinctive phenomenon, irreducible to knowledge generation, and therefore requiring its own theoretical treatment.

1.3 Further Options for the Epistemology of Transmission

Suppose we embrace the idea, as I do in this book, that knowledge transmission is indeed irreducible to knowledge generation. Suppose, in other words, that we embrace transmission anti-reductionism. How radical does such a position have to be? As I noted in the previous section, some philosophers have argued that the implications are quite radical – that taking transmission seriously requires a fundamental reorientation of epistemology. This question is related to a persistent issue in the epistemology of testimony and in social epistemology more generally: To what extent does taking the social dimensions of knowledge seriously require a revolution in epistemology itself?

Here is a different way to formulate that last question: Can knowledge transmission be understood using epistemology's traditional categories? Assuming that knowledge *generation* can be understood with traditional epistemological categories, can we give a unified account of knowledge transmission and knowledge generation? It should be clear that this is not the same question as either of our reductionism questions. Our first question about reduction asked whether testimonial knowledge, considered as a generative species, can be reduced to some non-testimonial species of knowledge. Our second question about reduction asked whether knowledge transmission can be reduced to knowledge generation. Suppose we answer no to both of these questions. We may still ask whether a unified account of knowledge generation and knowledge transmission is possible. That is, we can ask whether both can be understood using the same theoretical resources, within a single theoretical framework.

A clear example of a unified account would be a reliabilist one. Thus, it is open to the reliabilist to distinguish transmission from generation, but analyze both in terms of relevant reliable processes. The idea would be that the processes relevant to knowledge transmission are different from those relevant to knowledge generation, and in such a way that neither can be reduced to the other. Nevertheless, what makes for both successful generation and successful transmission is to be understood in reliabilist terms.

A clear example of a non-unified account would be a certain kind of trust theory. For example, consider a view that understands knowledge generation in traditional evidentialist terms, but holds that knowledge transmission essentially involves a relationship of trust between speaker and hearer. Moreover, on this view, trust does not enter into the explanation of knowledge transmission by way of some relation to evidence. Rather, trust is understood as a moral or quasi-moral relation, and precisely *not* in terms of some relation to evidence. On such a view, knowledge generation and knowledge transmission are to be understood in terms of different theoretical categories, and in that sense the view presents a non-unified account of knowledge in general.

Consider the structure of non-unified accounts. Like other forms of transmission anti-reductionism, such theories claim that there are two ways of coming to know – by generation and by transmission – and that neither is reducible to the other. But non-unified accounts make the further claim that there is no deeper theoretical unity between these two ways. On such a view there would be two ways of "coming to know," but these would not be species of a theoretically interesting genus. Such a "no common genus" view is consistent with more superficial forms of unity. For example, one might define knowledge as "properly held true belief," but then go on to give non-unified accounts of "properly held" for generated knowledge and for transmitted knowledge. For example, one might define knowledge generation in terms of proper evidence and knowledge transmission in terms of proper trust. Such a view would be "unified," but only in a nominal sense. In Chapter 4, I will argue that a unified account is indeed possible. The substantive epistemological theory that I will adopt for this purpose is broadly reliabilist. More specifically, it is "agent reliabilist" and virtue-theoretic.

1.4 Outline of the Remainder

The remainder of the book proceeds as follows. In Chapter 2, I introduce a general framework for approaching the epistemology of testimony and, in particular, the transmission of knowledge. The framework is "general" in that it is compatible with various substantive approaches in the theory of knowledge. For example, it is compatible with process reliabilism, evidentialism, and virtue epistemology.

An important idea developed in Chapter 2 is that of an *epistemic community*, understood as a collection of agents who share some set of information-dependent practical tasks, and who share norms for managing the informational needs associated with those tasks. Such a community, it is argued, will have two related concerns. On the one hand, there will be a concern to *acquire* quality information that is relevant to the community tasks. On the other, there will be a concern to *distribute* that information to those who need it. Furthermore, I will argue, in a well-designed epistemic community the norms governing information acquisition will be different from those governing information distribution. This is because the two functions answer to different dominant concerns. Briefly, the dominant concern of information acquisition is quality control – we want information that is good enough to act on, and that demands high quality along various dimensions. The dominant concern of information distribution, however, is to get information that is already in the system to those who need it.

The central idea, of course, is to understand knowledge generation in terms of information acquisition and to understand knowledge transmission in terms of information distribution. This very general idea already implies transmission anti-reductionism, insofar as the norms or

standards associated with information acquisition (knowledge generation) are different from the norms or standards associated with information distribution (knowledge transmission).

Because the general framework being defended in Chapter 2 is
informed by the metaphor of an economy, I label it the "information
economy" framework – or, when the context warrants, the "knowledge economy" framework. Because the framework models knowledge
generation and knowledge transmission on the phenomena of production and distribution in a material goods economy, the framework
could just as well be labeled the information economy "model" or the
knowledge economy "model." I will use all of these labels to refer to the
general framework presented in Chapter 2 and developed throughout
the book, letting context serve as my guide.

Whatever we call it, the reason for adopting this approach is its
explanatory power. In particular, the framework (a) explains a range
of cases in the testimony literature; (b) provides a principled understanding of the transmission–generation distinction; and (c) provides
a principled explanation of the truth behind various and conflicting
positions in the epistemology of testimony. As we will see below, the
framework also nicely integrates with other plausible positions in
epistemology, the philosophy of language, action theory, social science,
and cognitive science.[14]

Chapter 3 develops the framework presented in Chapter 2 by invoking two additional resources: the concept of a speech act from the
philosophy of language, and the concept of joint agency from action
theory. In the process, the chapter vindicates a prominent anti-
reductionist theme in the epistemology of testimony: that the interpersonal relation of trust plays an essential role in testimonial knowledge.
The central idea is that knowledge transmission essentially involves
a kind of joint agency, characterized by a special sort of cooperation
between speaker and hearer, and that joint agency essentially involves
relations of trust between the cooperating agents. In addition, the
chapter argues that the kind of joint agency involved in knowledge
transmission essentially involves the speech act of "telling." The central
idea is that a successful telling requires that the speaker intends to pass

---

[14] In this regard, Chapter 3 invokes resources from both speech–act theory and
     action theory, Chapter 4 invokes the concept of social norms as understood in
     the social sciences, and Chapter 6 invokes cognitive science's understanding of
     procedural knowledge.

on knowledge to the hearer, and that the hearer understands that this is the speaker's intention. It follows that a successful telling involves the kinds of "shared intention" and "common understanding" that are (a) characteristic of joint agency in general and (b) specific to knowledge transmission in particular.

In Chapter 4, this general framework is developed further by exploring two of its essential elements. In particular, the chapter further explores the nature of social environments and social-cognitive abilities. One central idea here is that social environments are "layered" in a way that creates various kinds of transmission channels. In particular, social environments are shaped in part by (a) interpersonal relationships, (b) social norms, (c) institutional rules, and (d) positive law. These various dimensions constitute a kind of "social space" that practical-cognitive agents must navigate. Such space is also "contoured," and in ways that affect the flow of information. A related idea is that practical-cognitive agents must embody various social-cognitive capacities, including linguistic capacities, mind-reading capacities, and what one might call "social sensibilities"; that is, awareness of one's location in social space.

Chapters 1–4 present and defend a general framework for understanding testimonial knowledge. Chapter 5 shows how that framework can be wedded to a virtue-theoretic epistemology so as to yield a unified account of knowledge generation and knowledge transmission. The chapter begins with the familiar virtue-theoretic idea that knowledge is a kind of success from virtuous or competent agency, as opposed to a mere lucky success. Knowledge is an achievement in that sense. But now we draw a distinction between the competent agency of an individual and the competent joint agency of two individuals acting together. The argument, then, is that knowledge generation is to be understood in terms of success due to the competent agency of the knower. Knowledge transmission is to be understood in terms of success due to the competent joint agency of speaker and hearer acting together.

Chapter 5 does not amount to a full defense of a unified virtue-theoretic position. That would require showing that such an approach is superior to others, including other unified approaches, such as process reliabilist or evidentialist ones. Nevertheless, the chapter illustrates the possibility of a unified virtue-theoretic account and goes some way toward demonstrating its plausibility. In doing so, it also addresses the most persistent and pressing objection to virtue epistemology – that it cannot give an adequate account of testimonial knowledge, and that, more generally, virtue epistemology is overly individualistic.[15] In that respect, the chapter does constitute a partial defense of a virtue-theoretic approach in epistemology.

The information economy framework presented in Chapter 2 exploits the metaphor of an economy, and in particular the idea that such an economy will have different norms and standards for the generation of knowledge and the transmission of knowledge. Chapter 6 explores an interesting way of extending the metaphor. In addition to the categories of generated knowledge and transmitted knowledge, each governed by the norms and standards appropriate to their distinctive function, we might allow that there is a third such category – that of "common knowledge." Common knowledge would be analogous to common or public property – roughly speaking, everyone gets to use it for free. On this extended model, there is knowledge that you produce for yourself, knowledge that someone gives you, and common knowledge that is available for everyone. The chapter considers this idea in relation to Wittgenstein's notion of hinge commitments, and in particular Wittgenstein's observation that some of our most deeply held commitments are neither "a result of investigation" (and so, not from generation) nor something that is typically asserted (and so, not from transmission).

Chapter 6 also looks at the notion of procedural knowledge in cognitive psychology and artificial intelligence, and argues that many of the distinctive features that Wittgenstein attributes to hinge commitments are also characteristic features of procedural knowledge. In particular, procedural knowledge is tacit in both theoretical and

---

[15] For examples of the individualism objection, see Jennifer Lackey, "Why We Don't Deserve Credit for Everything We Know," *Synthese* 158, 3 (2007): 345–361; and "Knowledge and Credit," *Philosophical Studies* 142, 1 (2009): 27–42; Sanford Goldberg, *Anti-Individualism: Mind and Language, Knowledge and Justification* (New York: Cambridge University Press, 2007); *Relying on Others: An Essay in Epistemology* (Oxford: Oxford University Press, 2010); and "The Division of Epistemic Labour," *Episteme* 8, 1 (2011): 112–125; Duncan Pritchard "Knowledge and Understanding," in Adrian Haddock, Alan Millar, and Duncan Pritchard, *The Nature and Value of Knowledge: Three Investigations* (Oxford: Oxford University Press, 2010); and Jesper Kallestrup and Duncan Pritchard, "Robust Virtue Epistemology and Epistemic Anti-Individualism," *Pacific Philosophical Quarterly* 93, 1 (2012): 84–103.

practical reasoning, and in that sense drives perception, inference, and action. This suggests a virtue-theoretic account of common knowledge, in terms of tacit knowledge that is constitutive of cognitive virtue. In this way, it is possible to preserve a unified account of generated knowledge, transmitted knowledge, and common knowledge.

Chapters 2–6 argue that testimony sometimes transmits knowledge. Chapter 7 asks whether testimony can transmit understanding as well. On the one hand, there is a widespread intuition that understanding *cannot* be transmitted by mere testimony. For example, it might seem that understanding involves "seeing something for oneself," and that this is inconsistent with grounding one's belief in testimony. On the other hand, it is plausible that good teaching at least sometimes *does* transmit understanding – for example, in a series of expert lectures – and that this kind of teaching can be understood as a kind of extended testimony. Chapter 7 argues that understanding can indeed be transmitted by the kind of extended testimony that one finds in standard educational settings. First, the chapter defends a neo-Aristotelian account of understanding as systematic knowledge of causes, where "causes" are understood broadly as various kinds of dependence relations. Second, it is argued that, so understood, the transmission of understanding can be understood as a special case of the transmission of knowledge. The information economy framework enters the argument in two ways. First, the framework helps to explain both the mechanisms by which understanding is transmitted by testimony in educational settings, and the intuition that it cannot be. Second, the framework helps to address an objection to the claim that understanding is a kind of knowledge.

Chapter 8 considers the widespread epistemic dependence that characterizes "big science," and uses the information economy framework to dispel the worry that such dependence is inconsistent with the standards for scientific knowledge. This, in turn, leads to a new argument against reductionism in the epistemology of testimony. The new argument goes like this: First, reductionism is shown to be untenable for scientific knowledge. On the contrary, contemporary big science shows in high relief that the norms governing scientific knowledge generation and the norms governing scientific knowledge transmission must be understood differently. Second, if reductionism must be rejected for scientific knowledge, then it should be rejected more generally. This second idea can be vindicated in two ways. First, anti-reductionism about scientific knowledge entails anti-reductionism about knowledge in general, since anti-reductionism is best understood as the thesis that *some* transmitted knowledge cannot be reduced to generated knowledge. Second, if anti-reductionism is required for scientific knowledge, then reductionism for non-scientific knowledge is unmotivated. By far, the most elegant position will be anti-reductionism about knowledge transmission in general.

Chapter 9 argues for a "social turn" in the philosophy of religion, by showing how the information economy framework can be fruitfully applied to several perennial issues in religious epistemology, including the problem of religious disagreement, Hume's critique of testimonial evidence for miracles, and the problem of divine hiddenness. More generally, the chapter argues, contemporary epistemology of religion assumes an overly individualistic account of knowledge and justification, including reductionist accounts of testimonial knowledge and evidence. By adopting recent advances in the epistemology of testimony and in social epistemology more generally, a social religious epistemology promises to enrich and expand the field.

Finally, the Appendix introduces a problem for any non-skeptical epistemology of testimony. The problem, briefly, is that knowledge seems to be transmitted right alongside garbage. That is, the same communication channels seem to transmit both knowledge and what is clearly not knowledge, such as superstition, prejudice, spurious explanation, and just plain error. For example, consider a culture that accepts a spirit theory of disease. Presumably, the medical professionals in such a culture will have plenty of medical knowledge grounded in good inductive evidence (e.g., knowledge about how certain illnesses progress, knowledge about which symptoms are contagious, etc.), and presumably this knowledge can be transmitted to their patients. But in such a culture, that knowledge will be transmitted right alongside garbage about spirits. In fact, a doctor might communicate, in the very same sentence, that a particular symptom is contagious *and* that a particular spirit causes it by jumping from body to body. But how can this be? How is it that knowledge can be transmitted right alongside garbage? Call this the "Garbage Problem" for the epistemology of testimony.

After describing the problem and arguing for its importance, it is ultimately suggested that the Garbage Problem should be understood as a kind of generality problem. Accordingly, the key to solving the problem is to describe transmission channels in terms of parameters at the right level of generality. This suggestion would be made good by a principled explanation of how to draw the parameters, and one that gives plausible verdicts regarding when knowledge is transmitted and when it is not. The Appendix ends by doing just that, in part by drawing on resources from previous chapters.

Here, then, is the general picture that will be developed and defended in the book: Knowledge generation and knowledge transmission constitute distinct phenomena, each irreducible to the other, and each necessary for a well-functioning epistemic community. Put differently, each is necessary for a well-functioning economy of knowledge. But although these distinct phenomena are irreducible to each other, they both can be understood within a unified theoretical framework.

In this respect, the overall argument of the book involves three distinct parts. The first, comprising Chapters 1–4, articulates and begins to defend a general framework for understanding the generation–transmission distinction, and by means of that, the transmission of knowledge. At this stage of the argument, we already get an anti-reductionist account of testimonial knowledge. More specifically, the framework itself entails transmission anti-reductionism. The framework leaves open the question about theoretical unification, however. That is, it leaves open whether we can have a unified account of knowledge generation and knowledge transmission.

The second part of the argument, comprising Chapter 5, shows that a unified approach is possible. In particular, it shows that a unified virtue-theoretic approach is possible. This second part of the argument further supports the information economy framework defended in the first part, insofar as non-unified theories that adopt the framework are theoretically inelegant, and to that extent costly. In other words, it counts in favor of the framework that it can be wedded to a unified epistemology of generation and transmission. This second part of the argument supports a virtue-theoretic approach in epistemology as well, insofar as it answers the most important objection facing that position.

Finally, Chapters 6–9 and the Appendix consider various ways in which our information economy framework can be further extended and applied. Thus, Chapter 6 considers how the framework interacts with Wittgensteinian hinge commitments, Chapter 7 explains how education can transmit understanding as well as knowledge, Chapter 8 explores an original argument for anti-reductionism, via contemporary "big science," and Chapter 9 applies the framework to the epistemology of religion. Finally, the Appendix articulates an important problem for any theory of knowledge transmission, and shows how resources from the theory defended in earlier chapters provide a way forward.

In its most general form, this multi-stage argument is best understood as an argument to the best explanation – it stands or falls on the explanatory power that the position brings, or fails to bring, to a range of issues, questions, and problems. Clearly enough, one might endorse parts of this multi-stage argument while rejecting others. My hope is that, at the very least, readers will here find a plausible way of understanding the generation–transmission distinction in the epistemology of testimony, one that cuts better at the joints than extant theories and formulations, and that weds nicely with other attractive positions in epistemology and beyond.

2 | *The Framework Presented*
Testimonial Knowledge and the Flow of Information

> This doctrine–in effect that knowledge can be transmitted down a chain of authorities–may strike people in opposite ways. To many it may seem so obvious as to be practically banal while to others it may seem quite shocking, since it seems to make knowledge–or at any rate some knowledge–far too easy ... (Welbourne, "The Transmission of Knowledge," 1)

> This idea [of transmitting knowledge] is closely connected with the idea of a *community* of knowledge. It is only to the extent that we think of ourselves as belonging to such a community that we can engage in acts of transmitting and receiving knowledge ... (Welbourne, "The Community of Knowledge," 303; italics original)

This chapter presents a general framework for thinking about testimonial knowledge and knowledge transmission. I call it a "framework" because it is not supposed to be a full-blown epistemology of these phenomena. Rather, it is intended to be compatible with various substantive epistemologies, such as evidentialism, reliabilism, virtue epistemology, etc.

This general framework employs the technical notion of an *epistemic community*, defined as a group of cognitive agents engaged in shared information-dependent tasks, and sharing norms for evaluating information associated with those tasks. One central idea is that such communities can be characterized as having two distinct needs: that of acquiring relevant, quality information, and that of distributing such information to those who need it. A second central idea is that the activities of information acquisition and information distribution should answer to different norms, by virtue of their respective functions. The strategy, then, will be to understand knowledge generation in terms of the norms governing information acquisition, and to understand knowledge transmission in terms of the norms governing information distribution.

Finally, a third idea that is essential to the framework is that testimonial exchanges can serve *either* the acquisition function or the
transmission function. Within an epistemic community, where cognitive agents are cooperating with respect to some information-
dependent task, testimonial exchanges are typically in the service of
information distribution. But not all testimonial exchanges involve
speakers and hearers involved in that sort of cooperation. On the
contrary, sometimes a hearer uses testimony to acquire information
from an uncooperative, or at least non-cooperating, speaker. Since
information acquisition and information distribution are governed by
different epistemic norms, these two kinds of testimonial exchange are
governed by different norms as well. The result is that only some
testimonial exchanges can be understood as transmitting knowledge –
i.e., those that satisfy the norms of information distribution.

Section 2.1 provides a motivation for this general framework. It does
so by reviewing a number of related problems as they arise in the
contemporary literature on testimony, and by constructing some dilemmas for any theory of knowledge that tries to resolve them. Here,
a common theme emerges: It can seem that any theory must make
testimonial knowledge either too hard or too easy, and that therefore
no adequate account of testimonial knowledge is possible. Section 2.2
develops the general framework described above by elaborating on its
essential elements in some detail. Section 2.3 applies the proposed
framework to the dilemmas constructed in Section 2.1. Again, the key
insight is that testimony sometimes generates knowledge and sometimes transmits it. The proposed model thereby explains why some
testimonial knowledge is indeed "easy," and some testimonial knowledge is indeed "hard."[1]

2.1 Some Problems in the Epistemology of Testimony

As we saw in Chapter 1, a foundational problem in the contemporary
literature on testimony concerns whether testimonial knowledge can be

---

[1] For some overviews of the relevant literature, see Greco, "Recent Work on
Testimonial Knowledge"; Jonathan Adler, "Epistemological Problems of
Testimony," in Edward N. Zalta, ed., *The Stanford Encyclopedia of Philosophy*
(Fall 2008 edition), available at: http://plato.stanford.edu/archives/fall2008/ent
ries/testimony-episprob; and Jennifer Lackey, "Knowing from Testimony,"
Philosophy Compass 1, 5 (2006): 432–448.

"reduced" to knowledge of another kind, such as inductive knowledge. Also in Chapter 1, we saw that there are two ways to be an anti-reductionist about testimonial knowledge in general. First, one can endorse source anti-reductionism, claiming that testimony constitutes an irreducible generative source, along with other such sources such as perception and induction. Second, one can endorse transmission anti-reductionism, claiming that transmitted knowledge does not reduce to generated knowledge. The literature on testimony does not make this distinction, however, talking only about reductionism more generally. In this section I will follow the literature in this respect. As it turns out, the distinction is not necessary to construct an important dilemma, and ignoring it allows us to capture a recognizable dialectic in the literature.[2]

A different problem in the contemporary literature *is* framed explicitly in terms of knowledge transmission. Specifically, does testimony merely "generate" knowledge, much as other sources of knowledge do, or does testimony serve an entirely different function – that of "transmitting" knowledge from one knower to another, *rather than* generating knowledge? Both sides of this issue can allow for transmission of a sort, defined in terms of our neutral characterization in Chapter 1. That is, both sides can agree that sometimes one person comes to know on the basis of testimony from a speaker who knows. The question at issue, however, is whether something special is going on in the case of transmission, marking it as a phenomenon that is distinct from generation and important in its own right.

Finally, there is a third issue that is prominent in the contemporary literature, and that is related to the first two. Specifically, is there something *distinctively social* about testimonial knowledge, over and above the superficial fact that it requires an exchange between two persons? In other words, is there something distinctively social in a way that is *epistemically* interesting?

Our three issues are related in at least the following way: If you are a reductionist about testimonial knowledge, then there is a clear sense

---

[2] Coady cites Hume's Section 10 of *An Enquiry Concerning Human Understanding* as the *locus classicus* for reductionism, and he cites Reid as the paradigmatic anti-reductionist (in Coady's terminology, "fundamentalist") about testimony. See Coady, *Testimony: A Philosophical Study*. For Reid's view, see *Essays on the Intellectual Powers of Man*, especially *Essay Two*, chapter 20 and *Essay Six*, chapter 5, in Thomas Reid, *Philosophical Works*, H. M. Bracken, ed., 2 volumes (Hildesheim: Georg Olms, 1983).

in which you must think that there is nothing special about knowledge transmission, and nothing interesting social about testimonial knowledge. That is, if testimonial knowledge reduces to other kinds of knowledge, then transmitted knowledge is just more generated knowledge, and testimonial knowledge is just more individual knowledge. It will be helpful, nevertheless, to consider our three questions separately and to consider some further ways in which they are interrelated.

2.1.1 Issue 1: Reductionism vs. Anti-reductionism

Can testimonial knowledge be "reduced" to some other kind of knowledge? Put differently: Is testimonial knowledge *sui generis*, requiring its own distinctive treatment, or is testimonial knowledge merely a species of some familiar kind? Sometimes the question is put in terms of epistemic sources, sometimes in terms of epistemic norms:

- Is testimony an irreducible *source* of knowledge, or can testimonial knowledge be accounted for in terms of other traditional sources of knowledge, such as inductive reasoning?
- Are there special *norms* governing belief based on testimony, or can the norms governing testimonial belief be reduced to the same norms governing other kinds of belief?[3]

The most straightforward form of reductionism, deriving from Hume, is that testimonial knowledge is merely a species of inductive knowledge.[4] Roughly, observation of previous cases yields general conclusions about the reliability of testimony, across various subject matters and in different circumstances. Testimony yields knowledge when the hearer applies these generalizations to a specific case, thereby

---

[3] See, for examples, the formulations by Coady, *Testimony: A Philosophical Study*; Peter Graham, "Liberal Fundamentalism and Its Rivals" in Jennifer Lackey and Ernest Sosa, eds., *The Epistemology of Testimony* (Oxford: Oxford University Press, 2006), pp. 93–115; and Adler, "Epistemological Problems of Testimony." Notice that the formulation in terms of sources implies that the issue is about source reductionism, whereas the formulation in terms of norms is more ambiguous.

[4] Coady, *Testimony: A Philosophical Study*. See also Elizabeth Fricker, "The Epistemology of Testimony," *Proceedings of the Aristotelian Society*, 61 (suppl.) (1987): 57–83; and her "Against Gullibility," in B.K. Matilal and A. Chakrabarti, eds., *Knowing from Words* (Boston: Kluwer, 1994), pp. 125–161.

concluding that the speaker in question is sufficiently sincere and competent so as to merit belief regarding what she says. As we have seen, different reductionist theories will cash out the details in various ways, but the general thesis that they share is that there is nothing epistemically special going on in testimonial knowledge. The bottom line is that testimonial knowledge is a species of inductive knowledge (or knowledge of some other familiar sort), and as such it must satisfy the standards for that sort of knowledge in general.

"Anti-reductionist" theories disagree. In effect, these theories insist that there is something special about testimonial knowledge. That is, there is something *epistemically* special, and in such a way that testimonial knowledge cannot be reduced to some other epistemic kind.[5] Again, different versions of the theory will cash out the details in various ways. For example, some theorists claim that a successful testimonial exchange involves a distinctive illocutionary act, one that underwrites a prima facie right to believe what is said. The analogy here is to the exchange of promises, which can yield a prima facie right to act on what is promised.[6] Other theorists talk about a non-evidential reason to believe,[7] and others about a distinctive grounds for entitlement.[8] The common theme, however, is that testimonial knowledge cannot be reduced to knowledge of a more general and familiar kind, and for that reason requires its own theoretical treatment.

The major criticism raised against reductionist theories is that they make testimonial knowledge too hard. For example, it is charged that the sort of inductive evidence that reductionists require is typically unavailable to the hearer. If testimonial knowledge really does require

---

[5] The qualification is necessary. Cf. Sanford Goldberg, "Reductionism and the Distinctiveness of Testimonial Knowledge," in Jennifer Lackey and Ernest Sosa, eds., *The Epistemology of Testimony* (Oxford: Oxford University Press, 2006), pp. 127–144. There, Goldberg points out that testimonial knowledge might be special or distinctive in an epistemologically interesting way, even if it can be reduced to some other kind of knowledge.

[6] For example, see Hinchman, "Telling as Inviting to Trust." Hinchman cites J.L. Austin, "Other Minds," in J.L. Austin, *Philosophical Papers*, 3rd edition (Oxford: Oxford University Press, 1979). See also Moran, "Getting Told and Being Believed."

[7] For example, see Hardwig, "Epistemic Dependence"; Angus Ross, "Why Do We Believe What We Are Told?" *Ratio* 28, 1 (1986): 69–88; Moran, "Getting Told and Being Believed."

[8] For example, see Tyler Burge, "Content Preservation," *The Philosophical Review* 102, 4 (1993): 457–488.

such evidence, then testimonial knowledge will be rare. But that is an unacceptable result, the criticism continues. This is because our reliance on testimony is ubiquitous, and so if we lack knowledge here then skeptical consequences cannot be contained.

A special case in this regard involves small children learning from their caretakers. Is it really plausible that small children are good inductive reasoners, in a way that would be required to account for their testimonial knowledge in such terms? There are good reasons for saying no. First, one might think that children lack the requisite reasoning *capacities* for making extensive inductive inferences. Second, and even if such capacities are granted, it is implausible to think that children have the requisite inductive *evidence*, that they have made the number and range of observations needed to make a quality inference, assuming they have the capacities to do so.[9]

The prospects for reductionism are daunting here. The options for responding include making a plausible case that small children are indeed in a position for relevant inductive knowledge, despite initial appearances. Another option is to deny that children have testimonial knowledge. Here, the idea is that knowledge comes later, after the relevant reasoning capacities and an inductive evidence base are better in place. Neither option is clearly attractive, however. For one, it seems that small children do learn from their caretakers, in the sense of coming to know what they are told. For example, the following exchanges seems unobjectionable:

Exchange 1

DAD: Where is Mom?
CHILD: At work.
DAD: Really? How do you know?
CHILD: She told me.

Exchange 2

CHILD: Frogs eat bugs!
MOM: That's right! How did you know that?
CHILD: My teacher told me.

[9] Cf. Coady, *Testimony: A Philosophical Study*, among others. For discussion, see Sanford Goldberg and David Henderson, "Monitoring and Anti-Reductionism in the Epistemology of Testimony," *Philosophy and Phenomenological Research* 72, 3 (2006): 576–593.

The prospects for reductionism are daunting for a second reason. Namely, a reductionist account of testimonial knowledge will have to bottom-out in non-testimonial knowledge only. But whether we attribute testimonial knowledge to children early or late, it is implausible that an adequate evidence base, itself devoid of testimonial knowledge, will be in place. What is plausible about attributing testimonial knowledge late is that, as children grow up, their knowledge does increase and so they have more to work with to use in their inductive inferences. What is not plausible, however, is that their knowledge increases in a way that makes it *independent* of the testimonial knowledge that the reductionist means to explain. Specifically, children learn about who they can trust and when largely *by being told* as much.[10]

Reductionist theories, then, seem to make testimonial knowledge too hard. The major criticism raised against anti-reductionist theories, on the other hand, is that they make testimonial knowledge too easy. Elizabeth Fricker articulates this objection:

> The solution [to the problem of testimonial justification] can take either of two routes. It may be shown that the required step – from "S asserted that P" to "P" – can be made as a piece of inference involving only familiar deductive and inductive principles, applied to empirically established premises. Alternatively, it may be argued that the step is legitimized as the exercise of a special presumptive epistemic right to trust, not dependent on evidence.[11]

> [The key element of a presumptive right thesis is] the dispensation from the requirement to monitor or assess the speaker for trustworthiness, before believing in it. Thus it may be called a [presumptive right] to believe *blindly*, or uncritically, since the hearer's critical faculties are not required to be engaged.[12]

Anti-reductionists typically respond along two lines. First, they emphasize the danger of skeptical results if one insists on the reductionist picture. Second, they associate reductionist demands for evidence with an overly individualistic (and insufficiently social) approach in epistemology. Reductionism, these authors insist, is wedded to an

---

[10] Here is a weaker position that might seem more plausible: Testimonial knowledge always requires evidence for speaker reliability, but such evidence need not be irreducibly non-testimonial. This position is still too strong in my opinion (we will see why below); but in any case, it would not count as "reductionism" in the sense that we are considering here.

[11] Fricker, "Against Gullibility," p. 128.   [12] Ibid., p. 144.

inappropriate ideal of the individual, autonomous knower.[13] Whatever truth there is in these rejoinders, however, the original objection seems to stand. Anti-reductionist theories seem to make at least some cases of testimonial knowledge too easy.

For example, consider a police investigator whose task is to question a potentially uncooperative witness. The investigator asks questions and the witness answers them, but clearly the investigator should not just believe whatever the witness says. On the contrary, she will employ skills learned and honed over a career to discern what is and is not believable in what the witness asserts. Moreover, it is plausible to think of these skills in terms of bringing to bear inductive evidence. Plausibly, a seasoned investigator will employ various well-grounded generalizations to determine whether the witness is telling the truth in a particular instance. Some of these generalizations might be well articulated – perhaps they are formulated explicitly in investigator guides and handbooks.[14] Others might be less well articulated, but still the result of relevant observations over time. In any case, it looks like nothing special in going on here, epistemically speaking. On the contrary, the effective investigator looks to be a good inductive reasoner.[15]

We have now seen some considerations against both reductionist and anti-reductionist approaches regarding the epistemology of testimony. Reductionist theories seem to make testimonial knowledge too hard, disallowing, for example, that children can come to know on the basis of testimony from their caregivers. Anti-reductionist theories, on the other hand, seem to make testimonial knowledge too easy, allowing

---

[13] For example, Welbourne, "The Community of Knowledge"; Hardwig, "Epistemic Dependence." See also John Greco, "Intellectual Humility and Contemporary Epistemology: A Critique of Epistemic Individualism, Evidentialism, and Internalism," in Mark Alfano, Michael Lynch, and Alessandra Tanesini, eds., *The Routledge Handbook of the Philosophy of Humility* (New York: Routledge, 2020).

[14] For example, John E. Hess, *Interviewing and Interrogation for Law Enforcement*, 2nd edition (New Providence, NJ: Matthew Bender and Company, 2010).

[15] The situation is in fact a bit more complicated than this, in that such an investigator might be an expert *perceiver* rather than a good *reasoner*, or in addition to being a good reasoner. Nevertheless, the present point stands. For either way, there is nothing epistemically special going on – that is, nothing that can't be understood in terms of the resources already available for understanding non-testimonial knowledge. For relevant discussions, see Greco, "Recent Work on Testimonial Knowledge"; and Goldberg and Henderson, "Monitoring and Anti-Reductionism in the Epistemology of Testimony."

that one can come to know simply by believing what one is told, and thus licensing gullibility. The fact is, different cases pull in different directions. Sometimes it seems that testimonial knowledge *should* be easy, whereas other times it seems that it should not be.

Consider now a range of cases, beginning with our seasoned investigator and ending with a small child.

Case 1. A seasoned police investigator questions a potentially uncooperative witness.

Case 2. A job applicant tells you that he has relevant previous employment.

Case 3. You ask a stranger in an unfamiliar city for directions to the train station.

Case 4. You ask your friend whether he intends to come to your party, and he says that yes, he does.

Case 5. A third-grade teacher tells his student that France is in Europe.

Case 6. A mother tells her small child that there is milk in the refrigerator.

As the cases progress, it becomes more plausible that the hearer can believe straight away what he or she is told – and that he or she knows thereby. Thus, in Cases 1 and 2 (the investigator and the job applicant), it seems clear that knowledge does require something akin to good inductive reasons. By the time we get to Cases 5 and 6 (student/teacher and parent/child), it is less plausible that basing one's belief on good inductive reasons is required for knowledge, and more plausible that the hearer can believe straightaway, or at least *almost* straightaway.[16] It is also more plausible that something epistemically special is going on in these cases – that testimonial knowledge depends on a relationship between speaker and hearer that is present in these cases but not in the first. Cases 3 and 4 (asking directions and your friend's party) seem somewhere in between.

Now we can formulate a dilemma for any theory of testimonial knowledge. Some cases suggest *a necessary condition* on testimonial knowledge – that the hearer needs something akin to good inductive

---

[16] It is implausible to think that *nothing at all* is required on the part of the hearer. The important point, in the present context, is that much less seems required than in the other cases.

reasons for knowledge, and that she must base her testimonial belief on such reasons. But other cases suggest *sufficient conditions* for testimonial knowledge *that do not include that necessary condition.* A single account of all the cases seems unavailable.

Here is another way to articulate the dilemma:

1. Either testimonial knowledge requires good inductive evidence on the part of the hearer or it does not.[17]
2. If it does not, then testimonial knowledge is too easy. There will be cases counted as knowledge that should not be.
3. If it does, then testimonial knowledge is too hard. There will be cases not counted as knowledge that should be.

Therefore,

4. An adequate account of testimonial knowledge is impossible: Any given account must make testimonial knowledge either too easy for some cases or too hard for others.

2.1.2 Issue 2: Generation vs. Transmission

We have seen that a related issue in the literature on testimony concerns whether testimony "generates" knowledge, much as other sources of knowledge do, or rather "transmits" knowledge from one knower to another. The natural view to take here, perhaps, is that testimony does transmit knowledge – testimonial knowledge begins with knowledge on the part of the speaker, and the function of testimony is to make the speaker's knowledge available to the hearer, to transmit it to the hearer. This natural view has in fact been a starting point for many authors writing on testimony and testimonial knowledge.[18]

More recently, however, that view has come under attack. For example, Jennifer Lackey considers the following Transmission Thesis, which she divides into two claims:[19]

---

[17] Read "good inductive reasons" this way: inductive reasons of sufficient quality to ground inductive knowledge.
[18] For example, see Austin, "Other Minds"; Welbourne "The Transmission of Knowledge"; Coady, *Testimony, A Philosophical Study*; and Ross, "Why Do We Believe What We Are Told."
[19] The following are paraphrased from Lackey, "Knowing from Testimony."

Transmission Thesis: Testimony transmits knowledge from speaker to hearer, rather than generates it.

Transmission Necessary (TN): H knows that p on the basis of testimony from S *only if* S knows that p.

Transmission Sufficient (TS): If S knows that p and H believes that p (in the normal way) on the basis of S's testimony, then (absent defeating evidence) S knows that p.

Lackey and others have put forward counterexamples to both claims of the Transmission Thesis. The most plausible counterexamples to TN concern circumstances in which the hearer is somehow in an epistemically superior position to the speaker regarding the facts around p. The speaker is in possession of a misleading defeater, or she is somehow Gettiered, and this prevents her from knowing that some p is the case. Being in a superior epistemic position, this does not prevent the hearer from coming to know that p on the basis of the speaker's testimony.

The most plausible objection against TS comes from Lackey, who notes that a reliable believer might nevertheless be an unreliable speaker. In Lackey's example, the owner of a whale-watching business testifies that whales have been sighted in the area and does so from knowledge. But the owner would have testified the same way even if there were no whales sighted (she is dishonest and trying to drum up business). Plausibly, one does not come to know that whales have been sighted on the basis of her testimony, even though she knows that whales have been sighted.[20]

I am sympathetic to both kinds of counterexample. Plausibly, both claims of Transmission Thesis are false. But what is really at issue here? What is natural and plausible about Transmission Thesis, even if the thesis as formulated is literally false? In Chapter 1, I suggested that it is something like this: In cases of knowledge transmission, the hearer comes to know, but not by coming to know "for herself." In such cases, rather, it seems that knowledge is made available *by* the speaker *to* the hearer, or transferred *from* the speaker *to* the hearer. And this is opposed to the hearer having to shoulder the usual epistemic burdens associated with coming to know.

[20] Lackey, "Knowing from Testimony," 436–437. See also Graham, "Transferring Knowledge"; and his "Can Testimony Generate Knowledge?" *Philosophica* 78 (2006): 105–127.

What does all that amount to, exactly? I suppose that we cannot say, short of providing a more substantive account of knowledge transmission. That task begins in Section 2.2, and continues in later chapters. But even short of such an account, it seems clear that at least some testimonial exchanges do involve something epistemically special going on – something on the order of relieving the "epistemic burden" of the hearer.

So, does knowledge transmission, conceived in this way, actually exist? Again, different cases pull in different directions. Recall our series of cases above. In Cases 1 and 2 (the investigator and the job applicant), it seems clear that nothing akin to knowledge transmission is going on. If the investigator or the interviewer come to know in these cases, they do so "for themselves" and by their own efforts. Put differently, the speakers in these cases do not relieve the hearers of the usual epistemic burdens associated with coming to know. In Cases 5 and 6 (student/teacher and parent/child), however, it is far more plausible that something like knowledge transmission – conceived as epistemically special – does take place. In these cases, it seems, the hearers *can* believe what they are told, and without the usual burdens associated with coming to know. Cases 3 and 4 (asking directions and your friend's party) seem somewhere in between.

All this confirms that the debate over transmission is closely related to the debate over reduction. For one, if this kind of knowledge transmission is possible, then reductionism is false. That is, transmitted knowledge will not be reducible to other, familiar kinds of knowledge. Likewise, the debate over transmission threatens a similar dilemma to that posed by the debate over reduction:

1. Either testimonial knowledge involves knowledge transmission or it does not.
2. If it does, then testimonial knowledge is too easy. A hearer can come to know merely by believing what a speaker says, and that is inconsistent with the epistemic burdens involved in coming to know.
3. If it does not, then testimonial knowledge is too hard. A hearer can never depend on a speaker to transmit knowledge, but must in every case come to know "for herself."

Therefore,

4. An adequate account of testimonial knowledge is impossible: Any given account must make testimonial knowledge either too easy in some cases or too hard in others.

2.1.3 Issue 3: Is Testimonial Knowledge Distinctively Social?

As we have seen, a third issue in the literature on testimony concerns the social character of testimonial knowledge. How are the social dimensions of testimonial knowledge to be understood? Of course, at least two people are involved in any testimonial exchange, and so testimonial knowledge is "social" in at least a superficial sense. But how, if at all, is the social character of testimonial knowledge more substantial than that? The deeper question, often in the background, is this: To what extent must traditional epistemology be revised in order to adequately accommodate the social character of testimonial knowledge?

This question raises many of the same issues above, now in slightly different terms. Consider: One way that testimonial knowledge might be distinctively social is that it involves something like knowledge transmission. The idea is that testimonial exchanges play that distinctive function in a community of knowers – testimony serves to transmit or distribute knowledge in a social system, as opposed to generating it or "producing it anew" in each believer. Any adequate theory of testimonial knowledge, this line of reasoning goes, must take this distinctive function into account and explain how it is possible. And if that is right, then it seems that testimonial knowledge cannot be reduced to other kinds of knowledge, in which a knower does "produce knowledge anew" and "for herself." Again, all of our issues are related, and all give rise to similar dilemmas for an epistemology of testimony.

More generally, the problem is this: Many cases suggest a necessary condition on testimonial knowledge – that testimonial knowledge requires something like basing one's belief on good evidence. But other cases suggest that testimonial knowledge is nothing like that. Rather, these cases suggest, testimonial knowledge is its own kind of animal, a distinctively social phenomenon that involves something like "passing on knowledge" rather than "producing knowledge." No approach we have seen so far handles all the cases well.

Here is another way to characterize the mess: If you opt for reductionism, you make it impossible to accommodate transmission in any interesting sense, and impossible to explain how testimonial knowledge is distinctively social; that is, distinctively social in a way that is epistemically important, as testimonial knowledge at least often seems to be. Accordingly, you make testimonial knowledge too hard. If you opt for anti-reductionism, you open up space for distinctively social epistemic phenomena, including an epistemically interesting phenomenon of knowledge transmission. But in doing so you create a disconnect between the requirements for testimonial knowledge and the requirements for knowledge of any other kind. Accordingly, you make testimonial knowledge too easy.

2.2 A Proposal for Making Progress

In Section 2.1, we looked at some issues that arise in the contemporary literature on the epistemology of testimony, and we articulated some dilemmas faced by any account of testimonial knowledge. In this section, we consider a proposal for moving forward. The key insight, as was said above, is that testimonial exchanges can be in the service of *either* knowledge generation *or* knowledge transmission. This simple insight explains why some cases of testimonial knowledge place significant evidential burdens on the hearer, while others allow a kind of epistemic division of labor, designed to take the usual burdens off the hearer. But what motivates thinking of testimonial knowledge in this two-faced way? We begin by looking at an important idea from Edward Craig, and then extending it accordingly. Section 2.3 argues for the proposed framework by demonstrating its explanatory power. For one, the framework allows principled resolutions of the dilemmas set out in Section 2.1. Second, the framework predicts and explains many of the interesting features that knowledge transmission is supposed to have.

We begin with an idea from Craig in his *Knowledge and the State of Nature*.[21] Specifically, Craig suggests that the central purpose of the concept of knowledge is to flag good sources of information.

any community may be presumed to have an interest in evaluating sources of information; and in connection with that interest certain concepts will be in use. The hypothesis I wish to try out is that the concept of knowledge is one of them. To put it briefly and roughly, the concept of knowledge is used to flag approved sources of information.[22]

---

[21] Edward Craig, *Knowledge and the State of Nature* (Oxford: Oxford University Press, 1990).
[22] Ibid., p. 11.

It comes as no surprise, Craig argues, that beings like us would have such a concept. Human beings are social, information-dependent creatures. That is, we have significant needs for actionable information, and we need each other to get it. The concept of knowledge, Craig proposes, addresses these needs.[23]

Some elaborations on that basic idea give us the resources for resolving the dilemmas articulated in Section 2.1. First, if Craig's idea is even broadly correct, then we should expect there to be at least two kinds of activity governed by the concept of knowledge. First, there will be activities concerned with *acquiring* or *gathering* information, or getting information into the community of knowers in the first place. For example, empirical observation serves to acquire information about physical objects in our environment, and introspection serves to acquire information about accessible mental states. Second, there will be activities concerned with *distributing* information throughout the community of knowers; that is, there will be mechanisms for distributing information that is already in the social system. For example, teaching in the classroom, testifying in court, and reporting in the boardroom all serve this distribution function. In sum, there will be activities that get quality information into the system in the first place, and activities that keep that information flowing. Let's call the first *acquisition activities* and the second *distribution activities*.

Second, we may note that the norms governing the acquisition activities play a "gatekeeping" function – they exert quality control so as to admit only high-quality information into the social system.[24] The norms governing distribution activities, on the other hand, answer to a distributing function – they allow high-quality information already in

---

[23] A number of recent authors have argued for a close relationship between knowledge and action. For example, see Timothy Williamson, *Knowledge and its Limits* (Oxford: Oxford University Press, 2000); Jeremy Fantl and Matthew McGrath, "Evidence, Pragmatics, and Justification," *Philosophical Review* 111, 1 (2002): 6–94; and *Knowledge in an Uncertain World* (Oxford: Oxford University Press, 2009); John Hawthorne, *Knowledge and Lotteries* (Oxford: Oxford University Press, 2004); and Jason Stanley, *Knowledge and Practical Interests* (Oxford: Oxford University Press, 2005).

[24] I adopt the phrase "gatekeeping" from Henderson, who uses it to describe a similar function. See David Henderson, "Motivated Contextualism," *Philosophical Studies* 142, 1 (2009): 119–131. See also David Henderson and Terence Horgan, "What's the Point?" in David Henderson and John Greco, eds., *Epistemic Evaluation: Purposeful Epistemology* (Oxford: Oxford University Press, 2015), pp. 87–114.

the system to be distributed as needed throughout the community of knowers. Insofar as testimony plays this distributing function, it serves to make information already in the system available to those who need it.

And now a third point, essential for our purposes: It is reasonable that the norms governing the acquisition of information should be different from the norms governing the distribution of information. Suppose we were writing the norms, or setting the standards, for these two kinds of activity. We should make it harder to get information into the system than we make it to distribute that information, once in. Again, that is because the dominant concern governing the acquisition function is quality control – we want a strong gatekeeping mechanism here, so as to make sure that only high-quality information gets into the community of information sharers. But the dominant concern governing the distributing function will be easy access – we want information that has already passed the quality control test to be easily and efficiently available to those who need it. Different norms or standards are appropriate to these distinct functions.

We may consider the case of scientific knowledge as an instance of this general picture. Any item of scientific knowledge must have its original source, presumably in reliable method. But eventually that knowledge spreads through a shared system of knowledge by means of various kinds of testimony. Through record-keeping, formal and informal teaching, journal articles, public lectures, media reports, and the like, what begins as knowledge for a few becomes knowledge for many. Moreover, the norms and standards governing the first kind of activity are different from the norms and standards governing the second. Quality control is exercised over both kinds of activity, to be sure, but in different ways. Hence, the norms governing the exchange of information through journals, seminars, etc., are distinct from those governing experiment design, statistical analysis, theory choice, etc. In the case of scientific knowledge, then, various institutional and social practices are in place so as to bring high-quality information into the relevant scientific community, and also to distribute it within that community. Different norms govern these different practices, each according to its distinctive purpose or function. What holds for scientific knowledge in this regard plausibly holds for knowledge in general.

Notice that on the account of knowledge that emerges, knowledge from testimony becomes paradigmatic. That is, it becomes paradigmatic

Information Acquisition

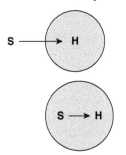

Information Distribution

Figure 2.1 Testimony in two roles.

of the second category of knowledge that we expect to find – knowledge grounded in the appropriate distribution of information. The account also predicts that testimonial knowledge (as such) should be ubiquitous.

We are now in a position to make a further suggestion, also essential for resolving the dilemmas articulated in Section 2.1. Namely, that testimonial knowledge *itself* comes in two kinds. In other words, it is plausible that testimony sometimes serves the distribution function of the concept of knowledge, and sometimes the acquisition function (Figure 2.1). The distribution function gives us the paradigmatic case, and gives us the most plausible treatment of Case 5 (student/teacher) and Case 6 (parent/child). But it is also plausible that testimony sometimes serves an acquisition function, bringing information into a community of knowers for the first time. This is the best treatment of Case 1 (investigator) and Case 2 (job applicant). This also explains why a student or a child, when in appropriate circumstances, can believe straightaway what a teacher or a parent tells her, and also explains why an investigator or interviewer cannot. In short, different norms govern the different kinds of testimonial exchange, some of which are at the service of information distribution within a community of knowers, others of which are at the service of information uptake for first use in a community of knowers.

2.3 Application to the Problems in Section 2.1

The present framework for thinking about testimonial knowledge, I have suggested, gives us resources for resolving the dilemmas constructed in Section 2.1. More generally, it allows us to resolve three issues that have dominated contemporary discussions in the epistemology of testimony. Let's take a closer look in that regard.

2.3.1 Reductionism

The present proposal is that some testimonial exchanges serve to get high-quality information into a community of information sharers for the first time, whereas others serve to distribute high-quality information that is already in the community. In the first kind of case, it is plausible that testimonial knowledge does reduce to knowledge of some other sort, such as inductive knowledge. I have already suggested that this is the most plausible interpretation of Case 1 (police investigator) and Case 2 (job applicant). In these cases, the hearer comes to know by exercising her good inductive reasoning, and the present account explains why that should be so. For here the speaker and hearer are not members of a "community of knowers" and they are not "information sharers," at least in the present context. Rather, the usual burdens for coming to know rest squarely on the hearer, and it would be inappropriate for her to rely on the speaker for the information in question. That is, it would be *epistemically* inappropriate; that sort of reliance would violate relevant norms and fail relevant standards.

Other cases of testimonial knowledge, however, more plausibly serve a distribution function. This is the more plausible interpretation, I suggested, of Case 5 (student/teacher) and Case 6 (parent/child), where it does seem that the hearer can believe straightaway, or almost straightaway, what he is told, and without violating relevant epistemic norms. Once again, the present account explains why. Specifically, in this kind of case the speaker and hearer *are* members of a community of knowers, and are appropriately in the role of information sharers. As such, the hearer's reliance on the speaker is appropriate in these cases, from an epistemic point of view. And since the norms governing this kind of exchange are specific to their purpose, testimonial knowledge in this kind of case cannot be reduced to knowledge of some other kind.

That is not to say, of course, that nothing at all is required on the part of the hearer in these cases. The important point, rather, is that something different is now required, given the different role that the hearer now occupies in the testimonial exchange. We may treat Case 3 and Case 4 accordingly. That is, there will be cases of information distribution where more or less is required of the hearer, depending on the more specific nature of the relevant social context, and of her role in the exchange. For example, a tourist asking for directions carries different burdens than a friend asking for an RSVP.

In effect, the present account implies that there are two kinds of testimonial knowledge, one of which can be reduced to knowledge of another sort, and the other of which cannot be. Accordingly, one might be tempted to say that a reductionist account of testimonial knowledge is correct for some cases, whereas an anti-reductionist account is correct for others. This is in fact too generous to the reductionist, however. That is because, properly understood, the reductionist claim is that *all* testimonial knowledge can be reduced to knowledge of another kind. The anti-reductionist claim, properly understood, is to deny this. Accordingly, the present account is anti-reductionist. More specifically, it is anti-reductionist about knowledge transmission, and therefore anti-reductionist about testimonial knowledge in general.

Finally, we may now review the dilemma that we formulated in terms of reductionism and anti-reductionism, and say explicitly how the present account responds to it. The first two premises of that dilemma were stated as follows:

1. Either testimonial knowledge requires good inductive evidence on the part of the hearer or it does not.
2. If it does not, then testimonial knowledge is too easy. There will be cases counted as knowledge that should not be.

Our response to the dilemma depends on how we read premise 1. Suppose we parse premise 1 this way: Either *all* testimonial knowledge requires good inductive evidence on the part of the hearer or *no* testimonial knowledge does. In that case we reject premise 1. That reading of the premise looks innocent so long as we are assuming that all testimonial knowledge should be treated the same way. On the present account, however, there are two kinds of testimonial knowledge, one of which carries the evidential burdens of inductive knowledge and the other of which does not.

Suppose we parse premise 1 as follows: Either *all* testimonial knowledge requires good inductive evidence on the part of the hearer, or it is not the case that *all* testimonial knowledge carries that requirement. On that reading we accept premise 1 but reject premise 2. In effect, premise 2 now assumes the following: If not all testimonial knowledge requires good inductive evidence, then no testimonial knowledge does. The present account rejects that assumption.

2.3.2 Knowledge Transmission

In Section 2.1, we considered the following Transmission Thesis: The function of testimony is to transmit knowledge from speaker to hearer, rather than to generate it. It was not clear how to understand that thesis, exactly, but we suggested that it was something like this: In cases of transmission, knowledge is made available *by* the speaker *to* the hearer, or transferred *from* the speaker *to* the hearer. And this was opposed to the hearer "producing knowledge anew," or coming to know "for herself." The present framework gives us a better understanding of knowledge transmission, and therefore a better understanding of Transmission Thesis. Specifically, we may now understand Transmission Thesis as follows: The function of testimony is to distribute quality information within an epistemic community, rather than to bring quality information into the community for the first time. Alternatively: The function of testimony is to distribute quality information that is already possessed by the epistemic community.

Accordingly, the present account endorses a qualified transmission thesis. Qualified, because on the present account not *all* testimony serves to transmit knowledge, even in cases where the speaker knows, and not *all* testimonial knowledge is transmitted knowledge. Nevertheless, the *distinctive epistemic function* of testimony is to transmit knowledge. That is what makes testimonial knowledge epistemically interesting in its own right, when it is.

2.3.3 Is Testimonial Knowledge Distinctively Social?

In Section 2.1 we said that issues concerning the social dimensions of testimonial knowledge were closely tied to issues concerning reduction and transmission. If testimonial knowledge is distinctively social, that is probably because it involves something like knowledge transmission, and for just that reason cannot be reduced to a different epistemic kind. We also said that a deeper question lies in the background: To what extent must traditional epistemology be revised, in order to adequately accommodate the social character of testimonial knowledge? In this context, we articulated the following dilemma:

1. If you opt for reductionism, you make it impossible to accommodate transmission and impossible to explain how testimonial
   knowledge is distinctively social; that is, distinctively social in
   a way that is *epistemically* important, as testimonial knowledge at
   least often seems to be. Accordingly, you make testimonial knowledge too hard.
2. If you opt for anti-reductionism, you open up space for both
   transmission and distinctively social epistemic phenomena. But
   in doing so you create a disconnect between the requirements
   for testimonial knowledge and the requirements for knowledge
   of any other kind. Accordingly, you make testimonial knowledge
   too easy.

Therefore,

3. No adequate account of testimonial knowledge is available.

I have urged that a proper understanding of reductionism and anti-
reductionism makes them exhaustive options. So, the conclusion
follows from the premises. The present account denies premise 2,
however. We opt for anti-reductionism, and in doing so we allow
for a disconnect between the requirements for testimonial knowledge
and the requirements for knowledge of any other kind. That is, we
allow for a disconnect between the requirements for *one kind* of
testimonial knowledge – transmitted knowledge – and the requirements for knowledge of any other kind. But we deny that this makes
testimonial knowledge too easy. On the contrary, the account makes
testimonial knowledge easy in cases where it should be easy, and hard
in cases where it should be hard.

Does this require a radical, or least significant, revision of traditional
epistemology? It does, insofar as it calls for two irreducible ways of
coming to know, answering to the two functions of acquiring and
distributing quality information in a community of knowers. On the
other hand, a unified theory of knowledge, along traditional lines,
might still be possible at a different level of abstraction.

I will use a generic reliabilist theory to illustrate.[25] First, suppose for
the sake of argument that the central claims of this chapter are correct:
(a) that the concept of knowledge serves a dual purpose in governing

---

[25] Chapter 5 argues in favor of a unified agent reliabilist view.

both the acquisition and distribution of quality information within a community of information sharers; and (b) that therefore the standards for knowledge are similarly dualistic, with different standards governing information acquisition and information distribution. Accordingly, (c) there are in effect two ways of coming to know, one satisfying the standards governing information acquisition and the other satisfying the standards governing information distribution. How might a reliabilist theory accommodate these conclusions?

One way to do so is to maintain that knowledge in general is true belief resulting from appropriately reliable cognitive processes, but to hold that "appropriate" reliability comes in two kinds. In other words, the kind of reliability required for knowledge generation is now understood differently from the kind of reliability required for knowledge transmission. A reliabilist theory that is modified along these lines will continue to face the usual problems for traditional reliabilism. For example, such a theory will face the generality problem regarding how relevant cognitive processes are to be circumscribed, and it will have to deal with Gettier problems in some way. But such problems will now be "split in two," requiring one solution for knowledge generation and perhaps another for knowledge transmission. For example, it is plausible that the considerations governing how knowledge-generating processes are to be circumscribed are different from the considerations governing how knowledge-transmitting processes are to be circumscribed, again with different considerations answering to the different purposes served by the two kinds of process. Likewise, it is plausible that the kind of luck that can infect reliable information acquisition, and thereby yield Gettier problems in that context, is different from the kind of luck that can infect reliable information distribution, and thereby yield Gettier problems there.

We may conclude that the implications for traditional epistemology are mixed. On the one hand, we need to admit two ways of coming to know, one answering to the standards appropriate for information acquisition and one answering to the standards appropriate for information distribution. On the other hand, at a higher level of abstraction, we might still think of the standards in question in reliabilist terms, or perhaps in other traditional terms. In any case, at least this much revision is required to accommodate the ubiquity of testimonial knowledge, and to appreciate its special function in a community of knowers.

3 | Joint Agency and the Role of Trust in Testimonial Knowledge

The framework presented in Chapter 2 already makes the notion of cooperation essential to the phenomenon of knowledge transmission. Specifically, it makes cooperation essential to the distinction between testimony in the service of information acquisition and testimony in the service of information distribution, and therefore essential to the difference between knowledge generation and knowledge transmission. This chapter develops the framework presented in Chapter 2 by invoking two additional resources: the concept of a speech act from the philosophy of language, and the concept of joint agency from action theory.

First, a number of philosophers have claimed that knowledge transmission essentially involves the speech act of *telling*, understood as a sub-species of assertion, but one that is specifically designed for sharing knowledge. For example, Elizabeth Fricker writes:

Tellings are a subset of assertions. In a paradigm and *felicitous* telling, the teller rightly takes herself to know that P, and seeks to share her knowledge with her intended audience ... Telling is the proprietary linguistic means ... of letting someone else know what one already knows oneself.[1]

This chapter endorses that idea and weds it to another – that of *joint agency*. Thus, recent action theory recognizes a special kind of action, one that can be characterized as "acting together." It is now standard that joint agency involves a network of shared intentions and common understanding between the participating actors, as well as specific kinds of interdependence. Section 3.1 argues that knowledge

---

[1] Elizabeth Fricker, "Second-Hand Knowledge," *Philosophy and Phenomenological Research* 73, 3 (2006): 596, italics original. Other philosophers who have emphasized the speech act of telling in testimonial knowledge include Hinchman, "Telling as Inviting to Trust"; Moran, "Getting Told and Being Believed" and his The Exchange of Words: Speech, Testimony, and Intersubjectivity (New York: Oxford University Press, 2018).

48 *The Transmission of Knowledge*

transmission can be understood as a kind of joint agency involving speaker and hearer, organized by the shared intention of "sharing knowledge," or "letting know," or "giving to know."[2]

One result of invoking these resources from speech act theory and action theory is that we better understand the kind of cooperation at issue in the transmission of knowledge. A second result is that we better understand the role of trust in testimonial knowledge. In this regard, the chapter offers a new defense of a familiar anti-reductionist claim: that testimonial knowledge essentially involves the hearer trusting the speaker. Importantly, the anti-reductionist claim is that trust has genuinely *epistemic* significance, as opposed to mere *psychological* significance. Section 3.2 argues that trust is indeed essential to testimonial knowledge, and in a way that is epistemically interesting. The argument is that trust is essential to joint agency in general, and joint agency is essential to knowledge transmission. It follows that trust is essential to one important way of *coming to know*.[3]

3.1 Telling, Joint Agency, and the Transmission of Knowledge

This section introduces two important resources for better understanding the special phenomenon of knowledge transmission. In Section 3.1.1, I argue that the transmission of knowledge involves a particular kind of *speech act*, one that we might think of as specially designed for the transmission of knowledge. In particular, the speech act of *telling* that p is tailor-made for sharing knowledge that p (or letting know that p, or giving to know that p). In Sections 3.1.2 and 3.1.3, I argue that the transmission of knowledge involves a special

[2] The question arises whether this way of understanding transmission is circular or otherwise uninformative, the worry being that the shared intention of "passing on" knowledge is too close – perhaps equivalent to – the idea of transmitting knowledge. Below I address these worries by providing a familiar kind of recursive definition – one that adds a recursive clause to an informative base clause.
[3] More exactly, and in keeping with the general framework presented in Chapter 2, I defend the claim that *some* testimonial knowledge – that gained by knowledge transmission – essentially involves the hearer trusting the speaker. The position is then this: Whereas the generation of knowledge may or may not involve joint agency in the acquisition of information, the transmission of knowledge *essentially* involves joint agency in the distribution of information. Accordingly, the transmission of knowledge essentially involves the kind of trust and interdependence that characterizes joint agency in general.

kind of *action* – a kind of action that may be variously characterized as "acting together" or "doing something together," and that has been fruitfully theorized in the recent literature on joint agency. Moreover, it is argued that, in knowledge transmission, the speech act of telling and the joint action of sharing knowledge are importantly related. Specifically, the characteristic intention of the relevant speech act of telling – that of *sharing knowledge* – is also the shared intention of the relevant joint action. That is, in successful instances of knowledge transmission, the speaker not only *tells* her audience that p, thereby manifesting her intention to share knowledge with her audience that p. In addition to this, her audience understands and shares this intention, and thereby becomes a participant in the joint action of sharing knowledge that p. Section 3.1.4 considers whether the account of knowledge transmission being offered here is circular.

3.1.1 Telling as Letting Know

It is standard in speech act theory that speaker intention is essential for specifying the kind of speech act that is being performed. For example, a speaker performs the speech act of promising (or commanding, or questioning) only if she intends to promise (or command, or question). It is also standard that, for a speech act to be *successful*, the speaker's intentions must be recognized and understood by the audience for what they are. This is easy to see in the case of betting. I have not *successfully* bet you $10 that my horse will win unless, among other things, you understand me as doing just that. Speech acts, then, share at least this much with other kinds of action – mere trying to φ does not make it so that one has φ'd. Rather, the world (and in this case the audience) must cooperate.

These general characteristics of speech acts are manifested by the particular speech act of *telling*, understood as a species of assertion. Here is an extended version of the passage from Fricker, quoted earlier:

Tellings are a subset of assertions. In a paradigm and *felicitous* telling, the teller rightly takes herself to know that P, and seeks to share her knowledge with her intended audience, whom she believes ignorant, or possibly ignorant, as to whether P. Telling is the proprietary linguistic means – often the only practicable way of achieving this, and almost always by far the easiest – of letting someone else know what one already knows oneself. The illocutionary act of telling is achieved when there is uptake: the intended audience correctly grasps the content and force of the speech act, recognizing that she is being told that

P. It is consummated when the audience trusts the teller, forming [the] belief
that P on her say-so . . . This type of action, telling, exists and has a rationale, in
our repertoire of mutually understood speech act types, in virtue of what is
achieved in a felicitous act of telling which is taken up and consummated.
Telling is a social institution for the spreading of knowledge.[4]

Here, Fricker mentions several important characteristics of *telling* in
particular, each of which will be important for our purposes. First, in
felicitous (i.e., proper) cases of telling, the speaker understands herself
to know what she tells, and intends that this knowledge be shared with
her audience. Second, Fricker says, telling is "the proprietary linguistic
means" for "letting someone else know what one already knows oneself." Here, Fricker uses a familiar and natural English locution –
"letting someone know" – to describe the illocutionary force of the
speech act of telling. That is, "letting someone know" naturally
describes what a speaker is *trying to do* when she tells someone that
such and such is the case.[5]

Third, Fricker says that there is appropriate "uptake" when "the
intended audience correctly grasps the content and force of the speech
act." And the act is "consummated" when the audience thereby forms
the appropriate belief on the basis of being so told. Finally, Fricker
claims that, so understood, "Telling is a social institution for the
spreading of knowledge." Endorsing this general idea, we might
now say: "Telling is a social institution for the transmission of
knowledge."

Richard Moran is another author who, in his account of testimonial
knowledge, gives pride of place to the speech act of telling, although
Moran characterizes the speaker's intention in terms of "giving

[4] Fricker, "Second-Hand Knowledge," 596.
[5] In this regard, the claim that *knowledge is the norm of telling* is more plausible
than the claim that knowledge is the norm of assertion in general. That is, if we
consider that telling is a species of assertion, and that its special function is to
share knowledge, then there is a clear explanation why knowledge would be the
norm for telling, but not for assertion more generally. Moreover, the linguistic
evidence that the knowledge norm is operative clearly supports the more
restricted thesis. In particular, it is often inappropriate in the face of assertion to
query the speaker with, "How do you know that?" or to criticize her with "You
don't know that." Think of cases of speculation and prediction, for example.
However, it is hard to think of cases of *telling* where these reactions are
inappropriate. (Fricker, however, endorses the more general knowledge norm of
assertion: "Second-Hand Knowledge," 594, including note 3.)

a reason to believe" rather than "giving to know." Nevertheless, Moran nicely emphasizes the kind of intersubjective dependence and mutual understanding involved in the successful uptake and completion of speech acts such as telling and promising.

In the following passage, Moran cites Thomas Reid for the insight that telling cannot be an individual action, but is rather a "social act" involving the participation of another person:

The simple act of telling involves an interlocking system of authority and dependence on, or deferral to, a role played by the other person. As Reid says, social acts of the mind are distinctive in that they "can have no existence without the intervention of some other intelligent being, *who acts a part in them* ... they must be expressed *to* another party who recognizes them for what they are and "acts a part" in their "completion."[6]

Tellings, then, like other social acts, are characterized by an "interlocking system of dependence" – one that includes another person's "recognizing them for what they are," and who thereby "acts a part in them." Likewise, telling involves a common or "shared" knowledge between speaker and hearer:

The speaker's knowledge of what she is doing in speech depends on this very knowledge being taken up and shared by her interlocutor; otherwise she will not in fact be doing what she announces in saying, "I apologize, accept, refuse, tell ..."[7]

It is precisely these features of interdependence and shared understanding that are also hallmarks of joint agency. We are in a good position, then, to see how the transmission of knowledge, now understood as executed by the speech act of telling, can also be understood as a kind of joint agency between speaker and hearer.

3.1.2 *Joint Agency, Group Agency, and Teamwork*

Think of joint action in terms of individual agents *acting together*, or *doing something together*. This is to be distinguished from what might be called "group action" in a technical sense – one that involves a *group agent* who is the subject of the action in question.[8]

---

[6] Moran, *The Exchange of Words*, p. 34.   [7] Ibid.

[8] For an overview of recent issues around group agency, see Deborah Tollefsen, *Groups as Agents* (Cambridge: Polity Press, 2015). Tollefsen nicely describes the

Group agency, in this special sense, involves one agent (a group) doing something itself. Joint agency, in the sense intended here, involves two or more individual agents doing something together. It is controversial whether group agency exists, insofar as it is controversial whether group agents exist.[9] It should not be controversial, however, that joint agency exists. Joint action, or acting together, is ubiquitous. What is controversial, or at least substantively interesting, is how we should understand joint agency – i.e., how it should be theorized.[10]

Much of the recent literature in action theory has been concerned with just this issue, and there has been excellent progress. In fact, just as there are some standard features of speech act theory – a kind of consensus that frames the debates over details – there is likewise a good consensus regarding the nature of joint action, or at least its characteristic features. The following analysis of knowledge transmission in terms of joint agency intends to stay close to this consensus. Before getting to that, however, let's look at an important precursor to the idea that knowledge transmission involves a kind of joint agency between speaker and hearer.

The precursor I have in mind is the idea that testimonial knowledge, or at least *some* testimonial knowledge, involves a kind of *teamwork* between speaker and hearer. Thus, in earlier work, I drew an analogy between testimonial knowledge and scoring a goal in soccer:

consider an uncontroversial case of credit for success: Playing in a soccer game, Ted receives a brilliant, almost impossible pass, and then scores an

---

distinction between joint (or "shared") agency and group agency: "Some philosophers are interested in explaining the ways that individuals can share intentional states such as belief and intention. These accounts, then, serve as a foundation for a theory of shared agency. Other philosophers are interested in group agency, the ability of a group *itself* to engage in purposeful action" (p. 5).

[9] For some defenses of group agents and groups agency, see ibid.; Philip Pettit, "The Reality of Group Agents," in C. Mantzavinos, ed., *Philosophy of the Social Sciences* (Cambridge: Cambridge University Press, 2009), pp. 67–91; and Christian List and Philip Pettit, *Group Agency: The Possibility, Design, and Status of Corporate Agents* (New York: Oxford University Press, 2011).

[10] One theoretical option here is that an adequate account of joint agency (in the intended sense) requires the admission of group agency (in the intended sense). The present point is that this is just that – one theoretical option. Recognizing the target phenomenon does not require it.

easy goal as a result ... My claim here, of course, is that the ... case is relevantly analogous to knowledge by expert testimony.[11]

The same analogy between testimonial knowledge and teamwork in sports appears in Sosa:

Compare the quarterback who shares the credit for his team's touchdown with the receiver, with the offensive lineman, especially those who made some crucial protective plays, etc. His touchdown pass depends importantly on him, it is true; but it also depends crucially on the work of others ... This I suggest as the right model for understanding how a belief might be apt even when it is more creditable to the testifier than to the recipient.[12]

And the same idea is developed at length by Adam Green in *The Social Contexts of Intellectual Virtue: Knowledge as a Team Achievement*:

Knowledge can be, and in the case of testimony is, akin to a team sport ... The skill that explains a given cognitive success ... often cannot be accounted for without including the skills of the testifier. Consider parallel credit attributions in soccer. There is a great difference between, on the one hand, scoring a goal as a result of breaking away on one's own and outfoxing the

---

[11] John Greco, "The Nature of Ability and the Purpose of Knowledge," *Philosophical Issues*, 17 (2007): 64–65. See also *Achieving Knowledge: A Virtue-Theoretic Account of Epistemic Normativity* (Cambridge: Cambridge University Press, 2010); and "A (Different) Virtue Epistemology," *Philosophy and Phenomenological Research* 85, 1 (2012): 1–26.

[12] Ernest Sosa, *Knowing Full Well* (Princeton, NJ: Princeton University Press, 2011), p. 28. Sosa makes a similar point, but this time in terms of group competence: "A quarterback may throw a touchdown pass, for example, thus exercising a competence. But this individual competence is only one part of a broader competence, seated in the whole offensive team, that more fully explains the successful touchdown pass, the apt performance of that quarterback. The pass receiver's competence may be crucial, for example, along with the individual competences of the offensive linesmen, and so on. If we think of animal knowledge as apt belief, and of belief as apt when correct attributably to a competence, then the fullest credit often belongs to a group, even a motley group. Seated in the group collectively is a competence whose complex exercise leads through testimonial links to the correctness of one's present belief. The correctness of one's belief is still attributable in part to a competence seated in oneself individually, but the credit that one earns will then be partial at best. The quarterback's pass derives from his competence, but its great success, its being a touchdown pass manifests more fully the team's competence. Similarly for one's testimony-derived belief." Ernest Sosa, *A Virtue Epistemology: Apt Belief and Reflective Knowledge*, vol. I (Oxford: Oxford University Press, 2007), pp. 94–95.

defense all by oneself and, on the other hand, scoring on a set play off of a corner kick.[13]

I still think that this basic idea is right: teamwork in sports is indeed analogous to what goes on in (at least some) testimonial knowledge; the former provides a "model" for understanding the latter, the two are "akin" to each other. In Section 3.1.3, I develop this general idea in two ways. First, I argue that the idea is true of one *kind* of testimonial knowledge, or one *way* of coming to know on the basis of testimony. That is, it is true of our target phenomenon in this book – the transmission of knowledge. Second, I propose that the category of joint agency is just what we need to explicate the analogy – to say more precisely in *what way* the transmission of knowledge is akin to teamwork. In fact, it is plausible that the category of joint agency can be used to analyze the concept of teamwork itself. That is, it is plausible that "teamwork" is just another word for "acting together" or "doing something together"; i.e., for the kind of cooperative activity that the category of joint agency intends to theorize.

Our next task, then, is to turn to the category of joint agency, and to show how it can be employed to theorize knowledge transmission.

3.1.3 Joint Agency and the Transmission of Knowledge

Suppose that two people are walking to the same restaurant at the same time, although neither is aware of what the other is doing.[14] This is compatible with the two persons walking side by side. Now imagine two people who are walking to the restaurant *together*. In this case, the two share an intention to walk to the restaurant together, and they share the knowledge that such an intention exists between them. This latter case is an example of *joint agency*.[15]

---

[13] Adam Green, *The Social Contexts of Intellectual Virtue: Knowledge as a Team Achievement* (London: Routledge, 2017), p. 14. See also his "Deficient Testimony is Deficient Teamwork," *Episteme* 11, 2 (2014): 213–227.

[14] See Margaret Gilbert, "Walking Together: A Paradigmatic Social Phenomenon," *Midwest Studies in Philosophy* 15, 1 (1990): 1–14.

[15] For a helpful overview, see Abraham Sesshu Roth, "Shared Agency," in Edward N. Zalta, ed., *Stanford Encyclopedia of Philosophy* (2011), available at: https://plato.stanford.edu/entries/shared-agency.

There are various accounts of joint agency in the literature, but there is broad agreement about its characteristic features.[16] First, and as already suggested, joint agency involves a "shared intention" on the part of the joint actors. That is, the participants in joint agency intend their participation, and understand their action, as something that they are doing together.[17]

A second characteristic feature of joint agency is that it involves what Michael Bratman calls "sub-plans."[18] If we are to do something together, such as walk to the restaurant, we must have some plan for carrying that action out together. For example, we are not walking together if you decide to take one route to the restaurant and I decide to take another. Bratman makes the point as follows:

In shared intention there will be a tendency to conform to a norm of compatibility of the relevant sub-plans of each. This is tied to the coordinating role of shared intention. If I intend that we go to NYC by driving, and you intend that we go by train, we have a problem. We will normally try to resolve that problem by making adjustments in one or both of these sub-plans, perhaps by way of bargaining ... each not only intends the shared activity, but also intends that this shared activity proceed by way of sub-plans of the participants that mesh in the sense that they are corealizable.[19]

---

[16] I will talk in terms of "characteristic features" so as to stay neutral regarding which features are *definitional* or *essential* of joint agency. The present discussion avoids such disputes by noting several features that are widely agreed to be characteristic of joint agency, at least in the sense of being typical or common. This will put me in a position to argue, below, that the transmission of knowledge involves joint agency, by arguing that transmission shares all of the characteristic features of joint agency. Importantly, that argument goes through even if not all of our characteristic features are essential features.

[17] In this regard, John Searle talks about "we intentions" and Christopher Kutz talks about "participatory intentions." In each case, the guiding idea is that joint agency involves some kind of special intention on the part of the joint actors, and that this marks an essential difference between acting together and acting individually. See Christopher Kutz, "Acting Together," *Philosophy and Phenomenological Research* 61, 1 (2000): 1–31; John Searle, "Collective Intentions and Actions," in Philip R. Cohen, Jerry Morgan, and Martha Pollack, eds., *Intentions in Communication* (Cambridge, MA: MIT Press, 1990), pp. 401–415.

[18] Michael E. Bratman, "Shared Cooperative Activity," *Philosophical Review* 101, 2 (1992): 327–341.

[19] Michael E. Bratman, "Shared Agency," in C. Mantzavinos, ed., *Philosophy of the Social Sciences: Philosophical Theory and Scientific Practice* (New York: Cambridge University Press, 2009), p. 48.

A third characteristic feature of joint agency is that it is *interactive*, in the sense that, if we are acting together, what I do in some sense depends on what you do, and what you do depends on what I do. For example, if we are walking together and one of us speeds up the pace, the other must speed up the pace as well. Likewise, it would be inappropriate for you to walk at a pace that I can't maintain. Gilbert puts the point as follows:

If Jack and Sue are indeed going for a walk together, and Jack has apparently drawn ahead without noticing what is happening, we can imagine Sue taking action in various ways. She might call out "Jack!" with a degree of impatience. She might catch up with him and then say, somewhat critically, "You are going to have to slow down! I can't keep up with you ... [This] suggests that Jack has, in effect, an obligation to notice and to act (an obligation Sue has also) ... each has a right to the other's attention and corrective action.[20]

As Bratman writes, in joint activity, "each is committed to, and appropriately responsive to, the coherent and effective interweaving of the ... agency of one another."[21]

Finally, joint agency involves a kind of interdependence – if we are doing something together, then neither of us can do the very same thing alone, or at least not in just the same way. Put differently, in joint agency each of the joint actors is doing some of the work of the joint action, doing his or her part in it. Suppose we are painting a house together. We are not really doing that together if I am doing all the painting. The point is less obvious in the case of walking to the restaurant together, but it still holds. Thus, I can't walk *with* you unless you do your part in responding to my interactions, or at least staying within the parameters of pace and path that I can manage.[22]

---

[20] Gilbert, "Walking Together," p. 3. Gilbert clarifies that she does not have in mind moral rights and obligations here. Rather, she thinks that such rights and obligations are generated by the joint agency itself: ..."if I am right, people out on a walk can *for that reason* be expected to recognize certain responsibilities and rights" (p. 4). Again, "It is doubtful whether the core obligations and entitlements in question are moral obligations and entitlements. At the same time, they are not merely a matter of prudence or self-interest. Importantly, they seem to be a direct function of the fact of going for a walk together" (p. 6). We need not further elaborate, or endorse, this aspect of Gilbert's view for present purposes. Here, I mean only to highlight the more general point that joint action has an interactive dimension.

[21] Bratman, "Shared Agency," p. 49.   [22] Gilbert, " Walking Together."

With these ideas in place, we are now in a position to argue that knowledge transmission essentially involves a kind of joint agency between hearer and speaker. First, the transmission of knowledge involves a communicative exchange, and it is plausible that communication in general involves the kinds of shared intention, shared understanding, and cooperation between speaker and hearer that are characteristic of joint agency.[23] Thus, in any communicative exchange, the speaker intends to be understood by the audience, and the audience understands that this is the speaker's intention. Moreover, speaker and hearer cooperate so as to achieve the intended result, each depending on the other to make appropriate contributions (communicative and interpretive) to the exchange.

In the case of knowledge transmission, however, joint agency goes beyond what is required for communication in general. Specifically, the transmission of knowledge involves the shared intention to impart relevant information. Thus, S transmits knowledge that p to H, on the account put forward above, only if S intends to inform H that p, H understands and shares this intention, and the two successfully cooperate so as to execute their shared intention successfully.

These considerations suggest a substantive account of knowledge transmission as follows:

(KT) Knowledge that p is transmitted from a speaker S to a hearer H just in case S successfully tells H that p.

And *that* happens just in case: (1) S knows that p; (2) S asserts that p with the intention of sharing knowledge that p with H; (3) H understands and shares S's intention; (4) S and H act jointly so as to bring about their shared intention (i.e., so as to "consummate" the speech act in condition 2).

By way of elaboration, the reference to joint action in condition 4 suggests that transmission need not be constituted by a "one-off" speech act; that is, an episodic or isolated assertion. Rather, there

---

[23] As is forcefully argued by Herbert H. Clark in *Using Language* (Cambridge: Cambridge University Press, 1996). Thanks to Deborah Tollefsen for informing me of Clark's work and its wide reception in linguistics and cognitive psychology. However, my own argument does not require Clark's thesis that all linguistic communication involves joint action. Rather, the point is that the speech act of *telling* does. Neither would Clark's more general thesis be sufficient for my argument, as will appear immediately below.

might be an integrated series of moves by both hearer and speaker aimed at pulling off the shared intention of passing along knowledge. That is, transmission might look like other extended joint action, and in fact often does.

For example, it is not uncommon for a hearer to ask a speaker for clarification, to redirect the speaker to a different question, to ask for some important detail or elaboration, or even to ask the speaker for her reasons. Likewise, it is not uncommon for a speaker to ask a hearer about what more specifically she needs to know, to provide the background information needed to make something else understood, or to redirect the hearer to a different question altogether. In all of these ways, and in others as well, testimonial exchanges are often more complicated than what is typically represented in the literature on testimony. This is important, because the false paradigm of testimony as involving a one-off assertion masks the extent of cooperation that is often involved in a speaker transmitting knowledge to a hearer. It is important to note, in this regard, that even in cases in which knowledge transmission *is* underwritten by a one-off assertion, this is against the background of shared intentions and common understanding in which speaker and hearer stand ready to cooperate as needed for a successful act of telling to be "consummated." So even when extended cooperation is not necessary, the potential for it is there if needed.

Also by way of elaboration, some further comments on clauses 2 through 4 are in order. Specifically, clause 2 refers to the speaker's intention to "share knowledge that p with H," and clauses 3 and 4 refer back to that intention. As suggested above, the intention could be variously characterized as the intention to "inform H that p," "let H know that p," or "give H to know that p." The reason that some such characterization is needed is to distinguish knowledge transmission from other ways that one might come to know via testimony. It is now commonplace in the literature, for example, that a hearer can come to know that the speaker has an alto voice, basing this on the *tone* of her testimony rather than its *content*.[24] But this would not be a case of telling, or of transmitting knowledge in the intended sense. Likewise, a hearer might come to know that a speaker is angry (or that she is talking, or that she is Irish), not by way of asserted content, but by

---

[24] Cf. Lackey, *Learning from Words*.

way of acquiring information that is otherwise encoded in the testimony offered.

There are also cases in which coming to know by testimony *does* exploit the content of what the speaker says, but again not in a way that constitutes knowledge transmission in the sense intended. There are two main cases of this. The first is Anscombe's case of the mistaken liar. In that case, one knows that the speaker will lie on the question whether *p*, but also that he is mistaken whether *p*. One may calculate, then, that since S testifies that *p* is true, *p* is true. As Anscombe points out, there is some sense in which one believes what S says "on the strength of his saying it," but this will not amount to knowledge transmission in the sense intended above.[25] This is explained, in part, by the fact that the speaker has no intention to share knowledge that *p* with the hearer, and, *ipso facto*, the hearer does not share that intention.

The second kind of case is more ubiquitous. Namely, there are all the more typical cases where coming to know from testimony is an instance of knowledge *generation* rather than knowledge *transmission*. Here, we can look back to cases presented in Chapters 1 and 2. For example, recall the case of the police investigator, where the speaker may be characterized as an "uncooperative" witness, and therefore precisely *not* holding the intention to share knowledge with her audience. But even in cases where a witness does have that intention, it will not (or should not) be shared by the investigator, and so clauses 3 and 4 will not be satisfied.

In fact, we should understand the account in such a way that clause 4 *could not* be satisfied by speakers and hearers in uncooperative contexts – that is, contexts in which an expectation of cooperation is inappropriate. Specifically, clause 4 should be understood as requiring that S and H *act appropriately* so as to bring about their shared intention, and this is impossible, given the norms that govern uncooperative contexts. As was argued in Chapter 2, and will be further elaborated in Chapter 4, the norms that govern testimonial exchanges in cooperative and non-cooperative contexts are for principled reasons different. Relevant to present purposes, the kind of trust that is appropriate in the context of information distribution (and so for

---

[25] G.E.M Anscombe, "What Is It to Believe Someone?" in *Faith in a Hard Ground: Essays on Religion, Philosophy and Ethics* (Charlottesville, VA: Imprint Academic Philosophy Documentation Center, 2008), p. 4. Anscombe attributes the example to Mary Geach.

knowledge transmission) is inappropriate in contexts of information acquisition.

Finally, I want to consider an objection to our claim that knowledge transmission involves the kind of shared intention characteristic of joint action. Specifically, even if a speaker has the intention of telling a hearer that p, the hearer cannot be said to "share" that very intention, because the hearer is not the one doing the telling. Likewise, even if S intends to "let H know that p," it could not be that H shares that very intention, insofar as H is not the one letting know.

In reply, it is important to note that "telling" (in the sense of "letting know") has the same ambiguity as "promising," "betting," and "passing a ball." In one sense of each word or phrase, it refers to the individual action of an individual actor. In another sense, however, each refers to a joint activity involving a shared intention, common understanding, etc. The distinction is easy to see in the case of passing a ball. On the one hand, there is Brady's individual action of throwing the ball, which he could do himself by throwing into a practice net. On the other hand, there is "passing the ball" in the sense of *completing a pass*, something that Brady and Gronkowski do together. In this sense, if Gronkowski does not catch the ball, then Brady was *trying* to pass the ball to Gronkowski but didn't.

The promising and betting examples are important, because they demonstrate a more general pattern in (a class of) speech acts that the present argument means to exploit. That is, there is an *individual action* sense and a *joint action* sense of "making a bet" and "making a promise." Moreover, a closer analysis of betting, for example, brings out that the joint action meaning is plausibly the more central one. Thus, I haven't "really" made a bet until you accept it. Likewise, I have not really made a promise, and incurred its attendant obligations, until you accept it. Just as one can refuse a bet, one can refuse a promise.

Likewise, I can say in frustration: "I tried to tell you that!" The implication is that I tried but failed. That wouldn't make sense if the single actor meaning was the only one. And again, it is plausible that the single actor meaning is parasitic on the joint action meaning. That is the real takeaway, it seems to me, of the relevant speech act theory. But the present argument does not need that stronger point. Rather, it is sufficient that there exists the joint action meaning of "telling," on the analogy with a joint action meaning of "betting" and "promising." It is in this sense that, in cases of knowledge transmission, speaker and hearer share the intention *that S tells H that* p, or *that S shares knowledge with H that* p.

3.1.4 Is the Account Circular?

On the present account, then, the joint agency that is essential to knowledge transmission inherits its shared intention from the speech act of telling. Thus, the speech act of *telling* is characterized by the intention of *sharing knowledge* with the hearer. For the speech act of telling to be successful, the hearer must understand and share the speaker's intention. In sum, the transmission of knowledge is constituted by a specific kind of joint agency, which is in turn constituted by a successful speech act of telling, both of which include the intention that the speaker share knowledge with the hearer.

This intentional structure might raise a worry about any substantive theory of knowledge that invokes KT. The worry is that such a theory, via KT, will necessarily employ the concept of *knowledge*, thereby making the theory circular or otherwise uninformative. For example, any substantive account of *coming to know* that invokes KT will thereby employ the concept of *sharing knowledge*, which is too close to the target concept of *coming to know*. Likewise, for any substantive account of *knowledge*: Any account of knowledge that employs KT will employ the concept of *knowledge*, and so there will be flat-out circularity.

This kind of worry can be addressed by recursive definition. Here we take a page from Alvin Goldman in his now classic paper, "What Is Justified Belief?"[26] There, Goldman defends a theory of justification that includes (1) a non-epistemic base clause, characterizing justification in terms of reliable processes; and (2) a recursive clause describing justification via a conditionally reliable process, such as inference or memory. Very roughly: A belief is justified if *either* (1) it is formed by a reliable process, or (2) it is formed by a conditionally reliable process that takes only justified beliefs as inputs. As is typical for a recursive definition, the base clause characterizes the target concept in an appropriately informative way. In the present case, *justified belief* is characterized entirely in non-epistemic terms. The base clause thereby makes

---

[26] Alvin Goldman, "What Is Justified Belief?" in George Pappas, ed., *Justification and Knowledge* (Boston, MA: D. Reidel., 1979), pp. 1–25.

the target concept available for use in a recursive clause. Together, the two clauses say essentially this: Take any belief that is formed by a reliable process. That belief is justified. Now, take any belief that is formed by a conditionally reliable process, and feed in justified beliefs as inputs. The resulting output belief is also justified. If we add a closure clause to the effect that these are the *only* ways for a belief to be justified, we end up with an informative account of justified belief.

This same strategy is available here. In the present case, a base clause defines knowledge generation in informative terms. This could be done in any number of ways, depending on one's substantive theory of knowledge. For purposes of illustration, I here use a simple process reliabilist view.

So, here is our base clause:

Generation: S knows that *p* if S's believing the truth regarding *p* is attributable to S's own reliable cognitive processes.

Here is our recursive clause:

Transmission: H knows that *p* if, for some speaker S, S and H satisfy the conditions specified in KT.

And here is the closure clause:

S knows that *p only if* S knows that *p* by Generation or Transmission.

Putting these clauses together, we get an informative account of knowledge. S knows that *p just in case* S knows either by generation or transmission, where each of these is understood, via recursive definition, in non-epistemic terms.[27]

3.2 The Role of Trust in Testimonial Knowledge

The recent literature in the epistemology of testimony has been much concerned with the role of trust in testimonial knowledge. More exactly: What is the *epistemic* role of trust, if any, in testimonial knowledge? This latter formulation emphasizes that the question is epistemological. That is, the question is whether trust plays some role, or makes some contribution, that is *epistemically* important or interesting. In this regard, some kinds of contribution would be clearly

---

[27] Chapter 6 considers a third route to knowledge.

not interesting. For example, suppose it turns out that trust is necessary for human beings to achieve some minimal level of psychological development, and that this minimal development is necessary for knowledge in general. Then it would turn out that trust is *psychologically* necessary for testimonial knowledge as well, but that would fall short of being epistemically interesting. Or suppose that some degree of trust is psychologically necessary for language acquisition. Then, again, trust would be psychologically necessary for testimonial knowledge, but in a way that is not interesting to epistemology *per se*.

Here is another way that trust might play a role in testimonial knowledge, but in a way that might still fall short of being epistemically interesting. Suppose that knowledge in general requires some kind of reliable process, and that a hearer's trusting the speaker contributes to the reliability of testimonial exchanges. For example, suppose that the hearer's trusting the speaker makes it more likely that the speaker will tell the truth.[28] In that case, trust would be "epistemically important" in a sense, but again not in a way that makes trust itself especially interesting. In effect, trusting the speaker would be just one way of fulfilling otherwise agreed-upon conditions for knowledge.[29]

This last point raises a question: *What would it take* for trust to be epistemically important or interesting? More specifically, what would it take for trust to make an epistemically interesting contribution to testimonial knowledge? So far, we have seen that it would take more than that trust is *psychologically* necessary for testimonial knowledge. Moreover, it would take more than that trust allows the knower to satisfy some otherwise agreed-upon condition for testimonial knowledge. In the latter case, trust would be contingently related to testimonial knowledge, so to speak, but would not be related to testimonial knowledge in any essential way. This suggests that "what it would take" for trust to be epistemically important is that trusting the speaker is somehow essentially related to testimonial knowledge. And this, in fact, is what some trust theorists at least seem to be claiming. That is,

---

[28] See Faulkner, *Knowledge on Trust*, for an argument to this effect.

[29] Here I have in mind Jennifer Lackey's objection to theories on which trust contributes to reliability and thereby explains justification. Lackey writes: "Thus, while the addition of [a reliability condition] places the Trust View on the epistemological map, trust itself turns out to be epistemically superfluous." Lackey, *Learning from Words*, p. 238.

they seem to be claiming that trust *itself* (rather than evidence or some other standard epistemic condition) is somehow essential to testimonial knowledge.[30]

This interpretation is in line with Lackey's dilemma for the "interpersonal view of testimony (IVT)," including trust theories. Lackey writes:

> Thus, we have seen that there is a general dilemma confronting the proponent of the IVT: either the view of testimony in question is genuinely interpersonal but not epistemological, or it is genuinely epistemological but not interpersonal. In the former case, the IVT will be novel but useless for an epistemology of testimony; in the latter case, the IVT will be epistemologically useful, but not interestingly different from its so-called competitors. The bottom line is this: interpersonal features cannot create justification or warrant epistemologically ex nihilo and hence there is no room for a genuinely interpersonal view in the epistemology of testimony.[31]

That is, there is no room for a view that makes interpersonal relations (such as trust) *themselves* essential to testimonial justification and knowledge, as opposed to underwriting some more properly epistemic condition, such as reliability, or sensitivity, or evidence, etc.

The theoretical categories invoked in this chapter, and the substantive account of knowledge transmission that results, provide resources for defending trust theories against Lackey's dilemma. In short, the argument is that knowledge transmission essentially involves joint agency, and joint agency essentially involves trust. Here is a further elaboration of the argument.

1. Knowledge transmission is an important epistemological phenomenon, and distinct from knowledge generation. In particular, knowledge transmission is not reducible to knowledge generation.
2. Knowledge transmission essentially involves joint agency. Specifically, knowledge transmission essentially involves the kind of cooperation and coordination between speaker and hearer that is the hallmark of joint agency.

---

[30] For some examples of trust theories, see Welbourne, *The Community of Knowledge*; John Hardwig, "The Role of Trust in Knowledge," *Journal of Philosophy* 88, 12 (1991): 693–708; Hinchman, "Telling as Inviting to Trust"; Faulkner, *Knowledge on Trust*.
[31] Lackey, *Learning from Words*, pp. 239–240.

3. Joint agency essentially involves trust between the cooperating agents.

Therefore,

4. Knowledge transmission essentially involves trust (2, 3).

Therefore,

5. An important and irreducible epistemological phenomenon essentially involves trust (1, 4).

Premise 1 of the argument was established in Chapter 2. Premise 2 was established in Section 3.1. The remaining issue, then, concerns premise 3. But that premise is easily established by employing standard accounts of trust in the relevant literatures. More exactly, we may take some standard accounts of trust and use those to construct a logically stronger account that can be used to support premise 3. That is, we may construct an account of trust that is objectionable, if at all, only because it is too strong. If, on that account, premise 3 is vindicated, then premise 3 would also be vindicated by weaker accounts.[32]

One feature of trust that is often noted is that it involves a relation of dependence – the trusting agent must somehow depend on that which is trusted. Some accounts invoke a general notion of dependence here, so as to make the account consistent with depending on an instrument or some other kind of non-person.[33] Other accounts have it that trust is essentially *interpersonal*, i.e. involving dependence on another person.[34] Since we are building a strong account, we will adopt the interpersonal view. Some accounts add that trust necessarily involves an expectation of success on the part of the person trusting. That is, trust involves the expectation that the trusted person will actually do what they are being depended on to do – that the trusted person is *dependable*, so to speak.[35]

---

[32] For a different argument that joint action essentially involves trust, see Hans Bernhard Schmid, "Trying to Act Together: The Structure and Role of Trust in Joint Action," in B. Kobow, H.B. Schmid, and M. Schmitz, eds., *The Background of Institutional Reality* (Dordrecht: Springer, 2013), pp. 37–55.

[33] Cf. Carolyn McLeod, "Trust," in Edward N. Zalta, ed., *The Stanford Encyclopedia of Philosophy* (Fall 2015 edition), available at: https://plato .stanford.edu/archives/fall2015/entries/trust.

[34] Ibid.

[35] For example, see Karen Jones, "Trust as an Affective Attitude," *Ethics* 107, 1 (1996): 4–25.

We may add other features to our account, making it even stronger. For example, we may add that, although the trusting person must have an expectation of success, there is no guarantee of success. A closely related feature is even stronger: In cases of trust, the trusted person does not have control over whether the trusted person fulfills expectations. This last clause is necessary, it is argued, to accommodate the idea that trust involves vulnerability to the person being trusted. Finally, one might think that trust involves depending on another person to do something *that one could not do oneself*. This seems too strong. For example, it seems that I can trust you to stop and buy groceries for dinner, even if I could stop and buy them myself. Nevertheless, we will accommodate the idea. We are looking to construct a logically strong account of trust, and it will not undermine our purposes if the account is too strong.

The next thing to see is that joint agency involves all of these features, and therefore entails even our strong notion of trust. More specifically, the joint agency involved in the transmission of knowledge has all of these features. Thus, in the context of knowledge transmission, the hearer depends on the speaker to do her part in sharing knowledge, and the speaker depends on the hearer to do his part. Moreover, each has the appropriate expectations of success associated with their shared intention. This follows from a point about action in general: that trying to ø entails some expectation that one will ø. Likewise, in cases of joint agency, and including the joint agency involved in the transmission of knowledge, there is no guarantee that the speaker will prove dependable (or that the hearer will, either), in part because the hearer does not have control over the speaker playing her part (or the speaker over the hearer playing hers).[36] Finally, in all cases of joint agency, the joint action is not something that a participating agent could have done herself. This follows from the fact that joint actions are individuated by their

---

[36] One might argue that in some cases of knowledge transmission the hearer does have control over the speaker. For example, perhaps the hearer has put a gun to the speaker's head. This sort of case raises issues about the nature of control. Accordingly, we may address such cases as follows. Either the gun to the head (or some such circumstance) places the speaker in the hearer's control or it does not. If it does not, then the "no control" clause remains satisfied. If it does, then we can treat the hearer's coming to know as a case of knowledge generation rather than knowledge transmission. That is, if H controls whether S tells the truth, then H can come to know by means of evidence that S is telling the truth.

shared intentions, and an individual cannot share an intention with herself.[37]

In conclusion, the familiar anti-reductionist claim that testimonial knowledge essentially involves trust is vindicated, at least in qualified form. The qualification is that *some* testimonial knowledge essentially involves trust; that is, the testimonial knowledge that is underwritten by knowledge transmission. In that sense, the trust between speaker and hearer that is essentially involved in the transmission of knowledge has *epistemic significance* as opposed to mere psychological significance. Moreover, these claims are vindicated in the context of an anti-reductionist account of testimonial knowledge. In Chapter 2, we argued that knowledge transmission is irreducible to knowledge generation because the norms governing the former are distinct from and irreducible to the norms governing the latter. This yielded an anti-reductionist account of testimonial knowledge in general, in that not all testimonial knowledge can be understood in terms of non-testimonial generative sources of knowledge, or even generative sources at all. Insofar as the joint action constitutive of knowledge transmission is irreducible to individual action, we have a second reason that knowledge transmission is irreducible to knowledge generation, and that therefore testimonial knowledge is irreducible to non-testimonial knowledge.[38]

---

[37] One might insist that an agent can share intentions with herself, perhaps by invoking the notion of past and future selves. But these kinds of case are controversial, and so not clearly relevant to cases of joint agency and knowledge transmission. But if they are relevant, then it is plausible that one can transmit knowledge to a future self. For example, through a diary, or some other "note to self."

[38] In fact, things are more complicated than this, in that it is an open possibility that some knowledge generation is constituted by joint agency. (This possibility is endorsed in Chapter 5.) More carefully, then, anti-reductionism about knowledge transmission is entailed if the specific *kind* of joint agency that is constitutive of knowledge transmission is irreducible to the kind of activity that underwrites knowledge generation. Whether joint action in general is reducible to individual action in general is a controversial question. According to Roth, reductivists include Michael Bratman, "Shared Intention," *Ethics* 104, 1 (1993): 97–113; *Faces of Intention: Selected Essays on Intention and Agency* (Cambridge: Cambridge University Press, 1999). Cf. Roth, "Shared Agency."

4 | *Social Norms and Social Sensibilities*

Chapter 2 presented a framework for thinking about the transmission of knowledge and about testimonial knowledge more generally. One central feature of the framework is that it distinguishes two ways of coming to know: by generation (e.g., via traditional generative sources such as perception and reasoning), and by transmission (e.g., via testimony from someone else who knows).[1] Another central feature of the framework is that one may come to know via testimony in either of these two ways. Thus, testimony sometimes generates knowledge, as reductionists suggest, via the familiar generative source of inductive reasoning. But testimony also serves as a vehicle for the transmission of knowledge, where this second way of coming to know is understood as a distinct epistemic phenomenon. A third feature of the framework, then, is that it is anti-reductionist about transmission; that is, the framework entails that the transmission of knowledge is not reducible to the generation of knowledge.[2] Anti-reductionism about transmission is achieved by understanding generation in terms of the norms associated with the acquisition of quality information for an epistemic community, and understanding transmission in terms of the norms associated with the distribution of quality information within that community. Because the norms governing acquisition and distribution answer to different purposes, it is implausible that either should be reducible to the other. In particular, it is implausible that the norms

---

[1] The framework leaves open whether there are non-testimonial means of transmission.
[2] The framework is consistent with, but does not entail, anti-reductionism about testimony as a generative source (see Chapter 1, p. 15). However, the framework does entail anti-reductionism about testimonial knowledge in general. That is because the defining thesis of anti-reductionism about testimonial knowledge is that not *all* testimonial knowledge can be reduced to other kinds of knowledge. But if testimonial knowledge resulting from transmission cannot be so reduced, then the more general anti-reductionist thesis is thereby entailed (see Chapter 1, p. 14 and Chapter 2, p. 43).

governing the distribution of quality information should duplicate the quality control imposed by the norms governing information acquisition.[3]

More generally, anti-reductionism about the transmission of knowledge has several important motivations, and each of these is captured by our framework as well. First and foremost, anti-reductionism relieves the hearer of the usual burdens associated with coming to know, thereby accommodating the important insight that testimony allows for an epistemic division of labor within epistemic communities. In particular, anti-reductionism relieves the hearer of the *evidential* burdens that would have to be in place if something like a reductionist picture were correct. For on the standard reductionist picture, testimonial knowledge is a kind of inductive knowledge, and therefore requires the same quality of evidence that is necessary for inductive knowledge in general. For closely related reasons, anti-reductionism about knowledge transmission is an important anti-skeptical resource. In short, the division of labor that anti-reductionism affords, precisely by lowering the burdens for transmitted knowledge, allows us to better account for the full range of knowledge that we think we have. Finally, and in related fashion, anti-reductionism about transmission allows us to explain a range of cases that would be otherwise mysterious. In particular, and as we have seen in Chapters 1 and 2, anti-reductionism can explain how small children can learn from their caretakers and, more generally, how evidentially impoverished hearers can nevertheless learn from speakers who know.[4]

Anti-reductionism about knowledge transmission, therefore, has strong motivations. But the position also comes with its own problems, and precisely because it has the anti-evidentialist features reviewed above. In this chapter, I want to focus on two problems along these lines. Each problem can be put in the form of a question.

[3] Chapter 3 offers a second reason why knowledge transmission is irreducible to knowledge generation; namely, that the kind of joint agency constitutive of knowledge transmission is irreducible to the kind of activity that underwrites knowledge generation (p. 67)

[4] Our present framework has the added benefit of explaining why, in some cases of testimony from a knowledgeable speaker, the hearer is nevertheless *not* in a position to know. This result is achieved because, according to the framework, not all testimonial transactions are governed by norms associated with information distribution.

The first is this: If the hearer's evidence does not explain the reliability of a testimonial exchange, then what does? The problem is pressing because we assume that knowledge in general requires de facto reliability, broadly understood.[5] In other words, we assume that knowledge must *in fact* be reliably formed. In the case of knowledge transmitted by testimony, we assume that the testimonial exchange must be reliable. But what, on an anti-reductionist account, explains why the testimonial exchanges that underwrite knowledge transmission *are* reliable? Notice that on the reductionist picture, we have a fairly straightforward answer to the question. Specifically, testimonial knowledge requires that the hearer *have good evidence* that the testimonial exchange is reliable. Interpreted strongly enough, this entails that, in cases of testimonial knowledge, the testimonial exchange *is* reliable. Clearly, that strategy is unavailable for an anti-reductionist account of knowledge transmission. But if hearer evidence does not explain the reliability of the testimonial exchanges that underwrite transmission, then what does?

Here is a second problem: Assuming that the testimonial exchanges that underwrite knowledge transmission are in fact reliable, what accounts for the hearer's *awareness* of reliability? Again, the problem is pressing because we assume that, for knowledge in general, the knower must have some sense that her knowledge is reliably formed. For example, for perceptual knowledge, we assume that the knower must have some sense that relevant perceptual appearances are reliable. We need not be evidentialist about this – we need not understand the knower's awareness of reliability in terms of evidence for reliability. That route threatens skepticism in now familiar ways. Nevertheless, we do need some kind of explanation here. And if the explanation is not in terms of the knower's evidence, then what is the alternative explanation? In the case of knowledge transmitted by testimony: What accounts for the hearer's awareness of the reliability of the testimonial exchange?

Finally, I want to emphasize a "meta-problem" for an anti-reductionist account. Namely, such an account must address our first two problems without falling back into evidentialism about testimonial

---

[5] For present purposes, we can put aside substantive issues regarding how the reliability requirement on knowledge should be stated; for example, in terms of cognitive processes, methods, faculties, etc., or in terms of actual track record, modal profile, etc.

knowledge. For it is precisely the anti-evidentialist aspects of the present model that allow for its most attractive features. That is, it is only the anti-evidentialism that allows for the division of epistemic labor, the anti-skeptical resources, and the explanation of cases.

In the remainder of the chapter, I want to argue that we can make progress on these problems by invoking the notion of social norms, and the related notion of "social sensibilities." In short, I want to argue that the nature of social norms, and in particular the ways that social norms structure our social environments, helps to explain the reliability of the testimonial exchanges that underwrite the transmission of knowledge. Second, the ways in which we internalize social norms, and the ways that such norms thereby govern behavior, help to explain our sensitivity to the reliability of testimonial exchanges. Moreover, by invoking social norms and the sensibilities that they engender, we can address our two problems without falling back into an evidentialist or otherwise reductionist framework for understanding testimonial knowledge.

To be clear, the present idea is not that social norms and our social sensibilities explain reliability and our sensitivity to reliability all by themselves. Rather, the claim to be defended is that they contribute important parts to the picture. To this end, Section 4.1 of the chapter considers the nature of social norms as they are understood in the social sciences, and considers some of the ways that social norms operate in our social environments. Section 4.2 considers some of the ways that social norms interact with epistemic norms, and how the social norms that structure a social environment can have important epistemic consequences. Sections 4.3 and 4.4 return to the two problems for anti-reductionism that were set out above, and show how the resources in Sections 4.1 and 4.2 can be used to make progress in resolving them.

4.1 The Nature of Social Norms

Philip Pettit characterizes social norms in terms of three essential characteristics.[6] First, social norms describe de facto regularities in

---

[6] Philip Pettit, "Virtus Normativa: Rational Choice Perspectives," *Ethics* 100, 4 (1990): 725–755. In the discussion that follows, I am indebted to Peter Graham's exposition of Pettit in Peter Graham, "Epistemic Normativity and Social Norms," in David Henderson and John Greco, eds., *Epistemic Evaluation: Purposeful Epistemology* (Oxford: Oxford University Press, 2015),

behavior. As Pettit writes, "if a regularity is a norm in a society, then it must be a regularity in which people generally conform; lip service is not enough."[7] As Peter Graham writes, "social norms articulate what's *normal*, what's *usually* done."[8] Second, social norms are prescriptions as well as descriptions. Thus, Pettit writes, "if a regularity is a norm, then people in the society generally approve of conformity and disapprove of deviance."[9] Put differently, social norms carry with them some kind of felt obligation or normative force: "[people] may believe, for example, that everyone ought to conform, that conformity is an obligation of some sort."[10] And third, social norms are descriptive at least in part *because* they are prescriptive. That is, the patterns of approval and disapproval associated with a norm effectively motivate conformity to the norm.[11] As Graham writes, "A social norm is genuinely a norm when genuinely *normative*, when the general belief that it *ought* to be done *motivates* compliance, in one way or another … Social norms are regularities *because* norms, regularities because *normative*."[12]

Social norms "motivate compliance" in two major ways. First, people who inhabit a social space are generally aware of what social norms are in place, and of associated rewards and punishments. But another important feature of social norms is that they are *internalized* by at least much of the population that they describe and govern. That is, at least much of the population endorses the norms as their own. Graham explains the idea as follows:

When we internalize a norm, we find it intrinsically motivating; our preferences change. We conform because we think it's the right thing to do, because we are supposed to do it. We want to do it. We may even deeply value compliance. Many internalized norms even come to be in part "constitutive of the selfhood or identity of individual adherents." Internalization then leads to compliance as an ultimate end, and not just as a means to avoid punishment.[13]

---

pp. 247–273. As Graham explains, Pettit's account of social norms articulates a general consensus in the social sciences (Graham, "Epistemic Normativity and Social Norms," p. 249).

[7] Pettit, "Virtus Normativa," p. 728.
[8] Graham, "Epistemic Normativity and Social Norms," p. 250.
[9] Pettit, "Virtus Normativa," p. 728.   [10] Ibid.   [11] Ibid., p. 730.
[12] Graham, "Epistemic Normativity and Social Norms," p. 251.
[13] Ibid., p. 253. In this regard, Graham cites Samuel Bowles and Herbert Gintis, "The Origins of Human Cooperation," in Peter Hammerstein, ed., *The Genetic and Cultural Evolution of Cooperation* (Cambridge: MIT Press, 2003),

Again,

> When internalized, I conformed to the norm *because it's the right thing to do*, because I positively value compliance, not (normally or just) because of the consequences of my actions or because of my other aims or desires. Internalized norms are then experienced as categorical, as what must be done, and not simply as what we should do given other aims or desires.[14]

As such, social norms govern more than our behavior. Once internalized, they govern our beliefs, emotions and even our desires as well. Put differently, social norms help shape our "social sensibilities"; that is, our sensibilities regarding how things are *in fact* done in a relevant social space, and also about how things are *supposed to be* done.

Social norms are often associated with the fairly superficial customs that can distinguish one culture from another; for example, norms of dress and norm of etiquette. But in fact, social norms are ubiquitous – they partially structure our social environments at virtually every level. Consider, for example, the interpersonal norms governing parent–child relations. One such norm, presumably a moral norm, is that parents ought to ensure the safety of their children. Clearly, this norm is also a social norm. Thus, it is certainly a regularity that parents care for the safety of their children, and certainly conformity to the norm is widely approved and violation widely condemned. Moreover, the norm is widely internalized. It is true that parents who do not look after the safety of their children are punished in various ways, both legally and socially. But it is also true that most parents endorse the norm in any case, and are motivated to conform to it independently of concern for reward or punishment. Accordingly, this interpersonal and moral norm has all the characteristic features of a social norm. In most – perhaps all – communities, it is a social norm.

pp. 429–443; *A Cooperative Species: Human Reciprocity and Its Evolution* (Princeton, NJ: Princeton University Press, 2011), p. 169; and Seumas Miller, *Social Action: A Teleological Account* (Cambridge: Cambridge University Press, 2001), p. 139.

[14] Graham, "Epistemic Normativity and Social Norms." Graham cites Chandra Sripada and Stephen Stich, "A Framework for the Psychology of Norms," in Peter Carruthers, Stephen, Laurence & Stephen P. Stich, eds., *The Innate Mind, Volume 2: Culture and Cognition* (Oxford: Oxford University Press, 2006): 237–256; and Cristina Bicchieri, *The Grammar of Society: The Nature and Dynamics of Social Norms* (Cambridge: Cambridge University Press, 2006), p. 43.

In the same fashion, it is easy to see that social norms are operative at other levels of the social environment as well. It is commonplace, for example, that social norms are constitutive of various social roles, such as friend, spouse, or mentor.[15] Think of the various expectations that we have, with their associated patterns of approval and disapproval, regarding how friends are supposed to treat friends, for example. Likewise, institutional rules often overlap with social norms, as does much of positive law. For example, we clearly internalize various norms regarding how co-workers are supposed to do their job, as well as how professionals are supposed to treat their clients. And we clearly internalize much of positive law, such as prohibitions against theft and murder. Institutional rules and positive law, then, commonly operate as social norms.

4.2 The Epistemic Import of Social Norms

We may think of epistemic norms on the analogy of moral norms. Whereas moral norms are rules prescribing morally appropriate behavior and proscribing morally inappropriate behavior, epistemic norms are rules prescribing epistemically appropriate behavior and proscribing epistemically inappropriate behavior. Examples of moral norms include *Be kind to others* and *Do not do gratuitous harm*. Examples of epistemic norms include *Base your beliefs on good evidence* and *Do not believe everything you are told*. Are some epistemic norms also social norms? Clearly yes. That is, some epistemic norms also describe regularities in behavior, reflect patterns of approval and disapproval, and are internalized in such a way as to drive behavior. The epistemic norm that *you should not believe everything you are told* is a case in point. In general, people do not believe everything they are told, they disapprove of others who do (or who stray too far in that direction), and they have internalized the norm as their own. That is, people generally agree with that rule, they generally act accordingly, and they do so independently of concerns about reward and punishment. Likewise, for many other epistemic norms. Think, for example, of how we endorse various

---

[15] See Cristina Bicchieri, Ryan Muldoon, and Alessandro Sontuoso, "Social Norms," in Edward N. Zalta, ed., *The Stanford Encyclopedia of Philosophy* (Winter 2018 edition), available at: https://plato.stanford.edu/archives/wi n2018/entries/social-norms.

patterns of good reasoning, and how we proscribe against wishful thinking, hasty generalizations, self-serving thinking, and the like.[16]

At least many epistemic norms, then, are also social norms. Moreover, many other social norms have epistemic content.[17] For example, the so-called knowledge norm of assertion – *Assert only what you know* – is plausibly a social norm. This is more clearly the case if we understand the norm in a more qualified way; something like: *Don't confidently assert flat-out, without appropriate qualification, things that you don't know to be the case.* People generally do follow this rule. And we certainly disapprove when the rule is violated; we call people out for it, we criticize them for it. Many other social norms also have epistemic content. For example: *You should give people the benefit of the doubt*; and *Don't act rashly*. Plausibly, rules such as these, or at least some version of them, are widely followed, endorsed, and internalized. That is, they function as social norms.

Finally, many social norms lack epistemic content, but they have indirect epistemic consequences. Consider, for example, two norms that many of us try to instill in our children: *Don't talk to strangers* and *Respect your elders*. Neither of these norms is explicitly epistemic, but each has consequences in terms of shaping relationships and, in particular, shaping epistemic relationships. Pertinent to present purposes, the two norms have consequences regarding information flow: They influence how information gets distributed within the epistemic community, and therefore influence the transmission of knowledge. Interestingly, the primary function of these two norms is not epistemic. The primary function of the norm regarding strangers is to promote safety. The primary function of the norm regarding elders is practical or moral. But the strangers-norm effectively shuts down channels of

---

[16] Cf. Graham, "Epistemic Normativity and Social Norms"; and David Henderson and Peter Graham, "Epistemic Norms and the 'Epistemic Game' They Regulate: The Basic Structured Epistemic Costs and Benefits," *American Philosophical Quarterly* 54, 4 (2017): 367–382. The latter argue that, in general, epistemic norms are social norms: "epistemic norms, in the context of a group that produces a shared stock of beliefs, are not simply individually held rules and methods that guide individual inquiry, but importantly become, in ways that we will explore, *social norms* for the *production* and *maintenance* of this public good" (p. 368).

[17] Here I rely on Mona Simion's distinction between epistemic norms and norms with epistemic content. See her "No Epistemic Norm for Action," *American Philosophical Quarterly* 55, 3 (2018): 231–238.

communication and therefore information flow. And the elders-norm effectively opens up such channels. As such, both norms have consequences for the transmission of knowledge within the communities in which they operate.

The point is fairly obvious in the case of the two norms we have chosen for illustration. But many social norms have similar effects in more subtle ways. Think, for example, of how the social norms governing friendships, family relations, work relationships, and neighborhood affiliations all have consequences for who talks to who, who is trusted (or mistrusted), and even whose voices are heard (and not heard) in the first place. Feminist and critical theory have long made similar points about the social norms governing race relations and gender relations, as well as other social norms that structure patterns of trust and authority within a community.[18] Social norms, then, affect information flow in various ways. They affect information output (who gets to say what), information availability (who hears who), and information uptake (who is believed, once heard). Once again, the primary function or purpose of such norms need not be epistemic, and often they are not – far from it. Nevertheless, such norms have important epistemic consequences regarding the flow of information, and therefore the transmission of knowledge.[19]

In various ways, then, the social norms that help structure our social environments can have important effects on information flow. In this regard, we can make an analogy between testimonial knowledge and perceptual knowledge. Just as natural laws structure the physical environment so as to determine the flow of information from world to mind, social norms structure the social environment so as to determine the

---

[18] For example, see Patricia Hill Collins, Black *Feminist Thought: Knowledge, Consciousness, and the Politics of Empowerment* (London: Routledge, 2002); Miranda Fricker, *Epistemic Injustice: Power and the Ethics of Knowing* (Oxford: Oxford University Press, 2007); and José Medina, *The Epistemology of Resistance: Gender and Racial Oppression, Epistemic Injustice, and the Social Imagination* (New York: Oxford University Press, 2013). For an extended discussion that employs the information economy framework defended in this book, see Krista Hyde, "A Virtue-Theoretic Account of the Epistemic Effects of Marginalization," (PhD diss., Saint Louis University, 2017).

[19] Social norms plausibly have consequences for the production of knowledge as well as its transmission. But our topic here is knowledge transmission, and so that will be my focus.

flow of information from mind to mind.[20] The result is an environment that is contoured so as to include various "information channels" – information pathways that both enable and constrain the flow of information.

Continuing the analogy, both perceptual and testimonial channels can be more or less *reliable*. Likewise, we ourselves can be more or less reliable, depending on how our perceptual and social sensibilities interact with those channels.[21] And here we have resources for making progress on the two problems set out at the top of this chapter. First, the various ways in which social norms affect the social environment help to explain why particular testimonial exchanges are in fact reliable and therefore able to underwrite the transmission of knowledge. Second, our "social sensibilities" – i.e., our sensibilities regarding how things are done (and are supposed to be done) in a social space – help to explain our sensitivity to the reliability of different testimonial exchanges. Moreover, we shall see, neither explanation requires that we fall back into evidentialism or reductionism about testimonial knowledge.

4.3 Reliability without Evidence

What explains, in cases where knowledge does get transmitted, the reliability of the testimonial exchange that enables knowledge transmission? The question can be sharpened. Not all testimonial exchanges are reliable. Speakers are sometimes insincere. Speakers are sometimes incompetent. Hearers are sometimes gullible. Presumably, when testimonial exchanges are unreliable, they do not underwrite testimonial knowledge. So, what explains the reliability of testimonial exchanges when they do transmit knowledge? As we saw above, evidentialists have an answer for this question. That is because evidentialists require that, in cases of testimonial knowledge, the hearer has *good evidence* of reliability. If we interpret this requirement strongly enough, then it explains why, in cases of testimonial knowledge, the testimonial

---

[20] This is not meant to imply that social norms cannot also influence the flow of information from world to mind. Clearly they can, such as when such norms determine who is allowed to occupy what space.

[21] Further details regarding how, exactly, we are to understand the kind of reliability required for knowledge will be discussed in the Appendix. The argument that follows is supposed to be independent of those details.

exchange *is* reliable.[22] As we also saw above, this answer is not available on the present model. So, what is the alternative answer?

The present suggestion is that, in cases of knowledge transmission, the reliability of the testimonial exchange is at least partly explained by the social environment. More exactly, it is explained (in part) by the social norms that structure the social environment, and the ways that hearer and speaker sensibilities interact with those norms. Some examples will help to illustrate this general idea.

First, consider a typical exchange between a mom and her toddler: A toddler asks mom if he can have some milk, and mom tells toddler that there is milk in the refrigerator. Intuitively, such an exchange transmits knowledge, at least in normal circumstances. How might we explain the reliability of the exchange? For present purposes, put aside any evidence that a toddler might or might not have about mother sincerity and/or competence. The present point is that we can explain the reliability of the exchange without invoking any evidence of the sort. On the hearer side, we have a child who has internalized norms about who to ask (and not ask) for information, and about listening to his mother in general. On the speaker side, we have a mom who has internalized norms of care and concern for her child, and these entail that she tells the truth about such matters as whether there is milk in the refrigerator, at least in normal circumstances. If that is not enough to explain the reliability of the present exchange, we can add further factors in the environment. What would grandmother think if mom lied to her child about such a thing? What would the neighbors think? The point is, there is no need to invoke hearer evidence to explain why this exchange, on this subject and in these circumstances, is a perfectly reliable one.

Next, consider a typical exchange between close friends. Mary asks Hank whether he is going to the party, and Hank replies that he is. Intuitively, such an exchange transmits knowledge in normal circumstances. Once again, put aside any evidence that Mary might have about Hank's sincerity and competence on the matter. The point is not that Mary would not have such evidence, but that we don't need to

---

[22] Moreover, the strong interpretation is a plausible one. For, more generally, it is plausible that in cases of knowledge grounded in evidence, the evidence cannot be misleading. Accordingly, in cases of testimonial knowledge that is grounded in evidence, the evidence for reliability is not misleading.

invoke it. What might explain the reliability of the exchange, *other than* the hearer's evidence?

On the hearer side, we now have an adult who has internalized general moral and interpersonal norms about truth-telling, and who therefore expects people to tell the truth – both in general, and especially regarding fairly trivial matters such as whether one intends to go to a party. Over and above this, we have a friend who has internalized standard norms of friendship, and who is therefore disposed to trust what her friend tells her. On the speaker side, we have another adult who has likewise internalized relevant moral norms and friendship norms, and who is therefore disposed to tell his friend the truth. If that is not enough to explain the reliability of the exchange, consider other aspects of the social situation. What would be the consequences if Hank were to lie in such a situation? What would Mary think, or do? What would their other friends think or do? For that matter, what would people think if Mary did *not* trust her friend to the tell truth here? The social norms in place largely determine these matters as well.

Finally, consider a typical exchange between doctor and patient: A doctor examines her patient, and then tells him that his condition is common and that a particular treatment will alleviate his symptoms. Over and above any evidence that the patient might have regarding the doctor's sincerity and competence, there are a host of social factors that contribute to the reliability of the exchange. First, there are general interpersonal and moral norms that are in place. For example, in general, people are socialized to show at least minimal care and concern, and people are socialized to expect these. Over and above that, there are relevant norms of professional ethics in place. And over and above these, there is relevant positive law. As we saw above, professional ethics and positive law will likely govern the doctor's behavior here because she herself endorses them – she has likely internalized them in a way that makes them her own. But even if that is not the case, her knowledge of associated rewards and punishment will surely have their effect. There are other social considerations as well. Happy patients recommend their doctors, and dissatisfied patients complain and gossip. Word gets around. And so, there are economic rewards and punishments in play, as well as professional and legal ones. Of course, everything that we have said about the doctor–patient exchange applies to lawyer–client exchanges, accountant–client exchanges, and a host of other professional exchanges as well.

In each of our cases, then, a combination of operative social norms, speaker and hearer sensibilities, and other features of the broader social environment helps to explain the reliability of the testimonial exchange. Moreover, they do so without invoking hearer evidence about the reliability of the speaker. Again, the point is not that hearers never have such evidence. Nor is it that such social factors can always explain the reliability of testimonial exchanges all by themselves. Rather, the present idea is that social norms and social sensibilities often contribute to the explanation of reliability. More specifically, they often help to explain the reliability of testimonial exchanges that transmit knowledge.

All of this is consistent, then, with social factors and hearer evidence working *in combination* to explain reliability. For example, it is consistent with hearer evidence playing a necessary but not sufficient role in explaining reliability. This might happen in two ways that are important for present purposes. First, it might be the case that hearer evidence is sufficient to explain the reliability of some testimonial exchanges but not others. And in fact, our framework explicitly accommodates this possibility, in that it allows that testimony sometimes generates knowledge in the standard reductionist way – that is, by means of inductive evidence about speaker reliability. Second, it might be that hearer evidence is essential in explaining why a particular testimonial exchange is reliable, but insufficient to do the job all by itself. In this kind of case, the hearer has some evidence of speaker reliability, and this goes part of the way toward explaining why the testimonial exchange is reliable. But a full explanation requires invoking social factors as well.[23]

It is important to note, however, that neither of these roles for hearer evidence would support reductionism about knowledge transmission or about testimonial knowledge in general. The first would not, because in that case hearer evidence would explain some testimonial knowledge but not all testimonial knowledge. In particular, it would not explain knowledge transmission. Likewise for the second way in which hearer evidence might combine with social factors so as to explain reliability. In the second kind of case, hearer evidence partially

---

[23] By a "full explanation," I mean one that cites a cause that is sufficient to explain the effect. This is in contrast to a "partial explanation," which cites a necessary but insufficient causal contributor.

explains the reliability of a particular testimonial exchange, but is insufficient to explain the reliability of the exchange all by itself. Reductionism, however, requires that hearer evidence is sufficient to do the job by itself. That is, on the standard reductionist picture, hearer evidence *by itself* explains the reliability of a knowledge-producing testimonial exchange. That is why testimonial knowledge is supposed to reduce to inductive knowledge.

This last point is worth emphasizing, because discussions in the epistemology of testimony often proceed as if the relevant question is whether, in cases of testimonial knowledge or justification, the hearer has *some* evidence that the speaker is reliable.[24] But that question distracts from what should be our central concern, which is whether hearer evidence is always *sufficient* to explain testimonial knowledge or justification.[25]

4.4 Awareness without Evidence

In Section 4.3, we addressed a question about the de facto reliability of knowledge transmission: Assuming that testimonial exchanges must be reliable if they are to underwrite the transmission of knowledge, what explains their reliability? The present section addresses a second question: In cases of knowledge transmission, what explains the hearer's *awareness* of reliability? Once again, the reductionist about testimonial knowledge has an easy answer here. Reductionists think that testimonial knowledge requires *evidence* of reliability, and so hearer awareness can be understood in terms of hearer evidence. That route is not available to the anti-reductionist, however, and so an alternative account is required.

The proposed account invokes the notion of social sensibilities. Recall that social sensibilities are sensibilities regarding "how things are to be done" – how things are done, and how they are supposed to be done, in a social space. These sensibilities are the result of an

---

[24] For example, anti-reductionism in the epistemology of testimony is often characterized as the position that testimonial beliefs have *default* justification, requiring no positive reasons *at all* on the part of the hearer. For example, see Fricker, "Against Gullibility" and Lackey, *Learning from Words*. For an overview, see my "Recent Work on Testimonial Knowledge" especially section 2.

[25] We return to this point in greater detail in Chapter 8.

internalization process in which we make the norms governing a social space our own. As Graham explains, "When we internalize a norm, we find it intrinsically motivating ... We conform because we think it's the right thing to do, because we are supposed to do it."[26] Also recall, internalized social norms govern not just our behavior, but also our emotions and beliefs. In particular, some social norms are also *epistemic* norms. Thus, we internalize norms specifying appropriate epistemic behavior. Likewise, we internalize other norms that are not explicitly epistemic norms, but that nevertheless guide how we believe, including who we believe and who we do not believe, on various topics and in various circumstances.

Putting this all together, our social sensibilities are normative sensibilities that govern, in part, who we believe and who we do not believe. As such, they are dispositions to trust (and distrust) what different people say, to accept (and reject) different testimonies, and even to participate (or not) in different testimonial exchanges. The present proposal is that these dispositions can constitute a kind of awareness of reliability – a kind of normative sensitivity to the reliability of various testimonial exchanges. To be clear, our social sensibilities can and sometimes do steer us badly wrong. In general, merely *having* a set of social sensibilities does not in any way guarantee that they are tracking reality. The point, rather, is that *when things go well* – when our sensibilities are *well-formed* – they reliably put us on to reliable testimonial exchanges. And when that happens, our well-formed dispositions manifest a kind of sensitivity to reliability. This need not amount to an *explicit* awareness of reliability – one that manifests in *beliefs* about the reliability of some speaker or another. Rather, such awareness can be implicit or tacit, manifested more by behavior than by belief.[27] But when a child listens to his mother rather than to a stranger, this typically manifests an awareness on the child's part that he *should* listen to his mother. And when an adult trusts his doctor rather than his friend regarding what medicine he should take, this typically manifests an awareness on the adult's part that he *should* listen to his doctor, and that he *should not* listen to his friend.

At this point a potential objection should be addressed. It might be thought that the "should" in our two examples is something like

---

[26] Graham, "Epistemic Normativity and Social Norms," p. 253.
[27] The topic of tacit knowledge is taken up further in Chapter 6.

a practical should rather than an epistemic one. Put differently, it might be objected that the "should" has nothing to do with believing what is true, and so nothing to do with sensitivity to reliability. In reply, we have already acknowledged that the primary function of a belief-norm need not be epistemic, and here we can acknowledge that the primary function of the resulting disposition need not be epistemic. But in the realm of belief, practical concerns and epistemic concerns do not easily come apart. And so even when the primary motivation for belief is practical or otherwise non-epistemic, it is unlikely that belief can manifest no concern for truth at all.

The point is sometimes made in terms of the "aim of belief."[28] Belief by nature aims at truth, it is said, and that is why it is impossible to believe *merely* for practical reasons, or *merely* on practical grounds. Accordingly, even if the primary motivation for a belief-norm or belief-disposition is not concern for the truth, no such norm or disposition can be entirely devoid of concern for the truth, on pain of not being a *belief*-norm or *belief*-disposition at all. As such, even those parts of our social sensibilities that are grounded in practical, moral, or other non-epistemic belief-norms, nevertheless manifest an awareness that trustworthy testifiers are reliable testifiers.

Finally, the point holds in the good case and the bad case. When things go well, one's sensibilities regarding who "should" be trusted track reality, and thereby put one in touch with reliable testifiers while avoiding unreliable ones. When things go badly, one's sensibilities regarding who should be trusted fail to track reality, and the result is that one fails to engage reliable testifiers and/or engages unreliable ones. As argued above, it does not much matter what the primary force of the "should" is. For any "should" that recommends belief must do so at least partly because the belief is likely to be true. Likewise, any "should" that recommends a source of belief must do so at least partly because the source is likely to be reliable. Accordingly, one's sensibilities in both the good case and the bad case will encode, in part, one's sensibilities regarding who is a reliable source. In the good case, one's sensibilities line up well with reality, in the bad case they do not.

---

[28] For a classic statement, see Bernard Williams, "Deciding to Believe," in his *Problems of the Self* (Cambridge: Cambridge University Press, 1973), pp. 136–151.

Next, consider a different line of objection. Namely, it might be thought that the "awareness of reliability" that is explained by the present account is too weak to support testimonial knowledge. That is, it might be thought that knowledge requires an explicit awareness that our testimonial sources are reliable, rather than the merely implicit or tacit awareness of reliability that is manifested in our belief-forming dispositions.

By way of replying to this line of objection, it is helpful to return to the analogy with perceptual knowledge. As we have already suggested, the de facto reliability of perception is largely explained by the interaction of perceptual "sensibilities" and the physical environment. That is, we are reliable perceivers insofar as the physical environment is structured in a way that, as a matter of fact, lines up with our perceptual dispositions. Turning to awareness of reliability, it is implausible that in every case of perceptual knowledge, this is to be explained in terms of perceiver evidence. For example, we think that very young children have perceptual knowledge. But it is highly implausible that young children typically have *beliefs* about the reliability of their perceptual beliefs, much less sufficient *evidence* for reliability – that is, evidence sufficient *by itself* to establish the reliability of their perceptual beliefs.

Putting small children aside, there are familiar skeptical arguments against the requirement that even adults have evidence sufficient to establish the reliability of perceptual beliefs. I won't rehearse such arguments here. Suffice to say, worries about circularity and regress make such a requirement on perceptual knowledge extremely implausible.[29] Nevertheless, there is a clear sense in which, in cases of perceptual knowledge, perceivers manifest an awareness of reliability. Namely, we form some perceptual beliefs, and not others. We trust some perceptual experiences, and not others. That is, we are disposed to make some transactions between experience and belief and not others, and these dispositions manifest a tacit awareness that some perceptual transitions are reliable and others not. That is, *when things go well*, our perceptual dispositions manifest a kind of sensitivity to reliability. In both the bad case and the good case, our perceptual

---

[29]   For extended treatment of this point, see my *Putting Skeptics in Their Place: The Nature of Skeptical Arguments and Their Role in Philosophical Inquiry* (New York: Cambridge University Press, 2000); and William Alston, *The Reliability of Sense Perception* (Ithaca, NY: Cornell University Press, 1993).

dispositions manifest our sensibilities regarding which perceptual transitions are reliable. In the good case, our sensibilities track reality.

A final objection challenges whether, even in the good case, hearers are sensitive to the reliability of testimonial exchanges. The thought is that, in many cases where we trust a reliable speaker, we would still trust the speaker even if she were not reliable. For example, even in the case where I believe my reliable doctor when she tells me that a particular medicine would relieve my symptoms, I would still believe her even if she were not reliable. Likewise, even in the good case where a small child trusts his mother and she is reliable, the child would still trust his mother even if she were not reliable. But if that is so, then there is no good sense in which hearers are sensitive to reliability even in the good case.

In reply to this objection, a clarification is in order. Namely, the present account of "awareness of reliability," or "sensitivity to reliability," is not properly understood on the model of standard sensitivity conditions in epistemology. Famously, a sensitivity condition on knowledge takes the following form:

If p were false, S would not believe that p.

Alternatively,

In the closest world where p is false, S does not believe that p.

If we were to model our account of "awareness of reliability" on such a condition, we would get:

If S were not reliable regarding p, H would not accept S's testimony that p.

The present objection shows that this interpretation of our "awareness of reliability" condition is too strong. But that is not the way that it is intended. Rather, a proper understanding of the condition can be modeled on standard safety conditions in epistemology. A standard safety condition has this form:

Not easily would S believe that p and p is false

Alternatively,

In the closest worlds where S believes that p, p is true.

Accordingly, the present account of "awareness of reliability" can then be interpreted this way:

In the closest worlds where H accepts S's testimony that p, S is reliable with regard to p.

Two qualifications of this reply are necessarily. First, the present formulation is only a very rough approximation. As with standard sensitivity and safety conditions on knowledge, this rough approximation would have to be significantly adjusted to be made plausible. A second, better approximation would be this:

In the closest worlds where S testifies to H that p and H accepts S's testimony, S is reliable with regard to p.

Second, any further approximations along similar lines would still fail to address a pressing problem in the neighborhood. Specifically, the present account is reliabilist, in the sense that it requires for the transmission of knowledge that transmission channels are reliable. As such, the account of knowledge transmission faces its own version of the generality problem for reliabilism, which in this case is to specify the parameters under which transmission channels must be reliable. Put differently, "awareness of reliability" in this context is shorthand for "awareness of reliability within relevant parameters, at relevant levels of generality." For clearly enough, it is not required for testimonial knowledge that a token testimonial exchange be reliable within *any parameters whatsoever*. It is not required, for example, that the speaker be reliable on every subject matter whatsoever. But neither is it sufficient for testimonial knowledge that a token testimonial exchange be reliable within *some* set of parameters, for example those specifying nearly exactly the situation that S and H are in, and so guaranteeing that S is perfectly reliable within that limited range. A more detailed account, then, would specify under what parameters, and at what level of generality, the reliability of transmission channels is to be understood.

The present reply does not mean to address such details.[30] Rather, the present point is only to correct a mistaken interpretation of the account as presented so far, which is to understand "awareness of reliability" or "sensitivity to reliability" on the model of standard sensitivity conditions on knowledge.

---

[30]   The generality problem is rejoined in the Appendix.

5 | A Unified Account of Generation and Transmission

Chapters 2–4 present and develop an anti-reductionist framework for the epistemology of testimony. The framework is anti-reductionist in its account of knowledge transmission, which it characterizes as irreducible to generation. In consequence of this, the framework is anti-reductionist about testimonial knowledge in general, since anti-reductionism about transmission entails that not all testimonial knowledge is reducible to non-testimonial knowledge.[1]

The question remains, however, whether the framework implies a non-*unified* account of knowledge in general. That is, even if knowledge transmission is distinct from and irreducible to knowledge generation, it remains an open question whether both can be theorized at some higher level of theoretical unity. A negative verdict in this regard would constitute a fairly radical approach to the theory of knowledge, implying that generated knowledge and transmitted knowledge cannot be understood in terms of common theoretical resources. Such an approach would be radical, but not without its supporters. As was suggested in Chapter 1, this is one way that some of the more radical theorists in the epistemology of testimony might be fruitfully understood. Their position would be that a proper account of testimonial knowledge and justification demands just such a radical departure from traditional epistemology, which either obscures or distorts the epistemic significance of testimony, and precisely because it is employs theoretical resources that are inadequate to the task.

In this respect, the present framework offers a somewhat irenic alternative. On the one hand, the framework accommodates the idea that, in order to adequately theorize testimonial knowledge, traditional epistemology must expand its resources to include theoretical categories from ethics, action theory, the philosophy of language, and

---

[1] As explained in Chapter 1, the framework is neutral with regard to reductionism at the level of generation. That is, it is neutral whether testimony is an irreducible generative source of knowledge.

social science. On the other hand, the framework is consistent with but does not entail theoretical disunity at some higher theoretical level. On the contrary, much of the discussion of Chapters 2–4 suggests that both knowledge generation and knowledge transmission can be understood within a general reliabilist framework.

In the present chapter, I want to develop the case for theoretical unity. More specifically, I want to argue that an agent-reliabilist approach in epistemology – a version of "virtue epistemology" – can be fruitfully wedded to the present theoretical framework, and in such a way that the two are mutually supporting. On the one hand, the framework gains support insofar as it is consistent with a theory of knowledge with significant and independent explanatory power. Put in more pessimistic terms, the absence of that possibility would constitute a significant theoretical liability. That is because, other things being equal, the inelegance of a disunified theory of knowledge carries significant theoretical costs. On the other hand, virtue epistemology benefits from such a marriage as well. In particular, the framework offers virtue epistemology resources for answering the most persistent and important objection that has been raised against it – that it is inadequate to account for testimonial knowledge, and inadequate to accommodate aspects of social epistemic dependence more generally. In effect, the objection is that virtue epistemology is inherently individualistic in its approach, and for that reason essentially flawed. By wedding to the present framework for thinking about knowledge transmission, virtue epistemology inherits resources for a decisive reply to that objection.

The chapter proceeds as follows. Section 5.1 rehearses some theoretical virtues of virtue epistemology, highlighting that position's significant explanatory power. Section 5.2 rehearses the most important objection to virtue epistemology – that it is inherently individualistic, and therefore cannot adequately theorize testimonial knowledge, or accommodate the social dimensions of knowledge more generally. Section 5.3 shows how virtue epistemology can be wedded to our framework for theorizing knowledge transmission, and in such a way as to overcome the objections in Section 5.2.

5.1 Some Theoretical Virtues of Virtue Epistemology

The driving idea of traditional virtue epistemology is that, in cases of knowledge, the knower's getting things right can be attributed to her own cognitive agency. More exactly, her getting things right can be attributed to her own *competent* cognitive agency. Another way to put the general idea, then, is that knowledge is a kind of success from competence, or success from ability.[2] Suppose that we think that intellectual virtues are a kind of intellectual excellence, ability, or competence. Then another way to put the general idea is that knowledge is a kind of success from virtue. If we understand success from ability as an *achievement*, then yet another way to put the general idea is that knowledge is a kind of achievement.[3]

This simple idea turns out to have considerable explanatory power regarding the nature, value, and scope of knowledge.[4] Regarding the nature of knowledge, the account yields the following diagnosis of standard Gettier cases. In cases of knowledge, S's arriving at the truth is due to her own competent cognition. More exactly: S has a true belief, S's belief is formed by competent cognition, and S has a true belief *because* her belief is formed by competent cognition. In Gettier cases, S has a true belief, S's belief is formed by competent cognition, but S does not have a true belief because her belief is formed by competent cognition. Rather, S's forming a true belief is merely lucky.[5] Consider the following two cases, which plausibly display this structure:

---

[2] Intellectual abilities or competences are here understood as abilities to reliably get things right, relative to some field or subject matter, and under appropriate conditions. For example, visual perception is an ability to form true beliefs about various features of middle-size objects (e.g., color, size), under appropriate lighting conditions, with an unobstructed view, etc. A number of authors have argued that knowledge is a kind of success due to ability, including Sosa, *A Virtue Epistemology*, vol. I; and his *Judgment and Agency* (Oxford: Oxford University Press, 2015); John Greco, "Knowledge as Credit for True Belief," in Michael DePaul and Linda Zagzebski, eds., *Intellectual Virtue: Perspectives from Ethics and Epistemology* (Oxford: Oxford University Press, 2003), pp. 111–134; *Achieving Knowledge*; and "A (Different) Virtue Epistemology"; Wayne Riggs, "Reliability and the Value of Knowledge," *Philosophy and Phenomenological Research* 64, 1 (2002): 79–96; "Why Epistemologists Are so Down on Their Luck," *Synthese* 158, 3 (2007): 329–344; and "Two Problems of Easy Credit," *Synthese* 169, 1 (2009): 201–216; and Linda Zagzebski, *Virtues of the Mind: An Inquiry into the Nature of Virtue and the Ethical Foundations of Knowledge* (Cambridge: Cambridge University Press, 1996).

[3] This is the central thesis of Greco, *Achieving Knowledge*.

[4] See Greco, *Achieving Knowledge* for extended discussion.

[5] See Greco, "Knowledge as Credit for True Belief" and *Achieving Knowledge*.

Perceptual Knowledge: A man with excellent vision looks out over a field and sees what he takes to be a sheep. In fact, what he sees is indeed a sheep, he perceptually recognizes it as such, and forms a true belief to that effect.

Gettiered Perception: A man with excellent vision looks out over a field and sees what he takes to be a sheep. Due to an unusual trick of light, however, what he takes to be a sheep is actually a dog. Nevertheless, unsuspected by the man, there is a sheep in another part of the field.[6]

In Perceptual Knowledge, S's true perceptual belief is attributable to his competent perception; that is, S has a true belief *because* S has exercised competent perception. In Gettiered Perception, S exercises competent perception and S ends up with a true belief, but S does not end up with a true belief because S has exercised competent perception. On the contrary, it is just good luck that there is a sheep in another part of the field, unseen and unknown to S. Suppose we think of *achievements* as successes that are attributable to competent agency, as opposed to mere lucky successes that are not so attributable. Then Perceptual Knowledge describes a cognitive achievement, whereas Gettiered Perception describes a mere lucky success.

The idea that knowledge is a kind of success due to competence – an *achievement* in that sense – also yields an elegant explanation of the *value* of knowledge. That is because, in general, we think that achievements are both intrinsically and finally valuable. That is, we think that achievements are both valuable "in themselves" and "for their own sake." By understanding knowledge as a kind of achievement, we can explain the value of knowledge in terms of the value of achievements more generally. In the same way, the account elegantly explains the *superior* value of knowledge over mere true belief, in terms of the superior value of achievements over mere lucky successes.[7]

The foregoing considerations regarding the *nature* and *value* of knowledge also have implications regarding the *scope* of knowledge. In particular, the idea that knowledge is a kind of achievement provides resources for responding to a variety of skeptical arguments. For

---

[6] Adapted from Roderick Chisholm, *Theory of Knowledge*, 2nd edition (Englewood Cliffs, NJ: Prentice-Hall, Inc., 1977), p. 105.
[7] Greco, "Knowledge as Credit for True Belief"; and *Achieving Knowledge*, especially chapter 6.

example, a number of skeptical arguments trade on the idea that our perceptual abilities cannot discriminate between real-world scenarios and various skeptical "dream" scenarios. For example, things would perceptually seem to me just as they do if I were the victim of a Cartesian demon or a prisoner in *The Matrix*. An implicit assumption of such skeptical reasoning is this: My perceptual abilities yield knowledge only if they *can* discriminate between real-world scenarios and skeptical dream scenarios. But the idea that knowledge is a kind of success from ability gives us traction against this sort of reasoning. Reflection on the nature of abilities or competences in general reveals that achievement-grounding abilities need not be infallible, and need not even be reliable in unusual or atypical environments.

Consider, for example, Derek Jeter's ability to hit baseballs.[8] Jeter has such an ability – he is one of the best hitters in the game. But this does not imply that he would get a hit any time that he swings the bat. Neither does it imply that he would be reliably successful in circumstances that are very different from those typical for playing baseball. Jeter would not have reliable success hitting the baseball in an active war zone, for example, where he would be too distracted. We may now apply these same considerations to our perceptual abilities. Knowledge requires success from ability, and perceptual knowledge requires success from perceptual ability. Presumably, we are reliable perceivers in normal perceptual circumstances and therefore often have perceptual knowledge. This does not imply that we never make perceptual mistakes. Neither does it imply that we would be reliably successful if we were in very different perceptual circumstances – if we were disembodied victims of a Cartesian demon or prisoners in *The Matrix*, for example. Therefore, the implicit assumption identified in the skeptical reasoning above – that my perceptual abilities yield knowledge only if they can discriminate between real-world scenarios and skeptical dream scenarios – is false, and reflection on the nature of achievement more generally gives us grounds for saying so.[9]

These anti-skeptical considerations are directly related to the idea that knowledge cannot be merely lucky. On the one hand, skeptical

---

[8] In what follows, I refer to Jeter *circa* 1999.

[9] See Greco, *Putting Skeptics in Their Place* and *Achieving Knowledge*. See also John Greco and John Turri, "Virtue Epistemology," in Edward N. Zalta, ed., *The Stanford Encyclopedia of Philosophy* (2015), available at: http://plato.stanford.edu/archives/sum2015/entries/epistemology-virtue/

arguments exploit the idea that knowledge is inconsistent with lucky true belief. One way to understand the skeptical reasoning above is in exactly these terms: If our perceptual abilities cannot discriminate between real-world perceptual scenarios and mere dreams, then any true perceptual beliefs we have are merely lucky, as opposed to due to our own perceptual abilities. The idea that knowledge is a kind of success from ability challenges that skeptical reasoning by deepening our thinking about the relationship between knowledge and luck, and once again, it does so by considering the relationships among luck, ability, and achievement more generally.

Specifically, we can agree with the skeptic that knowledge in particular, and achievements in general, are to be juxtaposed to mere lucky successes. But not just any kind of luck is inconsistent with achievement. For example, it is largely due to good luck that Jeter was born with the physical abilities that he was, and that he grew up in a place where he had the opportunity to nurture and exercise those abilities. But none of that is inconsistent with successes being attributable to Jeter's abilities, once given the opportunity to exercise them. More generally, success from ability is consistent with luck in acquiring one's abilities and luck regarding the opportunity to exercise them in an appropriate environment. And that is true of cognitive abilities as well. The moral of the story, then, is that the relationship between knowledge and luck is subtle and complicated, and the idea that knowledge is a kind of achievement gives us a basis for understanding that subtlety and complexity more clearly.

Finally, the idea that knowledge is a kind of success from competence or ability yields insight into the nature of epistemic normativity and epistemic evaluation, by understanding these within the context of a broader normative domain. That is, in any domain of human performance that allows for success and failure, we make a distinction between success due to competent agency and success that is merely lucky. The present account exploits this familiar distinction to understand epistemic normativity as simply a species of performance normativity more generally.[10] This final point is not unrelated to the considerations above regarding the value of knowledge, the superiority of knowledge over mere true belief, and the relationship between

[10] See Greco, *Achieving Knowledge*, especially chapter 1; Sosa, *Judgement and Agency*.

knowledge and luck. In all of these contexts, we get insight into the nature of epistemic normativity and epistemic evaluation by considering the contours of performance normativity more generally.

A virtue-theoretic approach in epistemology, then, has considerable explanatory power. Nevertheless, the view faces an important line of objection regarding the epistemology of testimony and regarding the social dimensions of knowledge more generally. We turn to that line of objection in Section 5.2.

5.2 The Standard Objection to Virtue Epistemology

The standard objection to virtue epistemology is that it is overly individualistic. By conceiving knowledge as an individual achievement of the knower, this objection claims, the view fails to accommodate important social dimensions of knowledge. In particular, it fails to accommodate the important ways in which the knowledge of individuals can depend on the cognitive contributions of others. Most obviously, much of our knowledge is due to the competent testimony of others. But then it is unclear why testimonial knowledge should be understood as an achievement of the *hearer*, as opposed to the *speaker*.[11] Put differently, in cases of testimonial knowledge, it is often the case that the hearer forming a true belief has little to do with her own cognitive abilities, and is attributable rather to the competent agency of the speaker. This is especially so, for example, in cases of expert testimony, where a novice hearer does little more than trust what the expert speaker says. There are various other ways in which our knowledge depends on the competent contributions of others as well. Let us call these various kinds of dependence on others "social epistemic dependence." The objection is that the achievement view ignores the importance of social epistemic dependence.[12]

In response to this line of objection, achievement theorists have noted that many of our cognitive abilities are *social* cognitive

---

[11] The earliest formulation of this objection, to my knowledge, is Lackey, "Why We Don't Deserve Credit for Everything We Know."

[12] For example, see Lackey, "Why We Don't Deserve Credit for Everything We Know"; and her "Knowledge and Credit"; Goldberg, *Anti-Individualism*; *Relying on Others*; and his "The Division of Epistemic Labour"; Pritchard, "Knowledge and Understanding"; Kallestrup and Pritchard, "Robust Virtue Epistemology and Epistemic Anti-Individualism."

abilities. In particular, it is by means of social cognitive abilities that a hearer competently participates in testimonial exchanges with a speaker, expert or no.[13] Moreover, just as perceptual knowledge requires a good fit between our perceptual faculties and our broader physical environment, testimonial knowledge requires a good fit between our social cognitive abilities and our broader social environment. For example, we rely on knowledgeable speakers, and we rely on the social institutions that both make them available to us and help us to monitor them for competence and sincerity.[14] In all these regards, then, the achievement view has resources for describing and explaining important aspects of social epistemic dependence.

Nevertheless, critics have insisted, there is an important sense in which our epistemic dependence on others is not fully appreciated by what has been said so far. To understand the point, we need to look at the standard objection more closely. To that end, let's consider the original formulation of that objection, due to Jennifer Lackey. Lackey considers the following example.

Chicago Visitor: Having just arrived at the train station in Chicago, Morris wishes to obtain directions to the Sears Tower. He looks around, randomly approaches the first passerby that he sees, and asks how to get to his desired destination. The passerby, who happens to be a Chicago resident who knows the city extraordinarily well, provides Morris with impeccable directions to the Sears Tower.

Even if Morris is appropriately attentive to the speaker, Lackey argues, and even if his reception of the speaker's testimony is appropriately discriminating, it seems right to say that he forms a true belief *because of the speaker's testimony* rather than because of his own efforts.

---

[13] For example, see Greco, "The Nature of Ability and the Purpose of Knowledge"; *Achieving Knowledge*; and "A (Different) Virtue Epistemology"; Riggs, "Two Problems of Easy Credit"; Benjamin McMyler, *Testimony, Trust, and Authority* (New York: Oxford University Press, 2011); and Jonathan Reibsamen, "Social Epistemic Dependence: Trust, Testimony, and Social Intellectual Virtue" (PhD diss., Saint Louis University, 2015).

[14] See Henderson and Horgan, "What's the Point?"; Henderson and Graham, "Epistemic Norms and the 'Epistemic Game' They Regulate"; John Greco, "Testimonial Knowledge and the Flow of Information," in David Henderson and John Greco, eds., *Epistemic Evaluation* (Oxford: Oxford University Press, 2015), pp. 274–290.

Alternatively, his true belief is attributable to the speaker's competent agency rather than his own.[15]

But why not say that Morris gains a true belief *both* in virtue of his own efforts (his own exercise of relevant abilities) *and* in virtue of the speaker's efforts? Lackey argues that this would ruin the earlier diagnosis of Gettier cases. For in Gettier cases, too, S gains a true belief *partly* in virtue of S's own efforts. Accordingly, Lackey's objection is best understood as a dilemma: Either (a) we understand the attribution of success to S's own agency strongly, in which case we cannot account for standard cases of testimonial knowledge; or (b) we understand the attribution of success to S's own agency weakly, in which case we lose our diagnosis of Gettier cases.[16]

A plausible way to understand the attribution of success to S's own competent agency is explanatory.[17] The idea is that, in cases of knowledge, S's cognitive competence *explains why* S has a true belief. In Gettier cases, something else explains why S has a true belief. Why, then, can't we use this same idea to explain testimonial knowledge? That is, why can't we say that, in testimonial knowledge, the hearer's competent agency (e.g., good listening, monitoring for signs of deception, etc.) explains why the hearer has a true testimonial belief? The problem is that the explanatory account harbors an ambiguity. To see it, consider the following dilemma, adapted from Lackey:[18]

1. The present account claims that, in cases of knowledge, S's competent agency explains why S has a true belief. But this is ambiguous between (a) S's competent agency is *the most important part* of the explanation why S has a true belief; and (b) S's competent agency is *one important part* of the explanation why S has a true belief.
2. If (a), then the account rules incorrectly on cases of testimonial knowledge, since in at least many such cases, S's competent agency

---

[15] Lackey, "Why We Don't Deserve Credit for Everything We Know"; and "Knowledge and Credit."

[16] Lackey characterizes her objection this way in Lackey, "Knowledge and Credit," p. 34.

[17] I have defended this view in several places, including Greco, "Knowledge as Credit for True Belief"; *Achieving Knowledge*; and "A (Different) Virtue Epistemology." A version of this view is also defended in Sosa, *A Virtue Epistemology*, vol. I

[18] Adapted from Lackey, "Knowledge and Credit."

is *not* the most important part of the explanation why S has a true belief.

3. If (b), then the account does not give an adequate diagnosis of Gettier cases, since in many of those S's competent agency *is* an important part of the explanation for S's true belief.

Therefore,

4. Either way, the account fails to rule correctly on some cases.

An initially promising response to Lackey's dilemma is to treat explanatory salience in qualitative rather than quantitative terms. More specifically, we may say that a success is attributable to S's own competent agency just in case S's agency contributes to that success *in the right way*, where "in the right way" means "in a way that would regularly serve relevant purposes." An example illustrates this rough idea:

Soccer: Playing in a soccer game, Ted receives a brilliant, almost impossible pass. With the defense out of position and the goalie lying prostrate on the ground, Ted kicks the ball into the net for an easy goal.

In the case we are imagining, it is the excellent performance of the passer that stands out. The pass was brilliant, its reception easy. Nevertheless, we might argue, the goal is attributable to Ted's competent performance as well. Whatever help Ted got, he did put the ball in the net, and he did it by playing the right way. That is hard to maintain if we are thinking in quantitative terms. That is, it is hard to maintain that Ted's contribution is very important in an explanation of the goal, especially when compared to the contribution of the passer. But notice the shift from a quantitative understanding of Ted's contribution to a qualitative understanding. We are now insisting that Ted was involved *in the right way* so as to attribute success to him. Compare this case with another: Ted is playing in a soccer game, but not paying attention. Never seeing the ball, a brilliant pass bounces off his head and into the goal. Here we do not attribute success to Ted's competent agency. He was involved in a way, *but not in the right way*.

A pressing question for this approach, of course, is how are we to understand "in the right way"? One natural suggestion is that "in the right way" means "in a way that would regularly serve soccer-relevant purposes" – that is, those purposes that are intrinsic to playing the game of soccer. In the first case, Ted's agency is involved in a way that would regularly serve soccer-relevant purposes, and that is why the goal is attributable to him as well as to the passer. In the second case, Ted's agency is not so involved, and so the goal is not attributable to him at all.

But what counts as "relevant purposes" when we make knowledge attributions? Chapter 2 argued that an important purpose of knowledge attributions is to govern the flow of quality information within a community of information sharers. This same idea can now be used to answer our present question: In cases of knowledge, S's competent cognitive agency contributes to her having a true belief "in the right way" just in case S's agency contributes in a way that would regularly serve relevant informational needs – that is, informational needs within the relevant epistemic community, associated with some relevant domain of action and practical reasoning.[19]

With these resources in hand, we might reply to Lackey's dilemma as follows. In cases of testimonial knowledge, but not in Gettier cases, S's competent agency contributes to S's believing the truth *in the right way* – that is, in a way that would regularly serve relevant informational needs. That is, in cases of knowledge, S's agency interacts with her environment, including sources of testimony, so as to produce true belief in regular, dependable ways. In standard Gettier cases that does not happen. S ends up with a true belief, and S's competent agency even contributes to that, but not in a way that can be regularly exploited, not in a way that is dependable or reliable. In this respect, we may say that standard Gettier cases involve something akin to a deviant causal chain. In such cases, S's competent performance is part of the total causal structure leading up to S having a true belief. But the route from performance to truth is deviant. In other words, it is not the sort of route that could be regularly exploited for relevant purposes.[20]

This approach is on the right track, but not yet fully adequate. The problem is that, as suggested above, the approach does not yet take adequate account of our epistemic dependence on others. To see the point, consider a remark by Sandy Goldberg. When thinking about testimonial knowledge, Goldberg suggests, we don't want to treat other

---

[19] See Greco, "A (Different) Virtue Epistemology," especially section 5.

[20] Barn Façade Cases must be handled differently than what I am here calling "standard" Gettier cases. See Greco, "A (Different) Virtue Epistemology," especially section 6.

people as "merely more furniture" in the environment.[21] But that is what the present approach does, it seems. That is because, for all that has been said so far, the virtue-theoretic approach makes no *principled* distinction between (a) the ways that, in perceptual knowledge, our perceptual abilities interact with the physical environment; and (b) the ways that, in testimonial knowledge, our social-cognitive abilities interact with the social environment. It is true that, in cases of testimonial knowledge, our social-cognitive abilities interact with other people – that is why they are *social*-cognitive abilities. But, for all that has been said so far, this seems more or less a contingent matter. As Goldberg might put it, those persons might as well be just more furniture in the environment. Accordingly, the present approach does not yet accommodate the point that, in cases of testimonial knowledge, our epistemic dependence on others is a kind of *interpersonal* dependence. To capture that essential point, we need to do better.

5.3 A Unified Virtue-Theoretic Account of Generation and Transmission

The central idea of the new view is this: The distinctive phenomenon of knowledge transmission is to be understood in terms of joint agency and the related idea of *joint achievement*. More specifically, transmitted knowledge is to be understood as a joint achievement attributable to the competent joint agency of a speaker and hearer cooperating in the context of a testimonial exchange. This central idea involves a significant revision to traditional virtue epistemology. For on the traditional view, the idea was that all knowledge constitutes an *individual* achievement. That is, all knowledge was understood as true belief attributable to the cognitive abilities of *the knower*. On the new proposal, there are in effect two ways of coming to know. First, one may come to know by means of one's individual competent agency. Second, one may come to know by means of one's competent participation in competent joint agency. In the second case, it is important to note, one's having a true belief is attributable to the *competent joint agency*, as

---

[21] In conversation. See also Sanford Goldberg, "A Proposed Research Program for Social Epistemology," in P. Reider, ed., *Social Epistemology and Epistemic Agency* (Lanham, MD: Rowman and Littlefield, 2017); and "'Analytic Social Epistemology' and the Epistemic Significance of Other Minds," *Social Epistemology Review and Reply Collective* 2, 8 (2013): 26–48.

opposed to one's competent participation in that joint agency. Put differently, in the second case one's own competent agency does not adequately explain one's success. Rather, one's success is explained by *one's cooperation with others,* and is in this sense a joint achievement (an achievement attributable to joint agency) *rather than* an individual achievement (an achievement attributable to individual agency).

Is it always the case that, in cases of knowledge, true belief is attributable *in some way or another* to the competent cognitive agency of the knower? The answer is yes. The notions of joint agency and joint achievement explain how a success can be attributable to a person's competent agency even if that agency is not primarily responsible for bringing about the success. The idea is that, when a success is *directly* attributable to the joint agency of S1 and S2 acting together, the success is *indirectly* attributable to both S1 and S2 individually, insofar as the individual agency of each contributed to the joint agency in the right way.

This is clear in a variety of non-epistemic cases. For example, in the Soccer example, Ted's individual agency contributes to joint agency in the right way, and that explains why the goal is (indirectly) attributable to Ted. NB: Ted's contribution to scoring the goal is only subsidiary – the pass was brilliant, the kick into the net easy. But that is enough for Ted to play an essential role in the joint agency that is directly responsible for the goal, and for attribution to indirectly accrue to him.

Here is another example. An orchestra performs a musical piece that heavily features the first violin. A successful performance is directly attributable to the joint agency of the orchestra playing together. If we are dishing out praise for the performance, we might naturally focus on the first violinist, and it is true that the successful performance is largely attributable to her. Nevertheless, the successful performance is also (indirectly) attributable to the second violinist, the flutist, the clarinetist, etc., insofar as they contribute to the performance in the right way. Once again, they play an essential role in the joint agency that is directly responsible for the successful performance, and that is sufficient for attribution to indirectly accrue to them.

And now we may make the same point with regard to the hearer in cases of knowledge transmission. It is true that, in many cases, the transmission of knowledge will be largely due to the competent agency of the speaker, but it is also true that the hearer must do his essential part for transmission to be successful. And that is sufficient for success to be (indirectly) attributable to the hearer's competent agency. But the point remains: In cases of knowledge transmission, the hearer's true belief is directly attributable to competent joint agency, that is, to speaker and hearer cooperation. Success is only indirectly attributable to the hearer, by way of her competent contribution to the relevant joint agency.

Finally, note that much of the foregoing discussion can be extended to knowledge generation as well. For once the new view is in place, it is easy to see that knowledge generation, as well as knowledge transmission, might sometimes be a joint achievement depending on joint agency. It is easy to see that knowledge generation might sometimes involve the kind of intentional cooperation that characterizes joint activity. For example, we can conceive of a research team that cooperates in an investigation that is too complicated for any one person to undertake alone. If that cooperation is structured in the right way, and if the knowledge so produced is attributable to that cooperation, we will have a case in which knowledge generation is a joint achievement.

The proposed view is of course lacking in many details. For example, there is more to say about how we should characterize the details of joint agency in general, what constitutes *competent* joint agency as opposed to mere joint agency, and how we should understand the specific details of the kinds of joint activity that can result in knowledge transmission and knowledge generation. But the general idea is now in view. Further details should be adjudicated according to the best theoretical results. For present purposes, however, I am interested in defending only the more general proposal. We can do that by considering (a) how the proposal addresses concerns about social epistemic dependence, and (b) how the proposal preserves the theoretical advantages of the original achievement view.

First, it should be straightforward that the revised view accommodates Goldberg's point that, in theorizing about social epistemic dependence, we should treat persons as persons, as opposed to merely more furniture in the environment. The present account does this by treating others on whom we depend as *agents*, and more specifically as agents with whom we cooperate in joint activity. The view also addresses concerns about epistemic individualism more generally. For one, the view continues to invoke social cognitive abilities and social environments in its account of knowledge. But more importantly, on the revised view knowledge is no longer understood solely in terms of individual achievement, but in terms of joint achievement as well.

How does the present approach handle Lackey's dilemma specifically? First, it continues to understand attribution for success in qualitative rather than quantitative terms: a success A is attributable to S's competence just in case S's competence contributes to A *in the right way* – that is, in a way that would regularly serve relevant purposes. Second, in cases of knowledge attribution, including cases of attributing testimonial knowledge, we understand "relevant purposes" in terms of relevant informational needs. We said that this approach falls short of being fully adequate insofar as it fails to capture the way in which social epistemic dependence is *interpersonal* dependence, or dependence on other persons *qua* persons. We are now in a position to develop the account in a way that addresses this flaw.

Specifically, we may now make a distinction between testimonial knowledge that results from knowledge generation and testimonial knowledge that results from knowledge transmission, and we may say that, in cases of transmission, the hearer depends on the speaker as a cooperating agent in joint activity. Again, in cases of knowledge transmission, the hearer's forming a true testimonial belief is attributable to the competent joint agency of speaker and hearer acting together.

Finally, the revised achievement view also preserves the theoretical advantages that we noted for the original achievement view. For example, it preserves the original view's basic approach to the nature and value of knowledge. First, knowledge is still understood as a kind of achievement, and achievement is still understood as success attributable to competent agency. We merely add that knowledge is sometimes a joint achievement, understood as success attributable to competent joint agency. This, in turn, preserves the achievement view's general approach to the value of knowledge: Knowledge is intrinsically and finally valuable because achievements in general are intrinsically and finally valuable, and we value knowledge over mere true belief because in general we value achievements over mere lucky successes. We need only add that we value joint achievements in which we participate (we value such achievements in and for themselves), and that we value such achievements over mere lucky successes.

For similar reasons, the revised achievement view straightforwardly preserves the original view's anti-skeptical resources, its approach to the relations between knowledge and luck, and its conception of epistemic normativity as a kind of performance normativity. In fact, the revised view potentially provides richer insights in all three respects, insofar as the notions of joint agency and joint achievement afford more resources than do the notions of individual agency and individual achievement alone.

5.4 Conclusion

In conclusion, the resulting view demonstrates the possibility of a theoretically unified account of knowledge generation and knowledge transmission. On the new account, generation and transmission remain irreducible to each other, but both are understood within a virtue-theoretic account of knowledge and epistemic normativity. This is an important point in favor of our framework for understanding the transmission of knowledge, in that a non-unified account would come at significant theoretical costs. Moreover, the resulting view demonstrates that the framework is consistent with an account of knowledge that has significant, independent explanatory power. Finally, the wedding of our framework to virtue epistemology has significant advantages for the latter as well, in that our framework gives virtue epistemology resources for answering the most important objection against it.

6 | *The Framework Extended*
Common Knowledge

In *On Certainty*, Wittgenstein calls our attention to what he takes to be an odd but pervasive phenomenon.[1] There is a class of propositions, he tells us, that have a kind of certainty to them, but which are never explicitly "learned" (152) or "taught" (153), or arrived at "as a result of investigation" (138). Nevertheless, Wittgenstein thinks, such propositions play an important role in our psychology. For although they are themselves "exempt from doubt," they provide a kind of "scaffolding" that allows doubting (and thinking in general) to take place (341).

Following Duncan Pritchard, let's call the psychological counterparts of such propositions "hinge commitments."[2] Here are some examples:

My hands don't disappear when I am not paying attention to them. (153)
There are physical objects. (35)
What has always happened will happen again (or something like it). (135)
Every human being has parents. (211)
Cats do not grow on trees. (282)

Section 6.1 explores the oddness of Wittgensteinian hinge commitments and raises some problems for giving an adequate account of them. Section 6.2 suggests a way of extending the framework defended in previous chapters in a way that solves those problems. By way of preview, the extended framework proposes that epistemic communities can be characterized as having three distinct concerns regarding the way they acquire and manage information: the

---

[1] Ludwig Wittgenstein, *On Certainty*, edited by G.E.M. Anscombe and Go Ho von Wright and translated by Denis Paul and G.E.M. Anscombe (Oxford: Blackwell, 1969). Numbers within parentheses designate entries to this work.

[2] Duncan Pritchard, *Epistemic Angst: Radical Scepticism and the Groundlessness of Our Believing* (Princeton, NJ: Princeton University Press, 2016)

acquisition of information, its distribution, *and its pooling for common use.* In different terms, the new framework recognizes generated knowledge, transmitted knowledge, and now *common knowledge*, where the latter is understood on the analogy of public property – knowledge that members of the community get for free, so to speak.[3]

One feature of this model that holds both advantages and disadvantages is that it is fairly radical. For one, it introduces a category of knowledge that has gone previously unrecognized by traditional epistemology. Worse, the new category of common knowledge threatens to defy unified theoretical treatment. For example, it is unclear how either reliabilism or evidentialism could account for knowledge that is neither "taught" nor arrived at "as a result of investigation." Section 6.3 addresses this worry by defending two theses. First, it is argued that Wittgensteinian "hinge knowledge" can be understood as what cognitive science calls *procedural knowledge*; that is, knowledge that is exercised in the performance of a task. Such knowledge need not be represented in the system, explicitly or otherwise, but is nonetheless manifested in the system's information processing. Second, it is argued that procedural knowledge, so understood, can be given a virtue-theoretic account. In short: S has hinge knowledge that *p* only if a commitment that *p* is constitutive of S's competent cognitive functioning.

The extended framework presents an interesting option in epistemology – one that involves a fairly radical departure from traditional epistemological categories, but that can be surprisingly well integrated into a virtue-theoretic approach.

---

[3] Whether hinge commitments count as knowledge is disputed among Wittgenstein's commentators. For example, Coliva, McGinn, and Moyal-Sharrock all say no. See Annalisa Coliva, *Moore and Wittgenstein: Scepticism, Certainty and Common Sense* (Basingstoke: Palgrave Macmillan, 2010); Marie McGinn, *Sense and Certainty: A Dissolution of Scepticism* (Oxford: Blackwell, 1989); Danièle Moyal-Sharrock, *Understanding Wittgenstein's on Certainty* (Basingstoke: Palgrave Macmillan, 2004). For several "epistemic readings" of hinge commitments, see Pritchard, *Epistemic Angst*, chapter 3, sections 4 and 5. But either way, hinge commitments fall within the proper domain of epistemology. Consider: not every deep-seated commitment functions so as to ground or frame knowledge. Accordingly, there is an epistemological question regarding which commitments are *appropriate* to play that role. Alternatively, in virtue of what properties are hinge commitments appropriate for grounding or framing knowledge? Any epistemology that assigns hinge commitments an important role will have to answer these questions, whether or not it holds that hinge commitments themselves qualify as knowledge.

6.1 The Oddness of Hinge Propositions, and Some Problems

Let us begin with some further examples of Wittgensteinian hinge commitments, and by noting some of their salient characteristics.

First, some hinge commitments are stated in the first person, although Wittgenstein notes that there is "nothing personal" about them. What he means is that *everyone* is supposed to know such things:

I am a human being. (4)
I have a brain.(4)
My hands don't disappear when I am not paying attention to them.(153)

Other hinge propositions are more explicitly general and shared:

There are physical objects. (35)
What has always happened will happen again (or something like it). (135)
Every human being has parents. (211)
Motorcars don't grow out of the earth. (279)
Cats do not grow on trees. (282)

This first characteristic of hinge commitments, then, is that they are in an important sense held in common: "There is something universal here; not just something personal"(440); "The truths which Moore says he knows, are such as, roughly speaking, all of us know, if he knows them" (100).

A second characteristic of hinge commitments is that doubting them does not make sense: "If someone doubted whether the earth had existed a hundred years ago, I should not understand" (231). Relatedly, they are as certain as anything that could be said in favor or against them: "I want to say: my not having been on the moon is as sure a thing for me as any grounds I could give for it" (111).

A further important feature of hinge commitments is that they are odd to assert. As such, they are not (typically) expressed, even in thought:

If I say "this mountain didn't exist half an hour ago", that is such a strange statement that it is not clear what I mean. (237)
I believe that I had great-grandparents, that the people who gave themselves out as my parents really were my parents, etc. This belief may never have been expressed; even the thought that it was so, never thought. (159)

It is also odd to assert that one knows them, or that one does not know them. Both "knows" and "does not know," Wittgenstein says, make no sense here.

I know that a sick man is lying here? Nonsense! I am sitting at his bedside, I am looking attentively into his face. – So I don't know, then, that there is a sick man lying here? Neither the question nor the assertion makes sense. (10)

Another feature characteristic of hinge commitments is that we do not arrive at them through reasoning or investigation:

For it isn't, either, as if [Moore] had arrived at his proposition by pursuing some line of thought which, while it is open to me, I have not in fact pursued. (84)
We don't, for example, arrive at any of them as a result of investigation. (138)
I cannot say that I have good grounds for the opinion that cats don't grow on trees or that I had a father and mother. (282)

Finally, neither are such commitments explicitly learned or taught:

I do not explicitly learn the propositions that stand fast for me. (152)
No one ever taught me that my hands don't disappear when I am not paying attention to them. (153)

Rather, they are a kind of background for judging what is true or false. Hence Wittgenstein's famous scaffolding analogy:

Perhaps it was once disputed. But perhaps, for unthinkable ages, it has belonged to the *scaffolding* of our thoughts (Every human being has parents). (211)

Likewise, the river-bed analogy and the hinge analogy:

It might be imagined that some propositions, of the form of empirical propositions, were hardened and functioned as channels for such empirical propositions as were not hardened but fluid ... The mythology may change back into a state of flux, the river-bed of thoughts may shift. But I distinguish between the movement of the waters on the river-bed and the shift of the bed itself; though there is not a sharp division of the one from the other. (96–97)
That is to say, the *questions* that we raise and our *doubts* depend on the fact that some propositions are exempt from doubt, are as it were like hinges on which those turn. (341)

Finally, Pritchard makes a point about hinge commitments that is related to many of the features canvassed above. Specifically, he argues that hinge commitments do not qualify as beliefs, insofar as they have a different functional profile. In particular, hinge commitments are not reasons-responsive, as beliefs proper are essentially. Thus, Pritchard writes:

given that our hinge commitments are *ex hypothesi* never the result of a rational process and are in their nature unresponsive to rational considerations, then they are not plausible candidates to be beliefs ... Beliefs, after all, are propositional attitudes that by their nature are responsive to rational considerations.[4]

I think Prichard is right on this point. Another characteristic feature of hinge commitments, then, is that they display a different functional profile from beliefs – that is, they play a different functional role in our cognitive economy, and therefore are not well understood as beliefs proper. This point will be important in Section 6.3, where it is argued that hinge commitments display the same functional profile that cognitive science ascribes to procedural knowledge.

So far, we have been considering what hinge commitments are like, focusing on the characteristic features that provoked Wittgenstein's interest in them as objects for inquiry. We now turn to some problems that an adequate account of hinge propositions ought to address.

First, there is what we might call "The Assertion Problem":

The Assertion Problem: Why are hinge commitments *themselves* odd to assert? Also, why is it odd to assert that one *knows* them (or that one does not know them)?

Second, there is what we might call "The Epistemic Problem":

The Epistemic Problem: If we do know hinge propositions, then *how* do we know them? And if we do know them, why are they so certain? Why is their epistemic status so high, even compared to other knowledge?

As Duncan Pritchard points out, it is not easy for traditional theories to say:

Consider, for example, the prospects of developing this account along process reliabilist lines. The difficulty is that it doesn't seem at all plausible to

---

[4] Pritchard, *Epistemic Angst*, p. 90

suppose that we know hinge propositions in virtue of forming the target beliefs via a reliable belief-forming process. Indeed, our hinge commitments do not seem to be the product of any specific kind of belief-forming process, but are rather part of the tacit intellectual backdrop against which we acquire our beliefs in non-hinge propositions ... It follows that it's going to be hard to tell even an epistemic externalist-friendly story about how one might have knowledge of hinge propositions ... our hinge commitments don't seem to have any epistemic pedigree in this regard.[5]

Pritchard's point can be easily extended to evidentialist theories. On what evidence are hinge propositions plausibly based? Accordingly, two major approaches in the theory of knowledge will have a hard time accounting for our knowledge of hinge propositions. On the other hand, we should note that the point is not clearly right for many hinge propositions. Thus, consider: Here is one hand (1); A sick man is lying here (10); That is a book (17); I have never been on the moon (111). It is at least plausible that we know these by perception and memory, and quite easily so. The harder cases for traditional theories to explain are ones like these: Every human being has parents (211); The earth existed long before my birth (233); The earth is a body on whose surface we move. And it no more suddenly disappears or the like than any other solid body (234); What has always happened will happen again (or something like it) (135); Motor cars don't grow out of the earth (279); Cats do not grow on trees (282). Pritchard's point does seem right with regard to these cases. That is, it is not at all clear what sort of reliable process, or what sort of evidence, grounds our knowledge *that cats do not grow on trees* and the like.

The Epistemic Problem can be refined. Given what we have already said, we can construct a dilemma for traditional theories of knowledge:

1. Any item of knowledge must be either *generated for oneself* via non-testimonial sources or *transmitted from others* by means of testimony.
2. Knowledge of hinge commitments (at least in the hard cases) is not *generated for oneself*, since one does not arrive at such propositions "by pursuing some line of thought" or "working it out."

---

[5] Ibid. pp. 76–77.

3. Knowledge of hinge commitments is not *transmitted* by means of testimony, because such propositions are not typically asserted.

Therefore,

4. There is no knowledge of hinge commitments (at least in the hard cases).

This is a dilemma for traditional theories of knowledge, insofar as they must accept the dilemma's first premise. But then it is hard to see how traditional theories can escape the skeptical conclusion. Put differently, it is hard to see how traditional theories can explain how we do have knowledge *that motor cars don't grow out of the earth, that cats do not grow on trees,* and the like.

Finally, consider a third problem for any traditional epistemic account of hinge commitments:

The Specialness Problem: Suppose that you do give an account of our knowledge of hinge commitments in traditional terms. But then you will have missed what is special about hinge propositions; i.e. you will have missed why they are special and interesting epistemically.

And so, any traditional epistemic account of hinge commitments will have a strike against it on just that score. It is this sort of consideration, perhaps, that has led some authors to propose non-epistemic accounts of hinge propositions. Thus, Marie McGinn understands our certainty of hinge propositions in terms of practical-linguistic certainty. Pritchard understands them as having merely psychological certainty, and Danièle Moyal-Sharrock describes them as having "animal certainty."[6] Non-epistemic accounts avoid the Specialness Problem, since they deny that we have knowledge of hinge propositions at all. On the contrary, they try to account for the special role of hinge propositions in non-epistemic terms. But Wittgenstein sees a cost for non-epistemic treatments: "And why shouldn't I say that I know all this? Isn't that what one does say?" (288) "So I don't know, then, that there is a sick man lying here? Neither the question nor the assertion makes sense." (10)

---

[6] See McGinn, *Sense and Certainty*; Pritchard, *Epistemic Angst*; and Danièle Moyal-Sharrock, "The Animal in Epistemology: Wittgenstein's Enactivist Solution to the Problem of Regress," in Annalisa Coliva and Danièle Moyal-Sharrock, eds., *Hinge Epistemology* (Leiden: Brill, 2016), pp. 24–47.

We have now seen that both traditional epistemic accounts and non-epistemic accounts of hinge commitments face formidable problems. In light of this, it is reasonable to consider a more radical epistemic strategy.

6.2 Extending the Information Economy Framework

Let's return to an idea that was prominent in Section 6.1: that our knowledge of Wittgensteinian hinge commitments, at least in the hard cases, seems not to be *generated* by the knower herself nor *transmitted* by testimony. That is, we seem not to arrive at these propositions "by pursuing some line of thought" or "as a result of investigation." But neither do we seem to learn them by testimony. "No one ever taught me that my hands don't disappear when I am not paying attention to them." Here are some examples of hinge propositions that seem to resist such analysis:

Every human being has parents. (211)
The earth existed long before my birth. (233)
Motor cars don't grow out of the earth. (279)
Cats do not grow on trees. (282)

Here now is a proposal, suggested by the information economy model that we have been defending in earlier chapters. In addition to the categories of generated knowledge and transmitted knowledge, each governed by the norms appropriate to their distinctive place in an epistemic community, we should allow that there is a third such category – that of *common knowledge*. Common knowledge would be analogous to common or public property – roughly speaking, everyone gets to use it for free. On this extended model, there is knowledge that you produce for yourself, knowledge that someone gives you, and common knowledge that is available for everyone.

Note that these categories correspond to three kinds of answer to the question, "How do you know?" Thus, one can answer:

a. I saw it myself; I figured it out.
b. Someone told me; I read it in a book.
c. It's common knowledge; everyone knows that!

Our information economy model says that the concept of knowledge functions so as to govern the flow of quality information within an epistemic community. As such, that model predicts two characteristics of common knowledge. First, that there should be some knowledge that is held in common; that is, that some information should be available to use for everyone at any time. Second, that there should be some knowledge that is for free; that is, that some information should be available without a corresponding epistemic burden. In sum, we should expect there to be common knowledge on the analogy of common property – by virtue of membership in the epistemic community, everyone gets to use it for free.

Does common knowledge, on this way of thinking, form a "natural kind"? That is, does all common knowledge share some essential property, which makes it common knowledge thereby? Probably not. Rather, common knowledge is a functional kind. It plays a particular role in a knowledge economy. Specifically, common knowledge is knowledge that we are happy to "spot" for free. We are happy to grant it, and take it for granted. Given this function, there are likely sub-categories of common knowledge. For example, knowledge so easy to gain that everyone either has it or should have it, and knowledge that has been so long held that everyone is aware if it or should be aware of it. The idea is that such knowledge can be freed up for common use without further concern for quality control. It is so well known, and so widely known, that we are happy to grant it to everyone.

If all this is right, then at least many of Wittgenstein's hinge propositions fall into the category of common knowledge. Here are some advantages of such an account. First, the account yields straightforward solutions to the Epistemic Problem and Specialness Problem. Specifically, it posits a third category of knowledge, common knowledge, and proposes that hinge propositions occupy this category. Accordingly, the information economy model both explains our knowledge of hinge propositions and explains why it is special. The account also solves the Refined Epistemic Problem by denying its first premise: that any item of knowledge must be either generated for oneself via non-testimonial sources or transmitted from others by means of testimony.

The account also yields solutions to the Assertion Problem. Here we can adopt the Gricean line that assertions of hinge propositions are true but inapt. Precisely because hinge propositions are known to be true by everyone, asserting them adds nothing informative to a conversation. This is so, at least, for most conversational contexts. But that is exactly how assertions of hinge propositions behave – they are odd or inapt except in very special circumstances, where they do make an appropriate contribution.

Another advantage of the account is that it straightforwardly explains all of the following features of hinge commitments:

- They are held in common (because they are known by everyone).
- Doubting them does not make sense (because they are so well known).
- They are as certain as anything that could be said in favor or against them (because they are so well known).
- They are odd to assert/not (typically) expressed or thought (because they are known by everyone and taken for granted).
- It is odd to assert that one knows them or that one does not know them (because it is granted that everyone knows them).
- We didn't arrive at these things by some line of thought/or by having good grounds/We didn't learn these things (because they are known by everyone and granted as known by everyone).
- They are the background for judging what is true or false (because they are known by everyone and taken for granted).

One significant *disadvantage* of our extended framework, it might be objected, is its lack of theoretical unity regarding the nature of knowledge. Specifically, the framework now proposes a third category of knowledge, subject to different norms and standards than both knowledge generation and knowledge transmission. Moreover, it is hard to see how this new category is to be reconciled with generated knowledge and transmitted knowledge at a higher level of theoretical unity. As we saw above, for example, it is not clear how reliabilism or evidentialism could provide a unifying theory. Such lack of unity, however, would constitute a significant theoretical cost.

Here is a different problem. The present approach is a non-starter if we don't in fact use hinge commitments in practical reasoning. In that case, the idea that they are used "for free" in the information economy would not apply, since they would not be used at all. But on the face of it, we don't use such propositions as *here is a hand* or *the world has existed long before my birth* in practical reasoning. As Wittgenstein suggests, it is plausible that hinge propositions are such that they "may never have been expressed; even the thought that it was so, never thought" (159).

One might think that hinge propositions are used as suppressed or implicit premises in practical reasoning. For example, suppose that I expect to see Danièle in the room but then don't find her there when I look. I might reason as follows: "I don't see Danièle in the room, so she must have stepped out." In so reasoning, am I relying on some hinge proposition serving as an implicit premise, for example *that physical bodies don't suddenly disappear*? Or suppose that I see some kittens in the yard, and I infer that the neighbor's cat must have had her litter. Do I rely on the implicit premise *that cats don't grow on trees*?

Both cases seem implausible. More likely, my reasoning is devoid of any such premises, even implicit ones. Upon not finding Danièle in the room, I infer directly that she has stepped out. Upon seeing the kittens in the yard, I infer directly that my neighbor's cat (or some other cat) has had a litter. The reliability of these and other inferences are contingent, guaranteed by external facts about the environment and the laws of nature rather than a battery of unnoticed assumptions. That is at least a plausible account of our inductive reasoning, and one that undermines the motivation for seeing hinge propositions as implicit premises in enthymematic reasoning.[7] But then, as suggested above, this constitutes a problem for the present account. For if we don't need hinge propositions for premises in our reasoning, or if we only rarely need them for such, then we lose a major motivation for locating them in a category of available common knowledge. Even worse, it becomes mysterious why they should be included in such a category at all, since their relationship to practical reasoning and action has now been severed.

Both problems for our extended framework are addressed in Section 6.3. The problem concerning practical reasoning is resolved by identifying Wittgensteinian common knowledge with procedural knowledge. The problem of theoretical unity is resolved by giving a virtue-theoretic account of procedural knowledge, and hence Wittgensteinian common knowledge.

---

[7] It has been argued that inductive reasoning must be characterized this way to avoid Hume's skepticism about induction. Specifically, if a regularity principle is required as an implicit premise in inductive reasoning, then Hume's skeptical argument goes through. See Greco, *Putting Skeptics in Their Place*; and James van Cleve, "Reliability, Justification, and the Problem of Induction," *Midwest Studies in Philosophy* 9, 1 (1984): 555–567.

6.3 A Virtue-Theoretic Account of Common Knowledge

This section proceeds as follows. Section 6.3.1 reviews the notion of procedural knowledge as it is understood in cognitive science. Section 6.3.2 makes the case that, at least in many cases, Wittgensteinian hinge commitments can be understood as manifestations of procedural knowledge so understood. Section 6.3.3 turns to a virtue-theoretic account of Wittgensteinian common knowledge.

6.3.1 Procedural Knowledge in Cognitive Psychology and Artificial Intelligence

Procedural knowledge is variously characterized in the cognitive sciences, including cognitive psychology and theories of artificial intelligence. But there are some common themes that suffice to describe the category for our purposes. Perhaps the most general characterization of procedural knowledge is "knowledge exercised in the performance of some task." Often enough, procedural knowledge is juxtaposed to other categories of knowledge, such as "declarative knowledge" and "propositional knowledge," and often it is characterized as "implicit knowledge" or "tacit knowledge." Consistent with all this, but by no means entailed by it, procedural knowledge is sometimes identified with "knowledge how." Given present purposes, we should remain as neutral as possible among these different characterizations. Accordingly, I will begin by using the most general formulation – procedural knowledge is the kind of knowledge that is exercised in the performance of a task – and I will remain neutral whether such knowledge is always explicit or implicit, propositional or no. As discussion proceeds, it will become apparent why the more specific characterizations of procedural knowledge reviewed above have been considered apt.

The next point to make is that, understood as knowledge operative in the performance of a task, procedural knowledge can be implemented in different ways. In each case, the commitment in question will be less explicit and more tacit, than the previous.

First, procedural knowledge can manifest as explicit knowledge of a rule, as when one follows a recipe in cooking or consults an instruction manual to change the oil in one's car. Such knowledge is certainly "exercised in the performance of a task," and so qualifies as procedural knowledge on our most general characterization, even if knowledge of said rule is explicit, declarative, propositional, etc.

Second, procedural knowledge can be understood on the analogy of programmed processing rules in a general-purpose computer. Programmed rules are not inputs of the system's processing, but rather drive its processing in the transition from inputs to outputs (Figure 6.1).

Third, procedural knowledge might be understood on the analogy of a hardwired processing rule, as in a classical computational system such as a calculator (Figure 6.2). In such a system, the processing rules are built right into the processor. For example, the rules of addition are built right into the wiring of a classical calculator. If you wanted the calculator to do something else – to follow some other rule in its processing – you would have to rewire it.

The procedural knowledge in our first case (following a recipe) is straightforwardly an explicit commitment of the system. The procedural knowledge in our second case (programmed rules in a computer) is also in some sense an explicit commitment of the system, in that it is a commitment that is explicitly written into its program. But even in our third case (the classical calculator), the rules of addition are reasonably understood as a "commitment" of the processing system, even if nowhere explicitly represented in the system. That is because the rules of addition are manifested in the system's processing patterns, and are in that sense an implicit commitment of the system. This constitutes a third way that procedural knowledge can be implemented.

As a final case, consider the learned processing patterns of a "trained up" connectionist network. In such a system, learned processing patterns need not be explicitly represented in the programming and need not be hardwired into the machinery. On the contrary, processing in

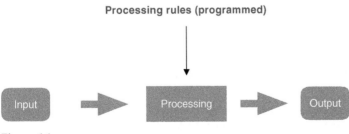

Figure 6.1

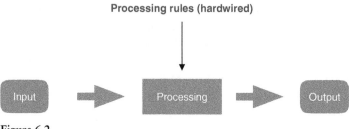

Figure 6.2

such a system takes place on the level of individual nodes and the connections among them, and often in such a way that does not invoke either programmed or hardwired rules. The system's commitments to learned processing patterns, rather, are manifested in what Horgan and Tienson call the "morphological content" of the system's connection weights.

Morphological possession of intentional content M is a matter of the cognitive system's being disposed, by virtue of its persisting structure rather than by virtue of any occurrent states that are tokens of M, to undergo state transitions that are systematically appropriate to content M – and to do so, at least much of the time, without generating a token of M during the process.[8]

Such content, Horgan and Tienson explain, need not be represented in the system either occurrently or dispositionally.

Morphological content differs from occurrent representational content (e.g., occurrent belief) because it involves the cognitive system's persisting structure, rather than occurrent tokening of M. Morphological content differs from dispositional representational content (e.g., dispositional belief) ... because the relevant dispositions associated with morphological content involve tendencies other than the tendency to generate token representations with that content.[9]

Here, then, we have yet another sense in which procedural knowledge might be implicit or tacit in a processing system. Such knowledge might be nowhere represented in the system, and may not be "built in"

---

[8] Terence Horgan and John Tienson, "Connectionism and the Commitments of Folk Psychology," *Philosophical Perspectives* 9 (1995): 132.
[9] Ibid.

to the system's hardware, either. Nevertheless, it is in an important sense a "commitment" of the system "exercised in the performance of a task," in that it is manifested in the system's information processing.

The next thing to note is that each of our four cases have either analogues or straight-out instances in human cognition. First, we follow recipes and instruction manuals, and thereby straightforwardly employ explicit and even conscious knowledge of certain rules in the performance of some tasks. Second, it is commonplace that we also internalize rules for performing tasks, so that explicit and conscious consultation of previously employed rules is no longer necessary. This can happen as one learns to cook, and so no longer needs the recipe, or learns to service one's car, and so no longer needs the instruction manual. It also happens when one internalizes the rules of chess, or the rules of grammar, etc. We can think of this kind of internalization on the analogy of programming. In effect, we can program ourselves to follow rules, and in a way that no longer requires that the rules be "inputs" to our thinking in the performance of a particular task.

Likewise, parts of our cognitive processing are hardwired, as in some parts of perception and in some forms of reasoning. It is now well known that the human mind is neither a "blank slate" nor unrestrictedly malleable, but rather comes with certain kinds of processing "built in" to the system. For example, this characterizes low-level perceptual processing, which famously resists learning from perceptual illusions, such as the Muller–Lyer illusion or the peripheral drift illusion.[10]

Finally, connectionist networks like the kinds described above are of great interest precisely because they are thought to model human cognition. The "nodes" and "connections" of artificial connectionist systems, of course, are supposed to have their analogues in the neurons and synapses of the human brain.[11] Plausibly, the human brain *is* a connectionist network.[12]

---

[10] For discussion of the peripheral drift illusion and evidence that it is the result of low-level perceptual processing, see A.L. Beer, A.H. Heckel, and M. W. Greenlee, "A Motion Illusion Reveals Mechanisms of Perceptual Stabilization," *PLoS ONE* 3, 7 (2008): e2741.

[11] William Bechtel, "Connectionism and the Philosophy of Mind: An Overview," in William Lycan, ed., *Mind and Cognition* (Oxford: Basil Blackwell, 1990).

[12] For an extended argument to this effect, see, Terence Horgan and John Tienson, *Connectionism and the Philosophy of Psychology* (Cambridge, MA: MIT Press, 1996).

In sum, procedural knowledge can be implemented in cognitive systems, including human cognitive systems, in a variety of ways. In Section 6.3.2, I argue that many of the cases that Wittgenstein identifies as hinge commitments can be plausibly understood as instances of procedural knowledge. Moreover, understanding the cases this way predicts several characteristic features of Wittgensteinian hinge commitments. In Section 6.3.3, I defend a unified epistemology of generated knowledge, transmitted knowledge, and Wittgensteinian hinge commitments.

6.3.2 Hinge Commitments as Procedural Knowledge

I begin with some specific examples of Wittgenstein hinge commitments, and I make some speculative suggestions about how these commitments might manifest procedural knowledge that is hardwired into human cognition. After that, I move to some more general considerations in favor of the thesis that hinge commitments manifest procedural knowledge.

Some Examples of Hinge Commitments

First, consider the proposition *that my hands don't disappear when I am not paying attention to them* (153). It is plausible to consider commitment to this proposition as manifesting procedural knowledge that is hardwired into human cognition. Specifically, it plausibly manifests a commitment to physical object permanence, a normal feature of human cognition that naturally develops at 4–7 months, and perhaps as early as 3.5 months.[13] For example, at roughly this age, infants will expect to see a moving object that passes behind a wall reemerge on the other side. Likewise, infants will be surprised if an object that is placed behind an occluding panel is not there when the panel is taken away.[14]

---

[13] Renée Baillargeon and Julie DeVos, "Object Permanence in Young Infants: Further Evidence," *Child Development* 62, 6 (1991): 1227–1246.

[14] There is some debate among researchers whether a commitment to object permanence should be considered "innate" or "learned," but all parties agree that such a commitment emerges in the course of normal development. For examples on each side, see Scott P. Johnson, Dima Amso, and Jonathan A. Slemmer, "Development of Object Concepts in Infancy: Evidence for Early Learning in an Eye-Tracking Paradigm," *Proceedings of the National Academy of Sciences of the United States of America* 100, 18 (2003): 10568–10573; and E.S. Spelke, K. Breinlinger, J. Macomber, and K. Jacobson, "Origins of Knowledge," *Psychological Review* 99, 4 (1992): 605–632.

Next, consider a more general proposition, that *there are physical objects* (35). Commitment to this proposition also plausibly manifests procedural knowledge of physical object permanence. In this context, we may recall G.E. Moore's account of the meaning of "external" in his "Proof of an External World," a paper that was of central concern to Wittgenstein as he was writing the notes that were eventually published as *On Certainty*. Moore ultimately analyzes "external" in terms of two features: (a) location in space and (b) independence from perception.[15] These are both features that are central to the characterization of physical object permanence.[16]

Next, consider the propositions that *every human being has parents* (211) and that *cats do not grow on trees* (282). Commitment to each of these propositions plausibly manifests essentialist and natural kind heuristics that frame much of human reasoning. In particular, human thinking about living organisms naturally manifests essentialist commitments about their characteristic properties, including origin. For example, we naturally see it as an essential characteristic of human beings that they have parents, and therefore we are constrained to think that *all* human beings have parents. Likewise, we are essentialist about animal and plant categories, and are thereby committed to the proposition that *cats do not grow on trees*.[17]

---

[15] G.E. Moore, "Proof of an External World," *Proceeding of the British Academy* 25 (1939): 273–300. Reprinted in G.E. Moore, *Philosophical Papers* (New York: Macmillan, 1959); see especially pp. 134–135.

[16] "When adults see an object occlude another object, they typically make three assumptions. The first is that the occluded object continues to exist behind the occluding object. The second is that the occluded object retains the physical and spatial properties it possessed prior to occlusion. Finally, the third is that the occluded object is still subject to physical laws: its displacements and interactions with other objects do not become capricious or arbitrary but remain regular and predictable." Baillargeon and DeVos, "Object Permanence in Young Infants," 1227.

[17] For example, see Susan A. Gelman, *The Essential Child: Origins of Essentialism in Everyday Thought* (New York: Oxford University Press, 2003). According to Gelman, "essentialism is a pervasive, persistent reasoning bias that affects human categorization in profound ways. It is deeply ingrained in our conceptual systems, emerging at a very young age across highly varied cultural contexts ... essentialism is the result of several converging psychological capacities, each of which is domain-general yet invoked differently in different domains. Collectively, when these capacities come together to form essentialism, they apply most powerfully to natural kinds (including animal and plant species, and natural substances such as water or gold) and social kinds (including race and gender), but not artifacts made by people (such as tables and socks)" (p. 6). For

Finally, consider a more general proposition, that *what has always happened will happen again (or something like it)* (135). This assumption about the uniformity of nature falls out of the natural kinds heuristic, which implies that natural objects are characterized by shared and stable clusters of properties. In this context, Howard Sankey writes,

> nature is, in fact, uniform. It is uniform in the sense that the fundamental kinds of things which exist are natural kinds of things, which possess essential sets of properties ... This is why, when we infer that an unobserved object will have a property which observed objects of the same kind have, we turn out to be right. For having such a property is just part of what it is to be an object of the same kind as the other objects.[18]

In this sense, Hume was right – we do not *reason* to the assumption that nature is uniform. Rather, we *presuppose* it in our reasoning. Moreover, this is a contingent fact about human psychology, rather than a necessary fact about reason or rationality.[19] What Hume did not consider is that such a commitment might nevertheless amount to a kind of knowledge.

Some General Features of Hinge Commitments

I have been defending the thesis that many of the commitments that Wittgenstein identifies as "hinge commitments" are plausibly what cognitive psychology and artificial intelligence call "procedural knowledge." We are now in a position to specify that thesis a bit more carefully. Specifically, Wittgensteinian hinge commitments are plausibly viewed as a subset of procedural knowledge: highly stable, widely shared procedural knowledge that results from either (a) species-wide hardwiring or (b) a shared cultural inheritance. This qualifies our thesis in two important ways. First, we include the latter

---

an extended argument that inductive inference is driven by essentialist and natural kind heuristics, see Hilary Kornblith, *Inductive Inference and Its Natural Ground: An Essay in Naturalistic Epistemology* (Cambridge, MA: MIT Press, 1993).

[18] Howard Sankey, "Induction and Natural Kinds," *Principia: An International Journal of Epistemology* 1, 2 (1997): 247.

[19] David Hume, *Enquiries Concerning Human Understanding and Concerning the Principles of Morals*, 3rd edition, L. A. Selby-Bigge, ed. (Oxford: Clarendon Press, 1975); and *A Treatise of Human Nature*, 2nd edition, L.A. Selby-Bigge, ed. (Oxford: Clarendon Press, 1978).

category (shared cultural inheritance) because not all human beings are plausibly committed to propositions such as *I have never been far from the earth's surface*[20] or *motorcars don't grow out of the earth* (279).[21] Nevertheless, such commitments, and their analogues, are both stable and widely shared within a particular culture. Second, not all procedural knowledge is widely shared. For example, much of it is the result of highly specific training, such as when a birdwatcher develops expert perception or an athlete develops procedural knowledge specific to her sport. Accordingly, Wittgensteinian hinge commitments can only be understood as corresponding to a *subset* of procedural knowledge; that is, the kind that results from either species-wide biological inheritance or broad cultural inheritance.

Next, I argue that understanding Wittgensteinian hinge commitments this way predicts several of their characteristic features. First, and perhaps most importantly, it predicts the unique functional contribution to our psychology that both Wittgenstein and Pritchard assign to hinge commitments. As we saw above, hinge commitments are supposed (a) not to derive from reasoning and investigation, but rather (b) to drive reasoning and thinking more generally. As Wittgenstein puts it, "the *questions* that we raise and our *doubts* depend on the fact that some propositions are exempt from doubt, are as it were like hinges on which those turn" (341). Accordingly, and as Pritchard emphasizes, such commitments are not themselves reasons-responsive: "our hinge commitments are *ex hypothesi* never the result of a rational process and are in their nature unresponsive to rational considerations" (90). This is why Pritchard thinks that such commitments "are not plausible candidates to be beliefs." Rather, beliefs "are propositional attitudes that by their nature are responsive to rational considerations" (90). Which is to say, beliefs are characterized by a quite different functional profile. But all of this is exactly as we would predict if such commitments are hardwired into our cognitive system. Or, alternatively, if they are internalized in learned habits of thought, and thereby manifest themselves in our cognitive processing, but not in the inputs of our questioning, reasoning, etc.

Another characteristic feature of hinge commitments, also described above, is that they are very stable. Again, this is nicely explained if such

---

[20] For example, Neil Armstrong is not. The proposition is cited as a certainty by G.E. Moore in "A Defense of Common Sense," in *Philosophical Papers* (New York: Macmillan, 1959), p. 33.

[21] Because not all human beings have the concept of motorcars.

commitments are built right into our cognition, or if they are internalized and thereby become habitual. This would also explain a further
feature of hinge commitments – that they are not typically articulated in
speech or thought. If such commitments manifest knowledge that is
tacit rather than explicit, then by definition, they will not show up
explicitly in our thinking, or at least not typically so. It remains possible
that tacit knowledge can be brought to consciousness with reflection,
but typically such knowledge will remain below the level of conscious
thought and linguistic assertion.

Finally, although hinge commitments are not typically asserted, and
therefore not explicitly learned or taught; they are nevertheless *held in
common*. This too is nicely explained if hinge commitments manifest
a particular kind of procedural knowledge; namely, the kind of procedural knowledge that results from biological or cultural inheritance. In
this sense, we can think of hinge commitments as constituting a class of
"common knowledge," and we may note that such knowledge comes
in two kinds: that which is species-wide and that which is group-wide.

So, should we think of hinge commitments as a kind of knowledge?
One reason to answer no is the idea that knowledge entails belief, and
hinge commitments are, on the present view, not a kind of belief. But
perhaps knowledge is wider than belief – perhaps other kinds of commitment can also be vehicles of knowledge. In fact, we are already
committed to this insofar as we recognize the categories of tacit knowledge and knowledge-how, and we assume that these cannot, in turn, be
understood in terms of belief. We might be happy, then, to count hinge
commitments as a kind of knowledge, although a very special kind of
knowledge, and one that does not entail belief.

That being said, it should be acknowledged that we often go from
implicit commitment to explicit belief. In doing so, we might go from
mere procedural knowledge to explicit declarative knowledge. As noted
above, we sometimes do exactly this via reflection on our implicit commitments. In addition to this, we can turn procedural knowledge into
declarative knowledge via both philosophical and empirical investigation. For example, one might come to explicitly believe that external
objects exist, either by considering philosophical questions in epistemology or ontology, or by empirically investigating the constraints of perceptual representation. This would allow a kind of middle position
between those who think that hinge commitments constitute a kind of
knowledge and those who think they do not. Specifically, we can say that

(a) hinge commitments are special in ways that make them unlike typical knowledge, whether we count them as a special kind of knowledge or not; but nevertheless, (b) the contents of hinge propositions *can come to be known*, via generation or transmission in the usual ways.

Finally, we should note a further consequence of our position: that the same person can have both a procedural commitment that *p* and a belief that *p* at the same time. This is because psychological states with different functional profiles can both have the content that *p*. Specifically, the same person might have both a procedural commitment that *p* and a reasons-responsive belief that *p*. This is plausibly the position that Moore was in when he reasoned to the existence of the external world. For similar reasons, it is possible that the same person has both a procedural commitment that *p* and reasons-responsive belief *that not-p*. This is plausibly the position that Berkeley was in when he reasoned to the conclusion that there are no mind-independent objects. In so concluding, Berkeley certainly failed to lose the procedural knowledge embedded in his faculties of perception.

6.3.3 A Unified Hinge Epistemology

A central commitment of virtue epistemology is that knowledge is success manifesting competent cognitive agency. That central commitment can be understood as a necessary condition on knowledge: A mental state counts as knowledge *only if* it manifests competent agency. This final section of the chapter argues that generated knowledge, transmitted knowledge, and "hinge knowledge" manifest competence (are attributable to competence) in different ways.

Consider first generated knowledge. The more specific formulation can be put this way:

Knowledge that *p* is **generated** in S only if S's believing the truth regarding *p* is attributable to S's competent cognitive agency.[22]

Consider a case of perceptual knowledge: S sees that there is a sheep in the field and thereby knows that there is a sheep in the field. In such a case, S's belief is formed by competent visual perception, S's belief is true, and S forms a true belief because her belief is formed by competent

---

[22] In Chapter 5, we considered that generated knowledge might be grounded in competent joint agency as well. Here I leave that possibility aside.

perception. Equivalently, S believing the truth regarding p is attributable to S's competent cognitive agency.

As we saw in Chapter 5, previous versions of virtue epistemology have treated this account of generated knowledge as equivalent to an account of knowledge in general. Our present approach departs from these previous versions. Specifically, we now recognize a special class of testimonial knowledge, understood as transmitted knowledge *as opposed to* generated knowledge. Hence,

Knowledge that p is **transmitted** from S to H only if H's believing the truth regarding p is attributable to S's and H's competent joint agency.

The accounts of generated and transmitted knowledge defended in earlier chapters employed the notions of information acquisition and information distribution within an epistemic community. Here, we exploited the metaphor of an information (or knowledge) economy, on the model of a material economy that includes both the production and distribution of economic goods. Section 6.2 extended the metaphor to include a kind of "common knowledge," on the analogy of public property. On such a model, "common knowledge" is knowledge that members of the community get for free, so to speak. In other words, it is knowledge that is neither generated for oneself nor transmitted from another person, but is rather available for everyone to use in common.

How might we understand such knowledge in a virtue-theoretic framework? In the previous section, we defended the thesis that hinge commitments are a subset of procedural knowledge: highly stable, widely shared procedural knowledge that is either (a) hardwired into the species or (b) an internalized cultural inheritance. A salient feature of such knowledge, we saw, is that it typically manifests as internal to cognitive processing, rather than as inputs or outputs of such processing, as beliefs do. More exactly, such procedural knowledge manifests in transitions from input to output, and is in that sense "constitutive" of cognition, rather than an input or output of cognition. Employing this same line of thought, we can give the following account of "hinge knowledge":

S has **hinge knowledge** that p only if a commitment that p is constitutive of S's competent cognitive agency.[23]

---

[23] Alternatively, a commitment that p **functions appropriately as a hinge commitment** of S only if a commitment that p is constitutive of S's competent cognitive agency.

The foregoing may be considered to be an anti-reductionist, unified account of generated knowledge, transmitted knowledge, and hinge knowledge (or appropriate hinge commitments). It is anti-reductionist, because each of our categories is deemed to require distinctive treatment, with none being reducible to another, or at least not plausibly so. The account is nevertheless unified, in that it is held together by a central theme – that knowledge in general is success manifesting competent cognition.

Other things being equal, a unified view seems preferable to a non-unified view. And as already suggested, it is hard to see how an evidentialist approach could give a unified account of either transmitted knowledge or hinge commitments. Regarding transmitted knowledge, the motivation for such a category is precisely that some testimonial knowledge resists treatment in evidentialist terms. Regarding hinge knowledge, it is hard to see how a commitment that is not reasons-responsive can count as knowledge in an evidentialist framework. The best option for the evidentialist, it would seem, is to reject the categories of transmitted knowledge and hinge knowledge altogether.

The prospects of a unified account seem even worse for an internalist approach, in that the kind of epistemic dependence characteristic of transmitted knowledge would seem to resist an internalist treatment. Likewise, the general inaccessibility of hinge commitments makes them a difficult target for an internalist framework. Once again, it seems that the better option would be to deny these categories altogether. Of course, denying the relevant phenomena rather than explaining them comes with significant theoretical costs. It does seem that there are different ways of coming to know, corresponding to our different ways of answering the question, *How do you know?* That is, it does seem that these are distinctive epistemic phenomena, and therefore something that an adequate epistemology ought to recognize and explain.

It is already widely recognized that a virtue-theoretic approach in epistemology has impressive explanatory power. To the extent that the approach adds explanatory power here, by allowing a unified epistemology of generated, transmitted, and "hinge knowledge," we have yet a further consideration in its favor.

7 | *Education and the Transmission of Understanding*

In Chapters 1–6, I have been arguing that testimony sometimes transmits knowledge. Can testimony transmit understanding as well? Here there are conflicting considerations. On the one hand, there is a widespread intuition that understanding *cannot* be transmitted by mere testimony. Roughly, the idea is that understanding involves grasping or seeing something "for oneself," and this is precisely what believing on testimony fails to achieve.[1] On the other hand, it is plausible that good teaching *can* transmit understanding, and that such teaching can at least sometimes be understood as a kind of extended testimony. Think of a series of history lectures, for example, or a biology course without a lab component. Is it plausible to deny that understanding, in history or biology, for example, can be transmitted in that kind of educational setting?

In this chapter, I want to argue that understanding can indeed be transmitted by the kind of extended testimony that one finds in standard educational settings. The argument will proceed in two stages. The first is to defend a neo-Aristotelian account of understanding as a systematic knowledge of causes.[2] More exactly, understanding is here understood as a systematic knowledge of modally strong *dependence*

---

[1] For example, see Linda Zagzebski, "Recovering Understanding," in Matthias Steup, ed., *Knowledge, Truth, and Duty: Essays on Epistemic Justification, Responsibility, and Virtue* (New York: Oxford University Press, 2001), pp. 235–251.

[2] In contemporary philosophy, the claim that understanding amounts to knowledge of causes is more popular in philosophy of science than in epistemology. On this point, cf. Stephen R. Grimm, "Is Understanding a Species of Knowledge?" *British Journal for the Philosophy of Science* 57, 3 (2006): 515–535. For example, Peter Lipton writes, "Understanding is not some sort of super-knowledge, but simply more knowledge: knowledge of causes." See his *Inference to the Best Explanation*, 2nd edition (New York: Routledge, 2004), p. 30. I defend a broadly Aristotelian account of understanding in "Episteme: Knowledge and Understanding," in Kevin Timpe and Craig Boyd, eds., *Virtues and Their Vices* (Oxford: Oxford University Press, 2014), pp. 285–302.

relations. Our contemporary notion of cause, as well as Aristotle's four causes, are examples of such relations. The second stage of the argument defends the claim that, so understood, the transmission of understanding can be understood as a special case of the transmission of knowledge. The idea is that the kind of systematic testimony that is characteristic of teaching in an educational setting can transmit a systematic knowledge of dependence relations in a domain – a domain such as history or biology, for example.[3]

The chapter is organized as follows. Section 7.1 reviews some characteristic features of understanding, taking special note of those features that seem to make the transmission of understanding impossible. Section 7.2 argues that a neo-Aristotelian account of understanding as knowledge of causes (or other dependence relations) nicely accommodates all of these features. Section 7.3 argues that understanding, so understood, can indeed be transmitted by the right kind of testimony in the right kind of setting. The information economy framework defended in previous chapters enters the discussion in two ways. First, the framework helps to address a recent objection, due to Jonathan Kvanvig, to the claim that understanding is a kind of knowledge. Second, the framework helps to explain both (a) the mechanisms by which understanding is transmitted by testimony in educational settings, and (b) the intuition that it cannot be.

7.1 Some Characteristic Features of Understanding

We begin by noting some salient features of understanding. These are features that are widely agreed to characterize understanding, and as such they are features that any account of understanding ought to accommodate. Even better, an adequate account should *explain why* understanding has these features – why understanding would be *expected* to have these features, if the account being proposed is correct.[4]

The first thing to note in this regard is that understanding is not *equivalent* to knowledge, since one can know that something is the case

---

[3] What I have primarily in mind here is *formal* educational settings, as in grade schools and universities. As we shall see below, however, the idea that such education is extended and systematic is more important than that it is formal.

[4] At the very least, an adequate account ought to explain why understanding *seems* to have these features, even if in the end the account claims that it does not.

without understanding why or how it is the case. For example, one can know that the cat is on the mat without understanding why the cat is on the mat. A closely related point is that knowledge can be isolated or episodic in ways that understanding cannot be. Thus, one can know individual or isolated facts about a subject matter, but understanding seems to come in larger packages. Understanding "hangs together" in ways that knowledge need not.[5]

Another widely recognized feature of understanding is that it can have different kinds of object. Thus, we often talk about understanding concrete objects, or parts of "the world," such as a particular ecosystem, or economy, or culture. But we talk about understanding abstract objects as well; for example, theories, equations, and problems. We also talk about understanding processes, models, graphs, and even people. Again, understanding can have a wide and diverse variety of objects.[6]

Another salient feature of understanding is that it is closely tied to explanation. To understand something is very close to being able to explain it. To explain something, in turn, is very close to seeing how it "fits together" with other things – how it came about from prior causes, for example, or how it otherwise "makes sense" given some broader context. Thus, understanding is closely related to explanation, and explanation is closely related to making sense of how things fit together.[7]

---

[5] This feature of understanding is noted by, among others, Jonathan Kvanvig, *The Value of Knowledge and the Pursuit of Understanding* (New York: Cambridge University Press, 2003); and Wayne Riggs, "Understanding 'Virtue' and the Virtue of Understanding," in M. DePaul and L. Zagzebski, eds., *Intellectual Virtue: Perspectives from Ethics and Epistemology* (New York: Oxford University Press, 2003), pp. 203–226.

[6] This feature of understanding is noted by, among others, Catherine Elgin, *Considered Judgment* (Princeton, NJ: Princeton University Press, 1996); Linda Zagzebski, "Recovering Understanding"; and Riggs, "Understanding 'Virtue' and the Virtue of Understanding."

[7] This feature of understanding is widely noted in the philosophy of science. See, for example, Peter Achinstein, *The Nature of Explanation* (New York: Oxford University Press, 1983); Wesley Salmon, *Scientific Explanation and the Causal Structure of the World* (Princeton, NJ: Princeton University Press, 1984); Philip Kitcher, "Explanatory Unification and the Causal Structure of the World," in Philip Kitcher and Wesley Salmon, eds., *Scientific Explanation* (Minneapolis, MN: University of Minnesota Press, 1989), pp. 410–505; James Woodward, *Making Things Happen: A Theory of Causal Explanation* (Oxford: Oxford University Press, 2003); Nancy Cartwright, "From Causation to Explanation

Finally, it is widely recognized that understanding is more valuable than mere belief, and even mere knowledge. Thus, at least typically, we prefer understanding why something is the case over merely knowing that it is the case. There is probably little consensus regarding why understanding is more valuable than mere knowledge, or exactly in what sense. But at least this much seems right: Understanding is valuable *in some important sense*, and is (at least often) *more valuable* than mere knowledge.

Here are some typical passages, taken from the recent literature on understanding, that highlight these features.

Understanding requires the grasping of explanatory and other coherence-making relationships in a large and comprehensive body of information. One can know many unrelated pieces of information, but understanding is achieved only when informational items are pieced together.[8]

understanding ... is the appreciation or grasp of order, pattern, and how things "hang together." Understanding has a multitude of appropriate objects, among them complicated machines, people, subject disciplines, mathematical proofs, and so on. Understanding something like this requires ... appreciation ... or awareness of how its parts fit together, what role each one plays in the context of the whole, and of the role it plays in the larger scheme of things.[9]

... understanding appears to be even more valuable than knowledge ... A head full of trivia and detail is an amazing thing, but nothing compared with the reach and sweep of a person of understanding, so if knowledge is a good thing, understanding is even better.[10]

According to many philosophers of science, for example, understanding is the good at which scientific inquiry aims. On this way of looking at things, what scientists want, when they begin their inquiries ... is to understand the world (or at least some part of it), where understanding the world involves something more than the acquisition of true beliefs. More generally, and looking outside of science, understanding is often said to be one of the great goods that makes life worth living.[11]

and Back," in Brian Leiter, ed., *The Future for Philosophy* (New York: Oxford University Press), pp. 230–245; Lipton, *Inference to the Best Explanation*.

[8] Kvanvig, *The Value of Knowledge and the Pursuit of Understanding*, p. 192.

[9] Riggs, "Understanding 'Virtue' and the Virtue of Understanding," p. 217.

[10] Kvanvig, *The Value of Knowledge and the Pursuit of Understanding*, p. 186.

[11] Stephen R. Grimm. "Understanding," in Sven Bernecker and Duncan Pritchard, eds., *The Routledge Companion to Epistemology* (New York: Routledge, 2011), p. 84.

It is at least widely agreed, then, that understanding has the following characteristic features:

- One can have knowledge without having understanding. One can know that something is the case without understanding why or how it is the case.
- Understanding cannot be isolated or episodic.
- Understanding can have different objects, such as economies, ecosystems, people, theories, stories, equations, and models.
- Understanding is closely tied to explanation.
- Understanding is closely tied to being able to answer "Why" and "How" questions.
- Understanding involves grasping coherence, or seeing patterns, or seeing how things "fit" or "hang" together.
- Understanding is in some important way valuable, and at least sometimes more valuable than mere knowledge.

Which of these characteristic features of understanding imply, or at least suggest, that understanding cannot be transmitted via testimony? It is not clear that any of them do, but perhaps the most obvious thought is that understanding cannot be isolated or episodic, while testimony can only deliver isolated and episodic content. Testimony, then, cannot deliver understanding. This worry is clearly related to other of understanding's characteristic features, such as its close relation to explanation, that it involves grasping coherence and patterns, and that it can take on complex objects such as ecosystems and economies. Each of these features, it might be thought, is incompatible with the limited content carried by testimonial assertions.

None of these concerns seem pressing, however, in that testimony need not be understood in terms of one-off assertions, delivering only limited content. As we have seen, testimony can sometimes be extended and systematic, as it is in standard educational settings, such as history and biology seminars. Importantly, this point need not be limited to *formal* educational settings. Here I am thinking of the kind of education through mentorship that is commonplace in any number of domains, both formally and informally.[12] In fact, extended and systematic testimony need not be limited to *educational* settings. For all that has been said, it is not clear why understanding could not be delivered by extended testimony

---

[12] For example, in business, in sports, and in martial arts.

from a family member or friend (e.g., regarding one's family history, one's relationships, etc.).

Nevertheless, there are other reasons for thinking that testimony cannot transmit understanding, even when the testimony is extended and systematic. One of these, we have seen, is that understanding must be gained "for oneself," perhaps through personal experience or "acquaintance" with the object of understanding, where these are understood to be incompatible with believing on the basis of testimony. Another thought is that understanding involves "knowledge-how," and that this practical mode of knowledge cannot be transmitted by testimony. We return to these concerns in Section 7.3.

7.2 Understanding as Systematic Knowledge

According to Aristotle, *episteme* consists in knowledge of causes. To have *episteme* is to know the cause of a thing. This kind of knowledge, in turn, is closely associated with having an explanation and with being able to answer *Why* questions. Thus, R.J. Hankinson writes, "to have [*episteme*] is to have explanatory understanding: not merely to 'know' a fact incidentally, to be able to assent to something which is true, but to know *why* it is a fact."[13] This suggests that Aristotle's *episteme* is at least close to the English "understanding." In the remainder of this section I will defend a broadly Aristotelian account of understanding, modeled on Aristotle's own account of *episteme*.[14]

To better understand Aristotle's own account, it is necessary to consider his theory of causation, or of what it is to be a cause. Famously, Aristotle thought that there are four kinds of cause: efficient, material, formal, and final. Aristotle's notion of *efficient cause* is closest to our contemporary notion of cause. Roughly, an efficient cause is a source or agent of change. For example, fire can be the efficient cause of the wood burning. An explosion can be the efficient cause of the house catching fire. But Aristotle recognizes other kinds of cause as well. A *material cause* is, roughly, the material out of which a thing is made. For example, the material cause of a house burning can be that it is made out of wood. Here again, we note the close connection between Aristotle's four causes and

---

[13] R.J. Hankinson, "Philosophy of Science," in Jonathan Barnes, ed., *The Cambridge Companion to Aristotle* (Cambridge: Cambridge University Press, 1995), p. 110.
[14] Here I draw from my "Episteme: Knowledge and Understanding."

the various answers we can give to *Why* questions. For example, someone might ask: "Why is that house over there in ruins?" In some contexts, we will be inclined to cite the efficient cause – there was a fire, or an explosion. But in other contexts we might cite the material cause – the house was made out of wood, or of straw. For example, that is why the first two houses are in ruins, whereas the third (made out of brick) is still standing.

Aristotle's notion of *formal cause* is that of a thing's "nature" or "essence" or "what-it-is." For example, we might say that "the cause" of the dog barking is *that it is a dog*. In other words, that's what dogs do – they bark! Notice that we are inclined to say such things in certain situations. For example, a guest sleeping at the farmhouse might be annoyed at the roosters crowing. The guest might ask, "Why do those roosters crow so early in the morning?" Here, a natural answer might be, "Well, they're roosters! That is what roosters do!" Lastly, a *final cause* is an end or goal. It is "that for the sake of which a thing is done."[15] The easiest place to see what Aristotle has in mind is in the case of human action. Thus, we commonly answer *Why* questions by citing what a person is trying to do or trying to achieve. For example, "Why is he running down the road?" "Because he is trying to lose weight" or "Because he wants to get home in time for dinner."

Notice, finally, that we can answer the same *Why* question by citing any one of Aristotle's four causes. Why did the house burn down? There was an explosion (efficient cause). It was made of wood (material cause). The owner wanted to collect on the insurance (final cause). We might even cite a formal cause here: "Sometimes houses burn down," said in answer to an insurance agent, trying to understand why this happened, just now, in this economy.

What do these various kinds of answers have in common? Put differently, what do Aristotle's four causes have in common? One way to think of it is that they each cite some kind of dependence relation. In other words, they each cite some way in which one thing can depend on another. Thus, the house burning down depended on there being an explosion. But it also depended, in various ways, on the house being made of wood, the owner wanting to collect insurance, and the fact that houses are the sort of thing that can burn down. Consider: Not everything

[15] Andrea Falcon, "Aristotle on Causality," in Edward N. Zalta, ed., *The Stanford Encyclopedia of Philosophy* (2011), available at: http://plato.stanford.edu/arc hives/fall2011/entries/aristotle-causality.

can burn down, and not everything that can burn down does burn down. To understand why this house burned down – to understand it fully – requires knowing how the house burning down depended on these various factors.

Notice that Aristotle's account already entails tight relations between (a) *episteme* (or understanding), (b) knowing the cause, (c) being able to cite the cause, (d) having an account or explanation, and (e) having the answer to *Why* questions. Next, I suggest that we can fruitfully update the Aristotelian account in three ways. First, we can replace Aristotle's four causes with a notion of dependence relations in general. As we have seen, all of Aristotle's "causes" are dependence relations – they are various ways in which one thing (or process, or event) can depend on another. But there are other dependence relations as well. For example, there are (a) part–whole or "mereological" relations; (b) logical and mathematical relations; (c) conceptual relations; and (d) supervenience relations of varying strength. This list is meant to be neither exclusive nor exhaustive. Rather, the substantive point is that there are many and various dependence relations, and understanding centrally involves knowledge of these. Think of a complex net of many and various modally strong dependence relations. According to the present account, to have understanding regarding some thing is to know its location in such a net.

One nice feature of this updated account is that it makes causal explanation (in our more restricted sense of "cause") a species of explanation in general. To have an explanation is to be able to cite appropriate dependence relations. To have a causal explanation is to be able to cite causal relations. In a similar fashion, the account makes scientific understanding and explanation a species of understanding and explanation in general, alongside mathematical understanding and explanation, philosophical understanding and explanation, and practical understanding and explanation.

Our second update to the Aristotelian account is to stress that understanding consists in a *systematic* knowledge of dependence relations. Put differently, understanding consists in knowledge *of a system* of dependence relations. This accommodates the plausible idea that understanding, unlike mere knowledge, cannot be isolated. It also accommodates the idea that understanding comes in degrees, in terms of both breadth and depth. Thus, we can think of "depth of understanding" in terms of "depth of knowledge," where the latter corresponds to knowledge of more fundamental dependence relations. Likewise, we can think of "breadth of understanding" in terms of "breath of knowledge," where the latter corresponds to knowledge of more diverse dependence relations.

Our third update is to allow that understanding can have diverse objects. In particular, it is plausible that understanding can have "non-propositional" objects, such as maps, graphs, pictures, and models, as well as "propositional" objects such as theories, narratives, and mathematical equations. All of these involve complex representations of dependence relations, or representations of complexes of dependence relations, and so sit comfortably with the idea that understanding involves a systematic knowledge of dependence relations.

Finally, we saw that an adequate account of understanding ought to explain the *value* of understanding. That is, it ought to explain why understanding is valuable, and why it is at least often more valuable than mere knowledge. Our neo-Aristotelian account does this straightforwardly. Specifically, it identifies understanding with a kind of knowledge, and so on the present account understanding inherits the value of knowledge in general. Moreover, understanding always involves a system of knowledge rather than mere isolated or episodic knowledge. But if more knowledge is (at least often) more valuable than less, then there is a straightforward sense in which understanding will be (at least often) more valuable than mere knowledge. Finally, understanding involves knowledge of an especially valuable sort; that is, understanding involves knowledge *why* and knowledge *how*, including knowledge how to live. Plausibly, these kinds of knowledge are often more valuable than other kinds of knowledge, or at least some other kinds of knowledge.

A neo-Aristotelian account of understanding as systematic knowledge of dependence relations therefore accommodates all of the characteristic features of understanding that we noted above. Such an account faces a recent objection, however. Specifically, Jonathan Kvanvig has argued that understanding, unlike knowledge, is compatible with certain kinds of epistemic luck. But then understanding cannot be a kind of knowledge, as our neo-Aristotelian account claims.

Let's consider Kvanvig's argument more carefully. First, it is now well-known that knowledge cannot tolerate certain kinds of luck – this is a lesson of the Gettier literature.[16] For example, recall the following Gettier case from Chapter 5.

Gettiered Perception: A man with excellent vision looks out over a field and sees what he takes to be a sheep. Due to an unusual trick of the light, however, what he takes to be a sheep is actually a dog. Nevertheless, unsuspected by the man, there is a sheep in another part of the field.[17]

Plausibly, the man in this case does not know that there is a sheep in the field, and precisely because his hitting on the truth here is "too lucky." Again, it is widely accepted that this is a lesson of Gettier cases. However, Kvanvig argues, understanding is not incompatible with luck in the same way that knowledge is. Whereas "lucky knowledge" is impossible, "lucky understanding" is not. More exactly, it is possible to have understanding even when one's true belief is lucky in a way that rules out knowledge. Kvanvig proposes the following case to illustrate:

Suppose you pick up a textbook on Native American History and read through a chapter documenting the Comanche dominance of the southern plains, until eventually you seem genuinely to understand why the Comanches dominated the southern plains. But suppose as well that while the book you happened to pick up is accurate, most other books on this topic are full of errors. If you had picked up one of these other books instead (and we can imagine that they are all within easy reach!), your beliefs about the Comanches would have been almost entirely false.[18]

Here is how Kvanvig diagnoses the case:

The basic idea here is that, though knowledge is incompatible with a certain kind of epistemic luck, understanding is not. Upon learning of the disturbed etiology of beliefs about the Comanches, as in the case imagined here, we might say that the person has true beliefs or even true justified beliefs, but no knowledge, if we have heeded our lessons from Gettier . . . But we needn't say the same thing about the claim of understanding. If the etiology were as

---

[16] Cf. Edmund Gettier, "Is Justified True Belief Knowledge?" *Analysis* 23, 6 (1963): 121–123; Linda Zagzebski, "What Is Knowledge?" in John Greco and Ernest Sosa, eds., *The Blackwell Guide to Epistemology* (Oxford: Blackwell, 1999), pp. 92–116; Duncan Pritchard, *Epistemic Luck* (Oxford: Oxford University Press, 2005).

[17] Adapted from Chisholm, *Theory of Knowledge*, p. 105.

[18] Adapted by Grimm, "Is Understanding a Species of Knowledge?" 519.

imagined, one would be lucky to have any understanding at all of the Comanche dominance of the southern plains. So such understanding would count as understanding not undermined by the kind of luck in question.[19]

Kvanvig's diagnosis of the case has intuitive pull. And if he is right that there is understanding but not knowledge here, then the neo-Aristotelian account must be rejected. There are two ways of resisting Kvanvig's diagnosis, however.

First, recall the point, made above, that understanding can take objects of various kinds. Elaborating on that now, we may note that understanding can take any of the following as its object:

a. A system of "real" relations, or relations "in the world." For example: an ecosystem, an economy, a machine, a historical event.
b. A representation of a real system. For example: a theory, a narrative, a model, a set of equations.
c. The relations between a real system and a representation. For example: relations between a model and the economy that it represents, relations between a theory and a causal process that it represents, relations between a diagram and a machine that it represents, relations between a narrative and the historical events that it represents.

In each of these cases, we can make a distinction between *the object* of understanding and *the vehicle* of understanding – that is, between the *thing* understood and its *representation*. In case (a), understanding will involve a representation of some part of "the world." In case (b), understanding will involve a representation of a representation. In case (c), understanding will involve a representation of a relation between a representation and the world.

With these distinctions in mind, however, we can now resist Kvanvig's conclusion that the person in his case understands Comanche history but does not know it. Notice that the term "history" is ambiguous between "actual history" and "historical narrative." That is, it is ambiguous between *real events* in the world and some *representation* of those events in narrative form. But then in no case are we forced to accept Kvanvig's claim that the person in his example has understanding without knowledge. On the contrary, we may continue

[19] Kvanvig, *The Value of Knowledge and the Pursuit of Understanding*, pp. 198–199.

to say that knowledge and understanding come and go together, and in just the way that the neo-Aristotelian account predicts. Regarding the historical narrative (the representation), S has both systematic knowledge and understanding. S knows how the story goes, and understands it. Regarding the representation-world relation, S lacks systematic knowledge. For example, S does not know that the story is true. But so too does S lack understanding that the story is true. Regarding the actual history, S again lacks systematic knowledge. For example, S does not know that the Comanches had superior weapons, and that this was a partial cause of Comanche successes in wars against other nations. That is Kvanvig's point. But so, too, we may now say, S lacks understanding here. The *appearance of understanding* is explained by S's understanding of the story; that is, the representation.

That, anyway, is *one* way to resist Kvanvig's conclusion that there can be understanding without knowledge. But there is another way as well. Namely, we can invoke the information economy framework to make the case that S *does* know Comanche history, as well as understanding it. That position is made available by claiming that published history books can act as transmission channels for historical knowledge. This second strategy requires more elaboration, of course. I will return to it at the end of Section 7.3.

7.3 The Transmission of Understanding

On the view of knowledge transmission defended in earlier chapters, the transmission of knowledge has its home in the context of epistemic communities. According to that view, such communities are faced with two different informational tasks, and, as such, testimonial exchanges within them are governed by two sets of norms or standards: those pertaining to the acquisition of high-quality information and those pertaining to its distribution. The transmission of knowledge, I have argued, is to be understood in terms of the information distribution task. On this picture, the norms and standards governing testimonial exchanges in the distribution role, and hence governing the transmission of knowledge, are themselves various, depending on additional factors regarding the social location of the speaker and hearer. In Chapter 4, we distinguished at least three kinds of relation that structure our social environments, and that enable successful testimonial exchanges in the distribution role. For lack of better labels, we may call them "interpersonal," "informal social," and "formal institutional."

Interpersonal relations depend primarily on the kind of interpersonal experience and "mind reading" that is more or less independent of particular social or institutional roles. Rather, there is a person-to-person connection that underwrites personal trust to one degree or another. This kind of interaction can take place between parents and children, siblings or friends, but also between strangers meeting for the first time. For example, one might trust one stranger to tell the truth but not another, based on quite limited interactions with the two persons. This is because, at times, even limited interaction can be sufficient to mind-read for sincerity and competence, especially in restricted circumstances and for a particular domain.

In contrast to "bare" interpersonal relations, *informal social* relations depend more on well-defined social roles, such as parent–child, sibling–sibling, neighbor–neighbor, and various kinds of friendship. Interactions in these roles will be governed by interpersonal skills, as above, but also by the social norms governing these specific relationships.[20] For example, it is necessary to mind-read in order to cooperate with one's neighbors in some neighborhood task, but how one cooperates (what expectations one has, what one is willing to sacrifice, etc.) will also be influenced by the social norms structuring the neighbor–neighbor relationship.

Here is one example of how the norms structuring social relations might enable the reliable distribution of quality information. We may suppose that in many cultures it is considered a matter of love and respect to go to one's parents for advice regarding childcare. Norms structuring the relationship thereby create a channel of communication from experienced parent to new parent. The information carried by that channel will likely be of high quality, given that the parent of a parent has had some success in the childcare domain. The channel itself will likely be of high quality as well, given the norms governing the communication of this kind of information between parent and child. Thus, the experienced parent will be highly motivated to provide sincere and competent advice, the new parent will be disposed to take that advice seriously, and both parties will be motivated to take care against misinformation and/or misunderstanding.

---

[20] For more on the epistemic significance of social norms, see Chapter 4.

The example shows how the interpersonal skills and social norms underwriting a successful testimonial exchange need not have an epistemic goal as their primary motivation. That is, neither the speaker nor the hearer need be motivated (at least not directly or primarily) by considerations about truth, knowledge, etc. On the contrary, the entire exchange might be explained in terms of the demands of the relationship, such as love and respect, or even guilt. Likewise, good neighbors might ask and give reliable information about bus routes, or other neighborhood practicalities, primarily motivated by the values of civility, helpfulness, and mutual cooperation that structure the neighbor-neighbor relationship.

Both interpersonal relations and informal social relations, then, have the effect of structuring exchanges of information between speaker and hearer. Moreover, both kinds of relation can contribute to the epistemic quality of such exchanges. In most testimonial exchanges, perhaps, both kinds of relations work together. For example, there are two reasons that one might trust a friend, one based on interpersonal interaction, and one based on the social relation. Thus, one might trust that a friend is telling the truth because "I know *her*." Alternatively, one might trust a friend because "That is how *friends* treat each other." And of course, one might trust for both reasons. Similarly, for parent–child trust, neighbor–neighbor trust, etc.

Finally, we saw in Chapter 4 that some relations are defined by more *formal institutional* roles. For example, teacher–student, doctor–patient, lawyer–client, and employer–employee relationships are largely governed by relevant institutional rules. Here again, the rules in question function in addition to or "on top of" the interpersonal skills and informal social norms discussed above. And here again, institutional rules can contribute to the quality of testimonial exchanges. For example, the doctor–patient relationship is underwritten by institutional rules that are designed to guarantee competency and honesty in practitioners. Likewise, for the lawyer–client and the employer–employee relationships. Such rules might take the form of government regulations, legal contracts, professional standards, or professional ethics. Together they provide additional structure to the social environment, often in ways that contribute to the epistemic quality of testimonial exchanges. Finally, as in the case of interpersonal skills and informal social norms, institutional rules need not have epistemic goals as their direct or primary motivation. For example, a particular lawyer might have little regard for the truth as such, a particular doctor might place little value on knowledge for its own sake. But in each case, there are institutional mechanisms in place to ensure honesty and competence in the relevant domains, thereby creating quality channels of information that can be exploited by patients and clients.

Also in Chapter 4, we noted an analogy to the flow of information in perceptual uptake. In cases of perception, a stable *physical* environment allows perception to exploit information-carrying signals. For example, a particular profile reliably signals *dog*, whereas a different profile reliably signals *cat*. This is not necessarily the case – the environment must be well suited to visual perception; that is, it must be enabling of the perceptual skills in play. A stable *social* environment plays the same role regarding the flow of information in testimonial exchanges. Just as natural laws construct a (more or less) stable physical environment, giving it the contours that it has, social norms construct a (more or less) stable social environment, giving it the contours that it has. Natural laws thereby underwrite regularities that can be exploited by perception. Social norms thereby underwrite regularities that can be exploited by testimony.

The case of small children is interesting here. Plausibly, small children have only limited skills for determining the sincerity and competence of speakers. That is, small children, left to themselves, can be somewhat gullible.[21] So how do children manage to learn from testimony as well as they do? The answer is that children are rarely left to themselves. On the contrary, we construct and monitor their social environments so as to keep them safe from insincere and incompetent speakers.[22] Put differently, we engineer environments that enable the transmission of knowledge that their care and upbringing require.

And now, clearly enough, we also engineer social environments to deliver a more formal education. In fact, formal educational institutions are designed to transmit knowledge as one of their primary motivations. And in fact, such institutions are designed to transmit *systematic* knowledge in various domains, such as physics, biology, history, economics, literature, philosophy, education, etc. Finally, in all

---

[21] The picture presented by empirical studies is mixed. For an overview of some relevant literature, see Paul L. Harris and Melissa A. Koenig, "The Basis of Epistemic Trust: Reliable Testimony or Reliable Sources?" *Episteme* 4, 3 (2007): 264–284.

[22] Cf. Goldberg, *Anti-Individualism*.

of these educational domains, the point is to transmit systematic knowledge of relevant *dependence* relations. The sciences, for example, transmit knowledge of relevant causal structures and processes. The humanities, for their part, transmit knowledge of other kinds of dependence relations, including relevant causal relations, but also teleological, normative, and metaphysical relations. History, for example, teaches the motivations, mechanisms, and broader conditions responsible for various historical events. Economics, for example, teaches rational choice theory and other mechanisms that explain economic activity.

I suggested that formal educational institutions are *designed* to transmit understanding. That is, they are designed to transmit systematic knowledge of relevant dependence relations. This is evident in various features of our educational institutions, including curricula that allow for sustained and in-depth study of a subject matter, and pedagogical strategies that allow for sustained and systematic presentation, exploration, analysis, and critique of relevant methodologies and content. Our formal educational institutions, moreover, are also embedded in broader social structures involving licensing, accreditation, peer review, market pressures, and informal reputation markers, all of which play a role in maintaining and signaling quality control.

All of these considerations, then, make it clear that formal educational institutions such as colleges, universities, and professional schools are designed for the transmission of understanding in relevant domains. But although that is one of the primary motivations of such institutions, it is not the only one. For such institutions are also in the business of *generating* knowledge, and at least as importantly, in the business of teaching their students how to generate knowledge. Put differently, our educational institutions are in the business of training their students to become fully participating members of various epistemic communities. That sort of training requires the transmission of relevant knowledge, for sure, but it also requires that students be trained how to generate knowledge themselves. It requires that students become *practitioners* in their chosen fields. And that is why a quality education does not *merely* transmit relevant understanding.

This feature of a quality education also explains the importance of acquaintance knowledge and knowledge-how. Acquaintance knowledge is more or less knowledge gained by first-hand experience, as opposed to knowledge gained by description, via a second- or third-party observer. Acquaintance knowledge, therefore, necessarily involves *generating* knowledge "for oneself." Moreover, a central feature of practitioners is knowledge-how. And in the present context, that means knowledge-how concerning the generation of knowledge. That is why a quality education involves components aimed at training for practice. Consider, for example, a chemistry course that includes a lab component. One might think that the purpose of running chemistry experiments is to "find out for oneself" or to "know for oneself" that particular chemical processes result in particular effects. But if that were the primary purpose of running such experiments, then the more the better, and failure to run other experiments would come with an associated cost in knowledge. But that is not what is going on in the lab component of a science course. The purpose of a lab component is not to learn the results of the experiments, but to learn *how to run* the experiments. That is, the purpose is to teach the kind of knowledge-how necessary to be a practitioner in the discipline.

Finally, it is easy enough to extend these same ideas to forms of *informal* education that are nevertheless extended and systematic. I argued above that interpersonal, informal social, and formal institutional relations all structure our social environments so as to create channels of information flow, some highly reliable. I also noted that these relations often operate in conjunction, so that formal institutional relations often overlap with informal social ones, and both of these often overlap with interpersonal relations. This is clearly so in the case of formal education, where the relationship between student and teacher is often a layered one, governed by formal institutional rules and policies, as well as positive law, but also by the more informal norms associated with teacher–student, mentor–mentee, and even friend–friend relations. But this is often the case for informal education as well; for example, in the many and various mentorship and apprentice relationships that take place outside the context of formal educational institutions, such as in business, professional trades, sports, martial arts, etc. In all of these contexts, it is clear enough that extended testimony can transmit knowledge of relevant dependence relations, and that in fact the relationship has been, at least in part, designed to do exactly that. It is also clear that such relationships are not designed to do only that. Among other things, they are designed for the student, mentee, or apprentice to learn relevant ways of generating knowledge themselves. A good education, whether formal or informal, is designed to do both of these things.

Return now to Kvanvig's Comanche case, and his objection that the person in that case understands Comanche history but does not know it. Understanding, Kvanvig concludes, is therefore not a kind of knowledge. The central idea behind that objection, recall, is that the person does not know in the case because his true beliefs about Comanche history are too lucky, depending as they do on reading one of many books, the only one of which reports reliably on the issue. One strategy for responding to the objection was to distinguish between different objects of understanding in the neighborhood, and to argue that knowledge and understanding do not come apart when we keep these various objects constant. In particular, I argued, we can make a distinction between the *historical narrative* portrayed in the book, which the person both knows and understands, and the *actual history* of Comanche dominance on the southern plains, which the person neither knows nor understands.

The present account of how education transmits understanding, however, makes available a different way of responding to Kvanvig's objection. Namely, that account makes it plausible to maintain that the person in Kvanvig's case both knows and understands actual Comanche history, because the person has been transmitted that knowledge and understanding by reading a reliable textbook. According to that account, the norms and rules that shape our educational institutions are *designed*, in part, to create reliable channels of information flow. Moreover, the function of such channels is to underwrite a useful division of intellectual labor; that is, they allow for knowledge to be transmitted independently of a hearer's ability to vindicate their reliability. That is, in part, why the framework offers an *anti-reductionist* account of knowledge transmission. The present proposal is that we can think of history textbooks as transmission channels on this model. By thinking of the *good* textbook in Kvanvig's example this way, we can explain how S knows Comanche history, and why S's true beliefs about Comanche history are "lucky" only in ways that knowledge can tolerate.

Whether the present proposal constitutes an adequate reply to Kvanvig's case depends on whether history books and other textbooks (i.e., those that are properly vetted, sanctioned, and published) can act as transmission channels in this way, and even in the kind of scenario

144   *The Transmission of Knowledge*

that Kvanvig describes. And that, in turn, will largely depend on further details regarding how we should understand the parameters of transmission channels more generally. This kind of issue is further addressed in the Appendix. For now, however, it is useful to note that Kvanvig's case, as the present proposal understands it, is in an important way structurally similar to *typical* cases of knowledge transmission on the anti-reductionist picture. That is, it is essential to the anti-reductionist picture that knowledge transmission partly depends on the "good luck" of being in a reliable transmission channel. In the typical case, there will be various actual and potential sources of testimony regarding some relevant item of information, some reliable and some not. Moreover, the hearer will often not herself be in a position to discriminate among these sources – to evaluate them for reliability – independently of a social division of labor that offloads at least some of that burden. Kvanvig's Comanche case can, from this perspective, be understood as merely one instance of this ubiquitous phenomenon.

7.4 Conclusion

This chapter has articulated and defended a neo-Aristotelian account of understanding – one that understands understanding as a systematic knowledge of dependence relations. So understood, it is plausible that understanding can be transmitted by the kind of sustained testimony characteristic of various formal and informal educational settings. In fact, I have argued, such settings are often designed for exactly this purpose. Nevertheless, a quality education strives to do more than transmit understanding. Importantly, such an education teaches students how to generate knowledge as well. Accordingly, the information economy framework defended here helps to explain how understanding can indeed be transmitted by the kind of systematic testimony that is characteristic of various educational settings. That same framework also helps to explain why not all testimony is apt for transmitting understanding, and why a quality education does more than transmit understanding.

8 | *Reductionism and Big Science*

In Chapter 1, I defined several versions of reductionism in the epistemology of testimony. In its most general form, reductionism claims that all testimonial knowledge can be reduced to non-testimonial knowledge. In Chapter 1 this was understood as a claim about species of knowledge: All testimonial knowledge can be understood as a species of some other kind of knowledge, such as inductive knowledge; testimonial knowledge does not require its own species within the knowledge genus. Anti-reductionism, in its most general form, is just the denial of this kind of reductionism. Also in Chapter 1, we saw that there are two routes to anti-reductionism so understood. First, one might embrace *source* anti-reductionism; that is, one might hold that testimony is its own generative source of knowledge, irreducible to other generative sources such as perception and induction. Second, one might embrace *transmission* anti-reductionism; that is, one might think that the transmission of knowledge is irreducible to the generation of knowledge. Of course, one might embrace both kinds of anti-reductionism. This book has defended *transmission* anti-reductionism, leaving open the question of whether *source* anti-reductionism is true as well.

The argument for transmission anti-reductionism has so far taken the form of an argument to the best explanation. More specifically, I have argued that our anti-reductionist framework (a) explains a range of individual cases; (b) solves various problems and puzzles in the epistemology of testimony; (c) explains a range of linguistic and behavioral phenomena; (d) explains what many alternative positions in the epistemology of testimony get right, or almost get right; and (e) integrates well with various plausible positions in epistemology, the philosophy of language, action theory, and the cognitive sciences.

In the present chapter, I offer a different argument against reductionism and in favor of anti-reductionism. The first part of the argument proceeds by considering the widespread epistemic dependence that characterizes contemporary "big science," and by arguing that anti-reductionism is *clearly* right in this context. More exactly, the argument is that adopting anti-reductionism is clearly necessary to avoid an implausible kind of skepticism about big science. The second part of the argument claims that, if anti-reductionism is necessary in the case of big science, then anti-reductionism is necessary more generally. This second part of the argument can be run two ways. The first is straightforward. The idea is that transmission reductionism is a thesis about the transmission of knowledge *in general*: It says that *all* knowledge transmission can be understood in terms of knowledge generation. But then, if the transmission of scientific knowledge cannot be so understood, then that is sufficient to reject the general thesis. A second route to the same conclusion is also available, however. The idea is that embracing transmission anti-reductionism about scientific knowledge but not non-scientific knowledge is inelegant and unmotivated. So, even if we were to restrict our anti-reductionism to the realm of scientific knowledge, we would lack good reason for doing so.

The remainder of the chapter proceeds as follows. Section 8.1 considers a skeptical argument directed at contemporary big science. That argument focuses on the nature and extent of the epistemic dependence that characterizes big science, and argues that scientific knowledge is incompatible with that sort of dependence. Section 8.2 argues that the skeptical argument can be avoided only by embracing anti-reductionism about knowledge transmission. Specifically, it is argued that skepticism is avoided only by rejecting the idea that the standards and norms governing the generation of knowledge in big science are the same as those governing the transmission of knowledge within big science. But since avoiding skepticism in this context requires embracing anti-reductionism, we should embrace anti-reductionism. Section 8.3 argues that the anti-reductionist conclusion of Section 8.2 generalizes: Anti-reductionism in the context of contemporary big science motivates anti-reductionism in general. Finally, Section 8.4 considers some objection to the line of argument presented in Sections 8.1–8.3.

8.1 A Skeptical Argument Directed at "Big Science"

In a seminal paper exploring the nature and extent of our epistemic dependence on other persons, John Hardwig describes a not atypical publication in particle physics.

approximately 50 physicists worked perhaps 50 man/years collecting the data for the experiment. When the data were in, the experimenters divided into five geographic groups to analyze the data, a process which involved looking at 2.5 million pictures, making measurements on 300,000 interesting events, and running the results through computers in order to isolate and measure 47 charm events. The "West Coast group" that analyzed about a third of the data included 40 physicists and technicians who spent about 60 man/years on their analysis.

Obviously, no one person could have done this experiment – in fact, [one of the researchers] reports that no one university or national laboratory could have done it – and many of the authors of an article like this will not even know how a given number in the article was arrived at.[1]

Hardwig continues,

the article's 99 authors represent different specializations with particle physics, but all are experimentalists, so none would be able to undertake the theoretical revisions which might be required as a result of this experiment and which provide a large part of the rationale for doing it. On the other hand, most ... theoreticians would not be competent to conduct the experiment – and neither the experimentalists nor the theoreticians are competent to design, build, and maintain the equipment without which the experiment could not be run at all.[2]

Hardwig's paper was published in 1985, the paper he is describing in 1983. Already at that time, then, the phenomena of "big science" was in full swing; that is, science in which "there is clearly a complex network of appeals to the authority of various experts, and the resulting knowledge could not have been achieved by any one person" and in which "each researcher is forced to acknowledge the extent to which his own work rests on the work of others – work which he has not and could not (if only for reasons of time and expense) verify for himself."

After describing the kind of epistemic dependence that characterizes much of contemporary science, Hardwig resists drawing skeptical conclusions. Rather, he says, "some very basic changes in our epistemologies are required."[3] In particular, "The epistemic individualism implicit in many of our epistemologies is thus called into question, with important

---

[1] Hardwig, "Epistemic Dependence," p. 347.   [2] Ibid., pp. 347–348.
[3] Ibid., p. 349.

implications for how we understand knowledge and the knower, as well as for our conception of rationality."[4] I will return to this last thought below. But first, I want to reconstruct a kind of skeptical worry that someone might have in reaction to the widespread epistemic dependence of big science. That worry can then be turned into an interesting skeptical argument, with an important epistemological lesson.

The worry goes something like this. It begins with an obvious thought: that scientific knowledge in general requires fairly high epistemic standards. These standards, we think, pertain to both (a) the quality of evidence required for scientific knowledge, and (b) the quality of evidential relations (support, confirmation) between evidence and conclusions. One might deny that this is an obvious thought if one denies that science gives us "knowledge" in the first place. One might think, rather, that science yields some other cognitive good, such as justification, or rational thought, or practically useful thought, etc. It is important to note, however, that our "obvious thought" does not claim that there *is* scientific knowledge. Rather, the thought is only that scientific knowledge would require high evidential standards. So this first thought, all by itself, should be acceptable to skeptic and non-skeptic alike.

A second thought is the one that we saw Hardwig emphasizing above: that big science requires widespread epistemic dependence among its practitioners. This dependence, we saw, includes both (1) internal dependence among researchers on the same working team; and (2) external dependence among different teams and researchers who use each other's work.

The notion of dependence at issue here might be characterized as follows:

S1 epistemically depends on S2 with respect to claim p just in case S1 takes p on trust from S2, where "taking p on trust" entails believing (accepting, assuming) that p in the absence of evidence that would be adequate for knowing that p.

On this understanding, S1 depending on S2 with respect to p entails that S1 herself lacks evidence that would be adequate for knowing that p. The present thought is that big science involves widespread epistemic dependence of this sort. In fact, we might *define* big science in terms of widespread epistemic dependence of this sort.

[4] Ibid., p. 336.

And now comes what is perhaps the essence of the skeptical worry: that the epistemic dependence required by big science is inconsistent with the evidential standards required for scientific knowledge. As Hardwig suggests above, "The epistemic individualism implicit in many of our epistemologies is thus called into question."[5]

Putting all this together, we may now formulate a skeptical argument directed at big science.

1. Scientific knowledge requires high epistemic standards. These standards pertain to both (a) the quality of evidence that grounds scientific knowledge; and (b) the quality of evidential relations (support, confirmation) between scientific evidence and scientific conclusions.
2. Big science requires extensive epistemic dependence among its practitioners.
3. The epistemic dependence cited in (2) violates the standards cited in (1).

Therefore,

4. Scientific knowledge from big science is impossible.

In the next section I will argue that our skeptical argument can be rejected by denying its third premise, and that doing so, in effect, amounts to embracing transmission anti-reductionism. In fact, I will argue, this is the *only* plausible way to reject the skeptical argument. Before turning to that line of argument, however, I want to pause here to discuss a methodological issue. In particular, I want to consider how our skeptical argument, and skeptical arguments in general, can be used to drive epistemological theorizing.

So, consider: We have before us a skeptical argument that begins with premises that, in isolation, seem innocent, but that when brought together lead to a seemingly absurd conclusion – that contemporary big science cannot produce knowledge. In this respect, our skeptical argument has the structure that Bertrand Russell attributed to philosophical problems in general: We begin with our "instinctive beliefs" (i.e., those that we find pre-theoretically plausible), and we come to recognize that they lead to an implausible conclusion. The philosophical task, then, is to decide what in our thinking we must "modify or abandon."[6]

---

[5] Ibid., p. 336.
[6] "Hence, by organizing our instinctive beliefs and their consequences, by considering which among them is most possible, if necessary, to modify or abandon, we can arrive, on the basis of accepting as our sole data what we

It is clear that our skeptical argument has the structure that Russell describes. The philosophical task, then, is to figure out what has gone wrong. Specifically, what premise of the skeptical argument can be rejected, what step in the reasoning can be resisted? My next point is that philosophical theorizing here may lead to a lesser or greater degree of satisfaction. First, and with a lesser degree of satisfaction, we might identify some premise or step in the reasoning that can be *plausibly rejected*. Or that, at least, can be more plausibly rejected than accepting the skeptical conclusion. This kind of response to the skeptical argument will be less than satisfying, however, insofar as it falls short of *explaining why* this is the correct modification in our pre-theoretical thinking. A more satisfying response to the argument provides exactly that kind of explanation, and it is in this way that the argument can drive substantive epistemological theory.[7] This is the kind of response that I will defend in Section 8.2, where I will argue that an adequate response to the argument requires a rejection of transmission reductionism.

The overall argumentative structure of the chapter, then, is this: Section 8.2 argues that an anti-skeptical response to the argument laid out above entails transmission anti-reductionism regarding scientific knowledge. More succinctly, rejecting skepticism about contemporary big science requires transmission anti-reductionism. Section 8.3 argues that this result should be extended to transmission anti-reductionism for knowledge in general, because this is the most theoretically elegant way to accommodate the lesson of Section 8.2.

8.2 What's Wrong with the Skeptical Argument? Big Science and Anti-reductionism

So, what's wrong with the skeptical reasoning laid out in Section 8.1? The argument is clearly valid, so long as we understand premise 1 as laying down a general condition on scientific knowledge. On that interpretation of the argument, premise 2 states a feature of contemporary big

instinctively believe, at an orderly systematic organization of our knowledge, in which, though the possibility of error remains, its likelihood is diminished by the interrelation of the parts and by the critical scrutiny which has preceded acquiescence." Bertrand Russell, *Problems of Philosophy* (Oxford: Oxford University Press, 1997), pp. 25–26.

7 I defend this methodology at length in *Putting Skeptics in Their Place*, especially in chapter 1.

science and premise 3 states that this feature is incompatible with the condition laid down in 1. The argument can be resisted, then, only if some premise is objectionable.

I have already suggested that premise 1 is obvious. It says only that scientific knowledge requires high epistemic standards. One might deny that this is obvious if one suspects that the premise is sneaking in some objectionable version of foundationalism, or empiricism, or some other philosophically controversial position. But premise 1 does nothing of the sort. For example, it says nothing about certain foundations, or theory-neutral data, or the like. Fill in the details as you like. So long as one agrees that scientific knowledge requires high epistemic standards *of one sort or another*, one should think that premise 1 is unobjectionable.[8]

Premise 2 is also obvious. It simply states a fact about contemporary big science. In fact, I suggested, we might define "big science" in terms of widespread epistemic dependence, as that notion is understood above. Premise 2, then, simply states the fact that contemporary science is big science, so understood.

Should we conclude that there is *nothing* wrong with the argument, and that its conclusion is therefore correct? One might be happy to do so if one thinks that science does not deliver "knowledge" in the first place. One might think, rather, that science yields some other cognitive good, such as justification, or rational thought, etc. But this line of thinking would be a mistake. For consider: The skeptical argument will run just the same way when you substitute your preferred value for "knowledge." As long as you think that science delivers some kind of cognitive good, and that the standards for that good are relatively high, then the skeptical argument will proceed in just the same way, but now to a skeptical conclusion that you are not willing to accept. So, even if you think that science delivers some cognitive good other than scientific knowledge, you are committed to thinking that the skeptical argument goes wrong somewhere.

That said, it remains implausible that contemporary big science never delivers knowledge. For even if our best theories do not themselves constitute knowledge, they seem clearly to produce knowledge. For example, we now know that there are black holes in deep

---

[8] More exactly, premise 1 is unobjectionable if interpreted as a claim about the generation of scientific knowledge, as I will below. If it is interpreted as a claim about all scientific knowledge, including transmitted knowledge, then our anti-reductionism will provide grounds for rejecting premise 1 as well as premise 3.

space, that some cancers are associated with genetic mutations, and that there are multiple kinds of radioactive decay. These concern the "outputs" of science. Moreover, it seems clear that science involves knowledge by way of inputs as well. For example, many of the various observations, data points, measurements, and calculations that drive scientific inquiry seem clearly to count as knowledge. So again, even if not everything that contemporary science uses or delivers counts as knowledge, it seems clear that there is plenty of knowledge involved.

The remaining option, of course, is to deny premise 3: that the epistemic dependence that characterizes big science violates the standards for scientific knowledge. That premise *is* controversial, and, importantly, far more implausible than the skeptical conclusion. At the very least, then, we have a clear strategy for rejecting the skeptical argument and thereby resisting its skeptical conclusion. In fact, however, we have much more than this. For we also have a ready *theoretical explanation* for why premise 3 is false. Namely, premise 3 implicitly assumes that the standards for transmitting knowledge are the same as those for generating knowledge.

Recall the driving idea behind premise 3 – that the epistemic dependence characterizing contemporary science violates the standards for scientific knowledge in general. The idea was that this kind of dependence violates the standards in play for the *generation* of scientific knowledge. That is, the kind of *sharing* of scientific knowledge that goes on in contemporary science was deemed inconsistent with the standards for *producing* scientific knowledge more generally. But this line of thinking assumes that the standards for sharing knowledge are the same as those for producing knowledge. And this is precisely what transmission anti-reductionism denies. Accordingly, transmission anti-reductionism *explains why* premise 3 is false. Put differently, that position gives us a theoretically principled reason for rejecting premise 3, and thereby resisting skepticism about contemporary big science.

Adopting transmission anti-reductionism, then, is sufficient for rejecting the skeptical argument presented in Section 8.1. I now want to argue that it is also necessary. We can see this by assuming transmission reductionism for scientific knowledge. That is, assume for the sake of argument that the standards for transmitting scientific knowledge among cooperating practitioners are reducible to the standards for generating scientific knowledge. If that is the case, then those standards are violated by cooperating practitioners of big science, and that is *obvious*.

To drive home the point, consider the example of a researcher (call her R) who uses the findings reported by an external lab (call it L) in her own research. In the typical case (really, in every case), R will not have done anything like scientifically adequate research into the reliability of L's results. R will not have, for example, designed blind studies or constructed statistical models to establish the reliability of L's results. Whatever the epistemic standards that R must meet in order to properly rely on L's results, those will not be the same standards that apply to R's original research. Which is just to say that the standards for the transmission of scientific knowledge are not the same as the standards for the generation of scientific knowledge.

Here is one more example. Suppose that a researcher (call her R1) uses findings reported in a scientific journal (call it J) in her own research. In the typical case (really, in every case), R1 will not have done anything like a scientifically adequate study into the reliability of J's results. R1 will not have, for example, designed scientifically sound studies evaluating the reliability of science journals, their editorial policies, their refereeing processes, etc. That is, she will not have done anything like the original research necessary to publish a respectable study on the reliability of science journals in general or of J in particular. But then, by hypothesis, by using findings published in J, she will have violated the norms governing the generation of scientific knowledge. Does that mean that she has violated any *relevant* epistemic norms? Only if the norms that govern her using the findings published in J are the same as the norms that govern her original research. But that is precisely what transmission reductionism claims and transmission anti-reductionism denies.

So again: If we assume that the standards for transmitting scientific knowledge are the same as those for generating scientific knowledge, then those standards are violated by cooperating practitioners of big science. In that case, premise 3 of the skeptical argument stands and the skeptical conclusion follows. We may conclude, then, that adopting transmission anti-reductionism for scientific knowledge is not merely *one* way to reject the skeptical argument, but the *only* way.

8.3 From Anti-reductionism in Big Science to Anti-reductionism More Generally

In Section 8.2 I argued that adopting transmission anti-reductionism is necessary for resisting skepticism about contemporary big science. In this section, I will argue that the conclusion generalizes. Specifically, if adopting transmission anti-reductionism is necessary for understanding contemporary scientific knowledge, then we should adopt transmission anti-reductionism for knowledge in general.

The first route to this conclusion is straightforward. Namely, transmission reductionism is a thesis about the transmission of knowledge in general: It states that all knowledge transmission can be reduced to knowledge generation. But if the transmission of scientific knowledge cannot be so reduced, then transmission reductionism is false. But suppose we restrict our transmission reductionism to non-scientific knowledge. This revised thesis would be that, although the transmission of scientific knowledge cannot be reduced to the generation of knowledge, the transmission of non-scientific knowledge *can* be. That is a possible position, but it would be inelegant and unmotivated.

For one, scientific knowledge is widely considered to be paradigmatic of knowledge in general. Our revised reductionism would now be in the position of denying this, claiming that there are two ways of coming to know for scientific knowledge (generation and transmission), but only one way for non-scientific knowledge. The revised position is additionally odd in that scientific knowledge is widely considered to be more restrictive than non-scientific knowledge. But our revised reductionism has it that scientific knowledge can tolerate the violation of appropriate standards for knowledge generation, but non-scientific knowledge cannot.

Our revised reductionist might argue that, in the case of scientific knowledge, widespread epistemic dependence is radical and obvious, but that this is not the case for non-scientific knowledge. Accordingly, whereas we are forced to embrace transmission anti-reductionism for scientific knowledge, no such theoretical move is required for non-scientific knowledge. On the contrary, this argument goes, transmission reductionism is theoretically preferable in that domain. In response to this line of argument, the first thing to note is that it is controversial whether transmission reductionism is preferable for non-scientific knowledge. In fact, Chapters 1–6 of the book have argued that it is not. But suppose, for the sake of argument, that we agree that transmission reductionism is a theoretically viable position for non-scientific knowledge. So long as we agree that transmission anti-reductionism is also a viable position for non-scientific knowledge, the clearly more elegant position is to adopt anti-reductionism for knowledge in general.

8.4 Objections

In this final section, I want to consider two avenues for resisting the arguments of Sections 8.2 and 8.3. I will argue that, in both cases, further consideration returns us to the conclusion that was established in Section 8.3 – that transmission anti-reductionism is the best theoretical option for understanding both scientific knowledge and knowledge in general.

First, one might insist that premise 1 of our skeptical argument is objectionable, and that therefore there is an alternative route to resisting that argument's skeptical conclusion. In particular, one might insist that not all scientific knowledge is grounded in evidence, and that therefore premise 1 is overly general. At most, this line of objection goes, only *some* scientific knowledge is so grounded. But if we reject premise 1 on these grounds, then we can avoid the skeptical conclusion without embracing transmission anti-reductionism about scientific knowledge.

For the sake of argument, let's agree that premise 1 is false when read as a general condition on scientific knowledge. In fact, this might be a natural position for the anti-reductionist to take. For example, we might naturally read premise 1 as a claim about the generation of scientific knowledge, rather than about scientific knowledge in general. And in that case, the anti-reductionist is actually committed to rejecting premise 1, as the objection suggests. The problem with this line of objection, however, is that we can revise the skeptical argument by replacing premise 1 with a premise that the objection must accept. And when we do, we see that transmission anti-reductionism is necessary for responding to the revised skeptical argument.

The revised argument would now go like this:

1b. *Some* scientific knowledge requires high epistemic standards. These standards pertain to both (a) the quality of evidence that grounds scientific knowledge, and (b) the quality of evidential relations (support, confirmation) between scientific evidence and scientific conclusions.

2. Big science requires extensive epistemic dependence among its practitioners.
3. The epistemic dependence cited in (2) violates the standards cited in (1b).

Therefore,

4. Scientific knowledge from big science is impossible.

But notice that when we replace premise 1 with premise 1b, the argument is no longer valid. For even if the epistemic dependence that characterizes big science violates the standards for some scientific knowledge, that is consistent with such dependence not violating other standards, also sufficient for scientific knowledge. Accordingly, to restore validity it is necessary to add a premise to the effect that extensive epistemic dependence violates all standards sufficient for scientific knowledge.

The revised argument would then look like this:

1b. *Some* scientific knowledge requires high epistemic standards. These standards pertain to both (a) the quality of evidence that grounds scientific knowledge, and (b) the quality of evidential relations (support, confirmation) between scientific evidence and scientific conclusions.
2. Big science requires extensive epistemic dependence among its practitioners.
3. The epistemic dependence cited in (2) violates the standards cited in (1b).
4. The epistemic dependence cited in (2) violates all other standards sufficient for scientific knowledge as well.

Therefore,

5. Scientific knowledge from big science is impossible.

But now the obvious culprit is the new premise 4. The revised argument is now clearly valid, and premise 1b is rendered innocent by the new reading. In any case, the present line of objection depends on it. Premises 2 and 3 also remain obvious, as before. The only premise to challenge, then, is premise 4. But what might serve as the theoretical basis of that challenge? Again, the only plausible answer is something like transmission anti-reductionism. That is, premise 4 assumes that the standards for coming to know in general are the same or similar to the standards cited in premise 1b. And that is exactly what transmission anti-reductionism denies.

Finally, we may drive home the same conclusion – that adopting transmission anti-reductionism is necessary for avoiding skepticism – by revising the skeptical argument so as to explicitly assume transmission reductionism. Our new skeptical argument goes like this:

1c. The *generation* of scientific knowledge requires high epistemic standards.
2. Big science requires extensive epistemic dependence among its practitioners.
3. The epistemic dependence cited in (2) violates the standards cited in (1c).
4. The standards relevant to the transmission of scientific knowledge are the same as those relevant to the generation of scientific knowledge (transmission reductionism).

Therefore,

5. The epistemic dependence required by big science is inconsistent with both the generation and transmission of scientific knowledge (1c–4).
6. If big science can neither generate nor transmit scientific knowledge, then scientific knowledge from big science is impossible.

Therefore,

7. Scientific knowledge from big science is impossible (5, 6).

The independent premises of this argument include 1c, 2, 3, and 6, all of which are unobjectionable. The argument is also valid. The remaining independent premise is premise 4, which amounts to a statement of transmission reductionism. The only way to avoid the argument's conclusion, then, is to reject premise 4 and embrace transmission anti-reductionism.

I will end by considering a different avenue for resisting the arguments of this chapter. Namely, one might think that our skeptical arguments could not force anti-reductionism about scientific knowledge, because Hardwig himself comes to a different conclusion on the basis of essentially the same considerations. Thus, in the face of the extensive epistemic dependence characterizing contemporary science (and characterizing our epistemic lives more generally), Hardwig comes to the following disjunctive conclusion:

Unless we maintain that most of our scientific research and scholarship could never, because of the cooperative methodology of the enterprise, result in knowledge, I submit that we must say that ... someone can know "vicariously" – i.e., without possessing the evidence for the truth of what he knows, perhaps without even fully understanding what he knows ... If the conclusion is unpalatable, another is possible. Perhaps that p is known, not by any one person, but by the community composed of A, B, C, D, and E. Perhaps D and E are not entitled to say, "I know that p," but only, "We know that p." This community is not reducible to a class of individuals, for no one individual and no one individually knows that p. If we take this tack, we could retain the idea that the knower must understand and have evidence for the truth of what he knows, but in doing so we deny that the knower is always an individual or even a class of individuals.[9]

And again:

Thus if the arguments of this paper are accepted ... [we must] either agree that one can know without possessing the supporting evidence or accept the idea that there is knowledge that is known by the community, not by any individual knower.[10]

Hardwig acknowledges the theoretical costs of his second option – that of embracing a community knower "not reducible to" individual knowers. But the present point is that Hardwig seems to be offering a different theoretical option than the one embraced above – a kind of metaphysical anti-reductionism, as opposed to epistemic anti-reductionism.[11] In response to this line of objection, I will argue that neither of Hardwig's disjunctive options for accommodating epistemic dependence are in fact alternatives to transmission reductionism.

This is easiest to see with his first option. In this regard, Hardwig makes a distinction between "good reasons for believing" a proposition and "evidence for the truth" of a proposition.[12] On this terminology,

<hr/>

[9] Hardwig, "Epistemic Dependence," pp. 348–349.   [10] Ibid., p. 349.
[11] Others embracing group knowers include Tollefsen, *Groups as Agents*, chapter 3; Pettit, "The Reality of Group Agents"; and List and Pettit, *Group Agency*.
[12] Hardwig, "Epistemic Dependence," p. 336.

one way to have good reasons for believing that *p* is to have evidence for the truth of *p*. But another way, Hardwig suggests, is having good reasons to believe that someone else has good reasons for believing that *p*. This latter respect, Hardwig says, involves an appeal to intellectual authority. Thus, Hardwig writes,

Suppose that person A has good reasons – evidence – for believing that p, but a second person, B, does not. In *this* sense B has no (or insufficient) reasons to believe that p. However, suppose also that B has good reasons to believe that A has good reasons to believe that p. Does B then, *ipso facto*, have good reasons to believe that p? If so, B's belief is epistemically grounded in an appeal to the authority of A and A's belief.[13]

Hardwig's first option for accommodating epistemic dependence embraces this suggestion. Likewise, this first option recognizes two ways of coming to know:

Suppose someone tells me something that is true without giving me evidence for its truth. Perhaps A tells me that laetrile does not cure cancer without giving me the studies that prove this, much less the concrete data on which those studies are based. But suppose I have good reasons to believe that A is an authority in the field of cancer research and so I believe what he tells me. Do I then know that laetrile does not cure cancer . . .?[14]

Hardwig's first option answers in the affirmative:

Unless we maintain that most of our scientific research and scholarship could *never*, because of the cooperative methodology of the enterprise, result in knowledge, I submit that we must say that p is known in cases like this . . . [W]e must also say that someone can know "vicariously" – i.e., without possessing the evidence for the truth of what he knows.[15]

As I have already suggested, Hardwig's first option for accommodating epistemic dependence is not an alternative to transmission reductionism. It is, rather, a version of it. In effect, the position is that there are two ways of coming to know. The first is to possess evidence for one's belief, which is to "think for oneself."[16] The second is to have good reason for believing that someone else knows, which is to "appeal to authority."[17] Moreover, these are decidedly different ways of coming to know, the idea being that one who appeals to authority does so

---

[13] Ibid.   [14] Ibid., pp. 334–335.   [15] Ibid., p. 348.   [16] Ibid., p. 340.
[17] Ibid., p. 348.

precisely because she lacks evidence for what she believes. Assuming that, when one comes to know by appealing to the authority of someone else who knows, this counts as knowledge transmission, Hardwig's first option amounts to a version of transmission anti-reductionism.

This is straightforward and, as I suggested, easy to see. What is less obvious is that Hardwig's second option for accommodating extensive epistemic dependence – adopting what I called "metaphysical anti-reductionism" – is likewise not an alternative to epistemic anti-reductionism. Consider: On Hardwig's metaphysical anti-reductionism, "no one individually knows that p."[18] Or again, "there is knowledge that is known by the community, not by any individual knower."[19] Accordingly, Hardwig's second option embraces a kind of skepticism about scientific knowledge. Specifically, it embraces the idea that individual scientists do not have scientific knowledge. More carefully, it embraces the idea that individual scientists do not have knowledge by way of contemporary big science. But then, in this sense, his second option is not an alternative anti-skeptical response to transmission anti-reductionism, because it is not an anti-skeptical response *at all*.

However, Hardwig considers a different version of his second option, inspired by Peirce's claim "that the *community* of inquirers is the primary knower and that individual knowledge is derivative."[20] But this version of the second option, if it is to avoid skepticism about individual knowledge, must be wedded to an account of the transmission of knowledge from group knower to individual knower. And that account will have to be anti-reductionist, since, by hypothesis, individual knowers do not meet the same standards for knowledge as group knowers. That is why Hardwig needed to introduce group knowers in the first place! And so, in the end, Hardwig's second option for accommodating extensive epistemic dependence does not constitute an alternative to transmission anti-reductionism.

---

[18] Ibid., p. 349.   [19] Ibid.   [20] Ibid.

9 | *Social Religious Epistemology*

In the latter part of the twentieth century religious epistemology underwent somewhat of a revolution, centered on an investigation into the epistemology of religious experience. This work perhaps cumulated in 1991 with William Alston's *Perceiving God*.[1] What made this a revolution was not the topic of religious experience – philosophers of religion had treated that topic extensively before. Rather, it was the methodology that Alston and others employed. In sum, these philosophers took advantage of recent developments in the epistemology of perception and perceptual experience in general, and applied them to the epistemology of religious experience in particular. The idea was this: recent work in the epistemology of perception made traditional skepticism about religious experience out of date, precisely because that skepticism traded on an inadequate and outdated understanding of the nature of perceptual evidence more generally.

A bit more specifically, the new approach to religious perception instituted a kind of anti-evidentialism and anti-internalism in religious epistemology. First, the new approach rejected the idea that perceptual knowledge should be understood on the model of a good inference from adequate evidence. As authors such as Alston and Alvin Plantinga forcefully argued, that model leads straight to skepticism about *physical object* perception, and so it is no surprise that it should lead to skepticism about religious perception as well.[2]

---

[1] William P. Alston, *Perceiving God: The Epistemology of Religious Experience* (Ithaca, NY: Cornell University Press, 1991).

[2] Alvin Plantinga, "Reason and Belief in God," in Alvin Plantinga and Nicholas Wolterstorff, eds., *Faith and Rationality* (Notre Dame, IN: University of Notre Dame Press, 1983), pp. 16–93. William P. Alston, "Christian Experience and Christian Belief," in Alvin Plantinga and Nicholas Wolterstorff, eds., *Faith and Rationality* (Notre Dame, IN: University of Notre Dame Press, 1983), pp. 103–134. I have argued that anti-evidentialism and anti-internalism are not unrelated, in that once an

161

Second, the new approach rejected internalist understandings of epistemic justification, long dominant in religious epistemology, in favor of more recent, externalist frameworks. Most famously, Alston developed a view of religious perception using a reliabilist framework, and Plantinga developed his own account using a proper function framework.[3]

The present chapter takes these recent developments in religious epistemology as its model. In short, just as Alston, Plantinga, and others initiated a kind of "externalist turn" in religious epistemology, I believe that it is now time for a "social turn." This is especially plausible with regard to the Abrahamic faiths, in which the role of testimony is clearly central. For example, consider in these traditions the importance of scripture, the role of prophets, and the centrality of religious authority, as well as the importance of the personal testimony of individual believers. This all suggests that an adequate religious epistemology must also be a social epistemology – that is, one that takes seriously our social epistemic dependence on others in the religious realm. This chapter constitutes a contribution along those lines.[4]

The chapter proceeds as follows. Section 9.1 considers three skeptical arguments regarding religious belief and testimonial evidence. The first two are versions of "the problem of religious diversity": How can religious belief be reasonable in the context of conflicting testimony regarding religious truths? The third is Hume's famous argument regarding testimonial evidence for miracles. The common theme here is that testimonial evidence seems

internalist approach is rejected, evidentialism loses much of its motivation. See my "Evidentialism and Knowledge," in Trent Dougherty, ed., *Evidentialism and Its Discontents* (Oxford: Oxford University Press, 2011), pp. 167–178; and chapter 4 of *Achieving Knowledge*.

[3] Alston, *Perceiving God*; Alvin Plantinga, *Warranted Christian Belief* (Oxford: Oxford University Press, 2000).

[4] Earlier attempts include my "Religious Knowledge in the Context of Conflicting Testimony," *Proceedings of the American Catholic Philosophical Association* 82 (2009): 61–76; and "Friendly Theism" in James Kraft and David Basinger eds., *Religious Tolerance through Humility* (Aldershot: Ashgate, 2008), pp. 51–58. See also Stephen Wykstra, "Toward a Sensible Evidentialism: On the Notion of 'Needing Evidence'," in William Rowe and William Wainwright, eds., *Readings in the Philosophy of Religion*, 2nd edition (San Diego, CA: Harcourt Brace Jovanovich: 1989), pp. 426–437.

inadequate to support reasonable belief in matters religious, especially in the context of conflicting evidence. On the contrary,
I argue, a better understanding of testimonial evidence, and especially the role of testimony in the transmission of knowledge,
allows straightforward, non-skeptical responses to these familiar
skeptical arguments.

Section 9.2 turns to the problem of "divine hiddenness." This is
not so much a skeptical challenge, at least not directly, but rather
a problem that arises internally in the theistic tradition. Namely, it is
the problem of explaining why an all-powerful and loving God is not
clearly present to all of creation. Put differently, it is the problem of
explaining nonbelief. A common response, both in the tradition and
among contemporary theistic philosophers, is that nonbelief signals
a cognitive and/or moral flaw in the nonbeliever.[5] Section 9.2 argues
that this "flawed atheist" response to the Problem of Divine
Hiddenness is inadequate insofar as that response looks for the
explanation of nonbelief only in the atheist.[6] From the point of
view of a social religious epistemology, however, explanations of
nonbelief might just as well be found in (a) the social relations
between believers and nonbelievers, and (b) the social environment
more broadly.

One purpose of the present chapter, then, is to show how our
knowledge economy framework can be used to make progress on
a range of perennial issues in the philosophy of religion. A second
purpose, however, is to make a more general case that social epistemology enriches religious epistemology. In particular, a "social religious epistemology" turns our attention to religious communities
and institutions, and shows how the moral and practical dimensions
of these can have epistemological significance. At the very least,
I want to argue, this kind of "social turn" allows a fresh theoretical
perspective on perennial issues in the field.

---

[5] For example, see Paul K. Moser, *The Elusive God: Reorienting Religious
Epistemology* (Cambridge: Cambridge University Press, 2008); Plantinga,
Warranted Christian Belief. See also the passage from Romans below.

[6] In fact, the terms "flawed atheist response" and "no-fault atheism" are too
restrictive for the positions I mean them to label, in that nonbelievers can
include agnostics as well as atheists. Nevertheless, I will continue to use
these labels, since "flawed nonbeliever response" and "no-fault nonbelief"
are not nearly as catchy.

9.1 Some Problems in Religious Epistemology: Three Skeptical Arguments

"The Problem of Religious Diversity" has been much discussed in religious epistemology.[7] Stated very generally, the problem is this: The plurality of religious traditions, and the attending fact of conflicting religious beliefs among traditions, seem to undermine the epistemic standing of religious belief in general, including one's own. Here are two ways that the general problem can arise.[8]

First, I might reflect that it is merely a historical accident that I was born into one religious tradition rather than another, and therefore merely an accident that I received the testimony about religious matters that I did. Moreover, the religious beliefs I have now are largely influenced by my receiving the testimony that I did. If I had been born into a different tradition, and received different testimony, then I would not have the same religious beliefs that I do now. In fact, it is plausible that I would have religious beliefs that *conflict* with those I have now. But then it seems too much an accident that I have the religious beliefs that I do. Even if I am lucky, even if I am born into the one true faith and I am handed down nothing but religious truths, it seems still just an accident that I am in that tradition and believe those truths. Let's call this "The Problem of Accidental Belief." The problem can be stated more formally as follows:

The Argument from Luck

1. When one forms a true religious belief on the basis of testimony from within a tradition, it is just an accident (just a matter of luck) if one forms a true belief on the basis of this testimony rather than a false belief on the basis of different testimony. In particular, if one had been born into a different testimonial tradition, then one would have formed different religious beliefs on the basis of different testimony, but it is just a matter of luck that one was born into his or her religious tradition rather than another.

[7] See, for example, Alston, *Perceiving God*, especially chapter 7; and Philip L. Quinn and Kevin Meeker, eds., *The Philosophical Challenge of Religious Diversity* (New York: Oxford University Press, 1999).
[8] For similar formulations and careful discussion, see Roger White, "You Just Believe that Because ...," *Philosophical Perspectives* 24 (2010), 573–615; and Tomas Bogardus, "The Problem of Contingency for Religious Belief," *Faith and Philosophy* 30, 4 (2013): 371–392.

2. Knowledge cannot tolerate that sort of luck or accident.

Therefore,

3. True religious belief based on testimony from within a tradition cannot count as knowledge.

Here is a second way that the problem can arise. I might reflect on the fact that I am nothing special when it comes to matters religious. I am not more intellectually gifted or more intellectually rigorous than the next person. In the language of contemporary epistemology, many of the people who hold religious beliefs that conflict with mine are my "epistemic peers." For example, many of those people base their religious beliefs on roughly the same sort of evidence on which I base mine – that is, on testimonial evidence from within their own traditions. Moreover, many of those people have the same evidence regarding religious diversity that I do – they are just as aware as I am about the diversity of religious traditions, and the diversity of testimony therein. But then who am I to stick to my guns in the face of disagreement? For that matter, who are *they* to stick to their guns? Shouldn't we *all* be more skeptical in the face of our common epistemic position?

Consider a non-religious case: I confidently believe, and think I know, that our dinner bill comes to less than $100. (Let's say I have just looked at the bill and added the total.) But then I find out that you, who are as well placed epistemically as I am, disagree. You confidently tell me that the bill has come to well over $100. Can I reasonably stick to my guns here? Can you? Shouldn't we now both lose our confidence, at least until the conflict can be explained and resolved? Let's call this "The Problem of Peer Disagreement."[9] Here is that problem stated more formally:

The Argument from Peer Disagreement
1. If my epistemic peers disagree with me on some issue, then it is unreasonable for me to continue believing as I do. I ought to lose my

---

[9] The epistemology of disagreement has been much discussed in the recent literature. For example, see Thomas Kelly, "The Epistemic Significance of Disagreement," in John Hawthorne and Tamar Gendler, eds., *Oxford Studies in Epistemology*, vol. 1 (Oxford: Oxford University Press, 2006), pp. 166–196; David Christensen, "Epistemology of Disagreement: The Good News," *Philosophical Review* 116, 2 (2007): 187–217; Adam Elga, "Reflection and Disagreement," *Noûs* 41, 3 (2007): 478–502; Bryan Frances, "Disagreement," in Duncan Pritchard and Sven Bernecker, eds., *Routledge Companion to Epistemology* (New York: Routledge, 2010), pp. 68–74.

confidence, or even suspend my belief, at least until the disagreement can be explained and resolved.
2. But many people who are my epistemic peers disagree with me on matters religious. In particular, my peers in different testimonial traditions do.

Therefore,

3. It is unreasonable for me to continue believing as I do in matters religious.

Finally, consider Hume's famous argument regarding testimony about miracles.[10] According to Hume, it is never reasonable to believe, on the basis of testimonial evidence, that a miracle has occurred. There has been much debate about how Hume's argument is supposed to go, but here is a plausible reconstruction.

First, suppose we are presented with testimony that some apparent miracle has occurred – let's say that someone has risen from the dead. According to Hume, reasonableness requires that we weigh this testimonial evidence against whatever other evidence we have that the event in question did not occur. That is the first premise of the argument. But since the event in question is an apparent miracle, that guarantees that our evidence against its occurring will be very good indeed. Here is the argument for that: If the event in question appears to be a miracle, then it must conflict with an apparent law of nature. But nothing could appear to be a law of nature unless we have very good evidence for it – unless we have *excellent* evidence for it, in fact. That is the second premise: that our evidence against the apparent miracle occurring will always be excellent.

Finally, Hume's third premise is that our evidence in favor of the event's occurring will always be less than excellent. That is because we already know that people often testify falsely about purported miracles occurring. Sometimes people lie. Sometimes they are self-deceived. Sometimes they just make a mistake. In sum, the track record is not very good. And in light of that track record, the testimonial evidence for the present case is not very good either. In any case, it won't be excellent. But now all Hume's premises are in place: Our testimonial evidence that an apparent miracle has occurred will never be as good as our evidence that it has not occurred. And so, we can never be reasonable in believing,

[10] From *Enquiry Concerning Human Understanding*, section 10, *Of Miracles*.

on the basis of testimonial evidence, that a miracle really has occurred. Here is the argument again:

Hume's Argument (Reconstructed)

1. In any case where we are presented with testimony that an apparent miracle M has occurred, we must weigh that testimonial evidence in favor of M's occurrence against our evidence that M has not occurred.
2. But if M is an apparent miracle, then M must conflict with an apparent law of nature L, for which our evidence must be excellent. (Our evidence for L, and hence against M's occurrence, must amount to excellent inductive evidence, or else L would not be an apparent law of nature.)
3. On the other hand, our testimonial evidence in favor of M's occurrence will always be less than excellent. (This is because testimony in favor of miracles has a less than excellent track record: We know of many cases where testimony that some miracle has occurred was false.)

Therefore,

4. In all cases where we are presented with testimony that some apparent miracle has occurred, our testimonial evidence in favor of M's occurrence will always be weaker than our inductive evidence against M's occurrence (from 1 to 3).

Therefore,

5. It is always unreasonable to believe, merely on the basis of testimonial evidence, that a miracle has occurred (from 4).

9.1.1 A Common Problem?

We have reviewed three arguments that threaten skepticism about religious beliefs based on testimony. The first is put in terms of knowledge, the second and third in terms of reasonable belief. Do our skeptical arguments have anything in common? Do they sound some common theme? Perhaps it is this: that testimonial evidence cannot give religious belief adequate support or grounding, especially in the context of conflicting evidence. Put differently, testimonial evidence is not "up to the task," epistemically speaking – it is inadequate to give us either knowledge or reasonable belief, at least in matters religious, at least in the sort of circumstances in which we actually find ourselves.[11]

But let's now take a step back. How should the epistemology of religious belief treat the evidence of testimony? One approach would be to treat religious testimony as a *generating source* of reasonable belief and knowledge. On that approach, the hearer (or receiver) of testimony is treated akin to an inductive reasoner. The task of such a reasoner is to gather the relevant evidence, to judge the quality of the evidence on either side, and to form one's beliefs accordingly. In this instance, the task would be to judge the quality of one's testimonial evidence, presumably by means of considering such factors as relevant track records, competing explanations of the nature and content of the testimony, etc. In short, the receiver of testimony would be akin to Hume's hearer of miracles, and epistemic assessment would proceed along roughly Humean lines. Of course, one might think that Hume has got the nature and/or the content of the inductive evidence wrong, and that adjustments to our assessments of the inductive evidence have to be made accordingly. But the rough idea would be in place: Testimonial evidence is a species of inductive evidence, and must be assessed accordingly.

An alternative approach, however, would be to treat religious testimony as having a *transmitting* function, on the model defended in previous chapters. On this approach, the hearer or receiver of testimony might arrive at reasonable belief, or even knowledge, by means of his or her location in a social context. Such location might be informal, as when knowledge is passed from individual to individual by means of interpersonal communication. Alternatively, the social location of speaker and hearer might be more formal, as when knowledge is passed from teacher to student by means of formal education. But in any case, religious testimony, or at least *some* religious testimony, would have the function of transmitting knowledge and/or reasonable belief, rather than generating it.

To be clear, there is no question of testimony *transmitting* religious knowledge (or reasonable belief) unless there is some way of *generating* such standings in the first place. This second approach to religious

---

[11] The sort of reasonableness at issue here is itself "epistemic," or the kind of reasonableness that is (among other things) required for knowledge. For ease of exposition, I will often talk below in terms of knowledge only. However, much of what is said applies to reasonable belief as well.

testimony, then, assumes that religious knowledge and reasonable belief are otherwise possible, and therefore possibly exists to be transmitted. That is an appropriate assumption in the present context, however, in that our three skeptical arguments mean to address the epistemic efficacy of religious testimony in particular. And it would be question-begging, in that context, to assume that religious knowledge or reasonable belief *in general* are impossible.

The point is easiest to see with regard to Hume's argument. It is no part of Hume's argument that those who *witness* a miracle do not thereby gain a reasonable belief that a miracle has occurred. For example, Hume's argument does not deny reasonable belief to someone who witnesses water turning to wine, or a man rising from the dead. Rather, Hume means to establish that one cannot come to reasonably believe such things *on the basis of testimony*. Moreover, it is clear that Hume does not think that this argument is trivial, as it would be if it is assumed that it is impossible to reasonably believe such things *at all*.

In similar fashion, the Argument from Luck concludes that testimony fails to ground religious knowledge because *that sort of grounding* is too lucky to give rise to knowledge. The Argument from Peer Disagreement concludes that religious belief is unreasonable *in the face of peer disagreement*, because peer disagreement provides a kind of defeater for one's justification. But again, those arguments would be trivial if they assumed that religious knowledge is impossible and that religious belief is unreasonable *in any case*. The skeptical arguments are better understood, then, as targeting the epistemic efficacy of testimony specifically. In one way or another, they argue that religious testimony is epistemically inefficacious, *even if* reasonable religious belief and/or knowledge might arise in some other way.

But given this understanding of the skeptical arguments, do the arguments establish their conclusions? I next want to argue that, in each case, the answer is no. That is because each of our skeptical arguments makes assumptions about the nature of testimonial evidence and the nature of testimonial knowledge that are controversial. More specifically, each fails to consider that religious testimony, like other testimony, might have a transmitting function rather than a generating function. The next task, then, is to evaluate each of the arguments with a transmission model in mind.

First, recall the Argument from Luck:

1. When one forms a true religious belief on the basis of testimony from within a tradition, it is just an accident (just a matter of luck) if one forms a true belief on the basis of this testimony rather than a false belief on the basis of different testimony.
2. Knowledge cannot tolerate that sort of luck or accident.

Therefore,

3. True religious belief based on testimony from within a tradition cannot count as knowledge.

If we consider the possibility of knowledge transmission, we may deny either of the argument's premises. Regarding premise 1, we may deny that when one receives testimony from within a tradition it is "just an accident" or "just a matter of luck" that one forms a true belief on the basis of that testimony. On the contrary, if the transaction in question constitutes an instance of knowledge transmission, it is underwritten by a reliable transmission of reliable information. That is, the transaction will involve knowledge on the part of the speaker, derived ultimately from some original source of knowledge, and then a reliable transmission of knowledge from speaker to hearer. In fact, the latter might involve social relations and social institutions designed specifically for that purpose, and so, again, the hearer's believing the truth on the basis of the speaker's testimony would be no accident.

Alternatively, we may deny premise 2 of the argument. That is, we may acknowledge that true belief on the basis of testimony involves *some sort of luck*; specifically, it involves the luck of being born into a particular tradition, and of occupying a particular social location within that tradition. But we may deny that knowledge cannot tolerate that sort of luck or accident. On the contrary, that sort of social inheritance enables testimonial knowledge, much as one's natural endowments enable knowledge through accurate perception and good reasoning.

Next, consider the Argument from Peer Disagreement. That argument depended on the following premise:

2. Many people who are my epistemic peers disagree with me on matters religious. In particular, my peers in different testimonial traditions do.

But on the present approach to testimonial evidence, premise 2 is false. That is because the notion of "epistemic peer" that is operative in that premise must be an appropriately strong one – it must require not only that peers are equally intelligent and equally conscientious, but that they share the same epistemic position regarding some claim that *p* more generally. For example, epistemic peers must share the same evidence regarding *p*. But on the present account, people in different testimonial traditions do not share the same epistemic position and do not share the same testimonial evidence, and so are not epistemic peers in the relevant sense.

One might think that simply being aware of another testimonial tradition, and being aware of the testimony within it, puts one in the same epistemic position as those who live within the tradition, at least with respect to the testimony in question. But that confuses (a) merely hearing or knowing about testimony with (b) receiving testimonial evidence. The latter, we have seen, requires situation in a reliable testimonial exchange. And that, in turn, requires participation in social practices and institutions that underwrite reliability. Put differently, receiving testimonial evidence requires more than being in the right time and place *geographically* – it requires being in the right time and place *socially*.

Finally, we return to the argument from Hume. That argument depended on the following premise:

3. Our testimonial evidence in favor of M's occurrence will always be less than excellent. (This is because testimony in favor of miracles carries a less than excellent track record: We know of many cases where testimony that some miracle has occurred was false.)

We may now see that Hume's support for premise 3 depends on treating testimony as a *generating source* of knowledge for the hearer. That is, it treats the hearer as an inductive reasoner, whose task it is to weigh her inductive evidence on each side of the issue and adjust her belief accordingly. But that is misguided in cases where testimony plays a *transmission* function. Put differently, the conditions for knowledge transmission are different from the conditions for knowledge generation by inductive reasoning. That being so, Hume cannot assume that one's testimonial evidence for a miracle will always be "less than excellent." For even if that evidence constitutes less than excellent *inductive* evidence, it might nevertheless constitute excellent *testimonial* evidence. That would depend on the

quality of the testimonial transaction, constituted by the quality of
the original source (perhaps the miracle was eye-witnessed) and the
quality of the social relations underwriting the testimonial exchange
(perhaps the exchange is between trusted friends, verified by reliable
authorities, etc.).[12]

We may conclude that all three of our skeptical arguments trade on
overly individualistic assumptions about the nature of testimonial
knowledge and testimonial evidence. In particular, all three implicitly
assume that testimony is epistemically efficacious only insofar as it
serves to generate knowledge (or reasonable belief) in the hearer.
Once we adopt a more social perspective – one on which testimonial
exchanges can be in the service of knowledge transmission – the arguments are robbed of their force. We next turn our attention to
a different kind of problem in the philosophy of religion.

9.2 The Problem of Divine Hiddenness

The Problem of Divine Hiddenness, we noted, is to explain nonbelief.
Given God's nature as all-loving and all-powerful, why should there be
nonbelief? Why does God not clearly reveal Himself to all?[13] These
questions are not primarily skeptical, but they can (and do) turn into
doubts, and even into an argument against God's existence. Here is one
reconstruction of that line of reasoning:[14]

The Argument from Hiddenness
1. If God exists, then He is all-loving, and so desires to be in a loving
   relationship with all created persons.[15]

---

[12] Hume cites a case involving such a verification process, but does not appreciate
its social significance. Cf. Hume, *Enquiry*, section 10.
[13] See, for example, Daniel Howard-Snyder and Paul K. Moser, "Introduction:
The Hiddenness of God," in Daniel Howard-Snyder and Paul K. Moser, eds.,
Divine Hiddenness: New Essays (Cambridge: Cambridge University Press,
2002), pp. 1–23; J.L. Schellenberg, *Divine Hiddenness and Human Reason*
(Ithaca, NY: Cornell University Press, 1993).
[14] Here I consider a relatively straightforward formulation of the argument. For
more careful formulations, see J.L. Schellenberg, "Divine Hiddenness and
Human Philosophy," in Adam Green and Eleonore Stump, eds., *Hidden
Divinity and Religious Belief: New Perspectives* (Cambridge: Cambridge
University Press, 2015), pp. 13–32; and Schellenberg, *Divine Hiddenness and
Human Reason*.
[15] Here is a more careful formulation from Schellenberg: "If God is perfectly loving
toward such finite persons as there may be, then for any capable finite person

2. If God exists, then He is all-powerful, and so does what is necessary to achieve what He desires.[16]
3. To be in a loving relationship with another person, one must reveal oneself to that person in the following sense: one must allow that person to know him/her. Put differently, one cannot remain hidden from the person.

Therefore,

4. If God exists, then He allows Himself to be known by all. He does not remain hidden from anyone (1, 2, 3).
5. But some people do not believe in God.
6. If some people do not believe in God, then God does not reveal Himself to all persons in the relevant sense: He does not allow Himself to be known by all.

Therefore,

7. God does not allow Himself to be known by all (5, 6).

Therefore,

8. God does not exist (4, 7).

Here we may note a structural analogy to the Problem of Evil.[17] In each case, we begin with assumptions about the nature of God, which in turn make the existence of evil (nonbelief) problematic. In effect, evil (nonbelief) demands an explanation: How is God's existence compatible with the thing at issue? And in each case, the question can turn into an argument against God's existence. The line of thought is that God's existence is *not* compatible with the existence of evil (nonbelief), but

S and time t, God is at t open to being in a positively meaningful and reciprocal conscious relationship (a personal relationship) with S at t" (Schellenberg, "Divine Hiddenness and Human Philosophy," pp. 24–25). As Schellenberg's formulation makes explicit, the premise makes a claim about created beings at a time, and about God's desire for a relationship with them at any such time that they exist. The remainder of the argument should be read accordingly.

[16] Again, a more careful formulation of the argument would have to include qualifications regarding the nature and scope of God's omnipotence. Since my treatment of the argument will not exploit any such qualification (or lack thereof), I will use this more straightforward formulation.

[17] For example, see J.L. Mackie, "Evil and Omnipotence," *Mind* 64, 254 (1955): 200–212; Alvin Plantinga, *God, Freedom, and Evil* (Grand Rapids, MI: Eerdmans, 1974).

since the existence of evil (nonbelief) is undeniable, we should conclude that God does not exist.[18]

9.2.1 The Flawed Atheist Response

Responses to the Problem of Divine Hiddenness continue the analogy. Thus, responses to the Problem of Evil generally follow one of two strategies. The first is to explain the existence of evil in terms of God's own intentions, for example to make possible some greater good, or prevent some greater evil.[19] The second is to find the explanation for evil in something external to God, for example the exercise of human free will.[20] The "flawed atheist" response to the Problem of Divine Hiddenness takes this latter route: Nonbelief is to be explained in terms of a moral and/or cognitive flaw on the part of the nonbeliever. As we saw, the response is as follows: The fact that some people do not know God, and do not even believe in God, can be traced to a flaw *in them*. That is, God does reveal Himself to all, but some people resist.

Here are some examples of this kind of response – the first from the apostle Paul, the next two from more contemporary authors.

Ever since the creation of the world his eternal and divine nature, invisible though they are, have been understood and seen through the things he made. So they are without excuse: for though they knew God, they did not honor him as God or give thanks to him, but they became futile in their thinking, and their senseless minds were darkened. (Romans 1: 20–21)

---

[18] Here is a contemporary update of the argument from evil: The "data" of human and animal suffering does not entail that God does not exist, but it makes the existence of God improbable. That is, the probability of God's existence on the data is low. An explanation of suffering e would, depending on one's strategy, allow the theist to deny that $P(G/d)$ is low, or affirm that $P(G/d\&e)$ is not low. Clearly, the Problem of Divine Hiddenness can be understood along probabilistic lines as well. See Daniel Howard-Snyder, *The Evidential Argument from Evil* (Bloomington, IN: Indiana University Press, 1996); William L. Rowe, "The Problem of Evil and Some Varieties of Atheism," *American Philosophical Quarterly* 16, 4 (1979): 355–341.

[19] Hick's "soul-making" strategy falls into this category. See, for example, John Hick, *Evil and the God of Love* (Basingstoke: Macmillan, 1966).

[20] The traditional "free will defense" includes this strategy as well as the "greater good" strategy. That is, free will is considered to be itself a great good, and the use of free will leads to unnecessary evil besides. For example, see Plantinga, *God, Freedom, and Evil*.

according to the A/C [Aquinas/Calvin] model this natural knowledge of God has been compromised, weakened, reduced, smothered, overlaid, or impeded by sin and its consequences ... here the A/C model stands Freud and Marx on their heads ... according to the model, it is really the *unbeliever* who displays epistemic malfunction; failing to believe in God is a result of some kind of dysfunction.[21]

Some people have a psychological attitude-set closed or even opposed to a divine redemptive program ... Their attitude-set, in guiding what they attend to and how they interpret what they attend to, obscures or even blocks for them the purposely available evidence of the reality of God. The volitionally sensitive evidence of God's reality is, I contend, actually available ... People need, however, appropriate, God-sensitive "ears to hear and eyes to see" the available evidence aright.[22]

It is hard to deny that there is something awkward about explaining nonbelief in terms of some moral or intellectual flaw in the nonbeliever. Of course, there are ways to soften the blow. We can quickly add that we are all sinners. Or we can make a distinction between original and personal sin, or distinguish between culpable and non-culpable flaws.[23] But even with these additions, the flawed atheist response remains less than ideal. The remainder of this section argues that the response is unnecessary.

9.2.2 No-Fault Atheism

By way of diagnosing what has gone wrong in the "flawed atheist" response, we may notice a common structure in two lines of thinking. Once again, we see an analogy to the Problem of Evil. Thus, the atheist thinks:

1. The evidence against God is overwhelming.
2. The same evidence is available to all, including the theist.

---

[21] Plantinga, *Warranted Christian Belief*, p. 184.
[22] Moser, *The Elusive God*, p. 112.
[23] Plantinga emphasizes the former: Original sin "carries with it a sort of blindness, a sort of imperceptiveness, dullness, stupidity. This is a cognitive limitation that first of all prevents its victim from proper knowledge of God and his beauty, glory, and love..." Plantinga, *Warranted Christian Belief*, p. 207. Stump emphasizes the latter possibility in Eleonore Stump, *Wandering in Darkness: Narrative and the Problem of Suffering* (Oxford: Oxford University Press, 2010).

Therefore,

3. The theist must be either ignoring or misevaluating the available evidence.[24]

Analogous thinking is behind the "flawed atheist" strategy:

1. Theists have ample evidence for God's presence.
2. The same evidence is available to all, including the atheist.

Therefore,

3. The atheist must be resisting the available evidence.

The strategy that I want to defend, and that our knowledge economy framework supports, is to reject the common premise – the assumption that theists and atheists have the same evidence available to them. Motivating this approach is the thought that knowledge of God falls into the category of knowledge of persons, and so we should adopt our best epistemology of persons as our epistemology of God. But knowledge of persons is typically via interpersonal perception and testimony – we typically learn about people from our experience of them, and from what they tell us about themselves and others.[25] And that kind of evidence is typically *not* shared or public, not available to all.

For example, persons typically self-disclose in a selective manner. There are many and obvious examples of this from both interpersonal perception and testimony. But this simple point does much to explain how theists and atheists can both be rational in their respective epistemic positions. That is, if God is like other persons in that God chooses to self-disclose in a selective manner, then that would explain how two persons could have different evidence regarding God's existence, and without tracing the difference in epistemic position to any flaw in the persons themselves. By way of illustration, consider the following case.[26]

---

[24] Cf. Rowe, "The Problem of Evil and Some Varieties of Atheism."

[25] By "interpersonal perception," I mean the perception of persons as persons. See Greco, "Friendly Theism"; Adam Green, "Reading the Mind of God (without Hebrew Lessons): Alston, Shared Attention, and Mystical Experience," *Religious Studies* 45, 4 (2009): 455–470; and Stump, *Wandering in Darkness*, especially chapter 4.

[26] Taken from Greco "Friendly Theism." A similar example is provided by Rowe himself.

Uncle Joe: It has been long taken for granted in your family that Uncle Joe is dead. Everyone knows the story of how his plane went down in the Atlantic, no survivors were ever found, etc. But one day you are on a business trip in Chicago and you clearly see Uncle Joe crossing the street. The two of you make eye contact, there is a look of recognition on his face, and then he gives you the slip in the crowd. The next day you go back home and report to your family that Uncle Joe is alive – that you saw him in Chicago. You are certain of what you saw, but your family reacts with skepticism.

Good Friend: You have a very good friend that you have trusted for years and who has always been honest and truthful. While you are talking with a colleague, your friend comes up to you and tells you something that is hard to believe – that he was just outside minding his own business, and a perfect stranger walked up and handed him a $20 bill.

In the Uncle Joe case, it is perfectly reasonable for your family to think that you are somehow mistaken, while it is perfectly reasonable for you to believe that you are not. Depending on the quality of your perception and their contrary evidence, it might very well be that you *know* that Uncle Joe is alive, and yet unreasonable for your family to believe that he is. Likewise, in the Good Friend case, it might be perfectly reasonable for you to believe your friend, while it is perfectly reasonable for your colleague to disbelieve him. Depending on the quality of your relationship, it might very well be that you *know* that your friend is telling the truth, and yet unreasonable for your colleague to believe that he is.

And now the important point is this: There is no need to attribute a cognitive flaw to anyone in the two cases. Put differently, there is a readily available "no-fault" explanation for nonbelief. To some extent, in fact, the present point of view makes nonbelief expected. This is because variability in epistemic position is typical in cases of interpersonal knowledge.

More needs to be said, however. This is because at least one author who embraces the flawed atheist response also endorses the idea that our knowledge of God is through interpersonal experience. Thus, Paul Moser has emphasized that our evidence for God is "volitionally sensitive" and therefore precisely not a kind of public or shared evidence that is available to all persons in the same way.[27] Likewise, Eleonore Stump has emphasized the "second-personal" nature of our experience of God.[28] Stump has not addressed the Problem of Divine Hiddenness directly, but what she says about interpersonal experience of God might be used to fuel the "flawed atheist" response. For example,

> Given divine omnipresence, the only thing that makes a difference to the kind of personal presence ... that God has to a human person is the condition of the human person herself ... If Paula wants God to be significantly present to her, what is needed to bring about what she wants depends only on her, on her being able and willing to share attention with God.[29]

On the current line of thinking, God's self-disclosure is not selective in the way that human self-disclosure can be, and therefore the analogy to human-to-human interpersonal relations breaks down at a crucial point. Since God's self-disclosing experience is not selective, the explanation for "deafness" or "blindness" to God's self-disclosure must remain with the nonbeliever.[30]

On the present view, then, the traditional response to divine hiddenness remains essentially in place:

1. Theists have ample evidence for God's presence in terms of interpersonal experience.
2. That evidence is available to all in the relevant sense; that is, it is equally available to all who are open to it.

---

[27] For example, see Moser, *The Elusive God*; and his *The Evidence for God: Religious Knowledge Reexamined* (Cambridge: Cambridge University Press, 2010).

[28] Stump, *Wandering in Darkness*.

[29] On Stump's view, someone might fail to be "able and willing" to enjoy a second-personal experience of God, but through no fault of her own. For example, such failing might be due to non-culpable psychological brokenness. See ibid.

[30] Again, proponents of the "flawed atheist" response can avoid attributing personal blame to the nonbeliever. The cause of the flaw might be original sin rather than personal sin, or the flaw might have some other non-culpable cause. The present point is that a "no-fault" response need not attribute any flaw to the nonbeliever, whether culpable or non-culpable. Better, a no-fault response need not *explain nonbelief* in terms of some flaw in the nonbeliever. Presumably, we are all flawed in some ways or others. The present point is that flaws in the nonbeliever need not be cited in the explanation of nonbelief; they need not be, in that sense, explanatory "difference makers."

Therefore,

3. If an atheist does not have the experience of God that theists do, then they must not be open to it.

So, is the traditional response right after all? Again, it is helpful in this context to emphasize a social approach, and in particular the notion of interpersonal evidence. One thing about interpersonal evidence, whether through interpersonal perception or testimony, is that self-disclosure is not only selective, but also *intentional*. In other words, people often *choose* or *decide*, sometimes for good reason, to self-disclose some things but not others, at some times but not others, to some people but not others. But the intentional nature of self-disclosure allows us to deny that experiential evidence of God must be available in the relevant sense – at all times available to all persons who are open to it. It is consistent with God's nature that, as other persons typically do, God has *good reasons* for selective self-disclosure.[31]

In response, one might agree that God is indeed free to restrict His self-disclosure, but argue that He would not choose to do so. Human beings do so choose, but God's goodness and love for us is such that He would not. But now we are back in a familiar dialectic – one that we know well from the Problem of Evil. Thus, we can now (a) posit possible greater goods to explain God's selective disclosure; or (b) plead skepticism about God's intentions, what God would choose, etc. That is, we can adopt either the "greater goods" response or the "skeptical theism" response, or some combination thereof, exactly as is available regarding the Problems of Evil.[32] And of course, the

---

[31] In effect, the present response denies premise one of the Argument from Hiddenness above, at least when that premise is read this way: If God exists, then He desires to be in a loving relationship with all created persons at every time that they exist. Recall Schellenberg's formulation of the relevant premise: If God is perfectly loving toward such finite persons as there may be, then for any capable finite person S and time t, God is at t open to being in a positively meaningful and reciprocal conscious relationship (a personal relationship) with S at t. Alternatively, the present response denies premise three, now read this way: To be in a loving relationship with another person, God must allow that person to know Him at every moment that the person exists. The present response claims that, consistent with God's all-loving nature, God might for good reasons choose to self-disclose in a more restricted way.

[32] For example, see Michael Bergmann, "Skeptical Theism and Rowe's New Evidential Argument from Evil," *Noûs* 35, 2 (2001): 278–296.

usual responses to these responses are also available. Plausibly, this will play out, for better or worse, just as it does in the Problem of Evil.[33] I like the odds here. That is, it seems to me that the usual responses to the Problem of Evil are good ones, and that they work equally well in the present context.

I do not mean to argue, of course, that no atheist is correctly diagnosed by the "flawed atheist" response. That would require insight into the deep psychology of particular nonbelievers, and I make no claim of competence there. The present point, rather, is that an adequately social epistemology does not *require* the traditional explanation of nonbelief. It makes other explanations available, and even expected. That is in itself a substantial conclusion, in that many philosophers would seem to disagree, and many epistemologies of religious belief would not allow for it.

But there is a further benefit of the present response to divine hiddenness. Namely, it raises interesting issues for religious epistemology by interacting with more general issues in social epistemology. In the remainder of the chapter, then, I want to revisit some of the implications of our knowledge economy framework, and to apply these to the Problem of Divine Hiddenness in particular.

First, according to our framework, various social relations shape our social environments and thereby underwrite the transmission of knowledge. The first thing to see is that all of these relations – interpersonal, social, and institutional – shape religious communities as well. Thus, at times religious testimony occurs in the context of an interpersonal relationship between hearer and trusted speaker. At other times, testimony occurs in the context of more well-defined social roles, such as when parents talk to their children about their shared faith. And of course, religious institutions are organized so as to produce religious testimony in various contexts, including formal education, preaching, ritual, and many other religious and cultural practices. Clearly, then, our knowledge economy framework has application in the domain of religious belief in particular.

In what follows, we may consider some further implications of the framework that are relevant to present purposes.

---

[33] It is important to note that Schellenberg argues otherwise. See J.L. Schellenberg, "The Hiddenness Problem and the Problem of Evil, " *Faith and Philosophy* 27, 1 (2010): 45–60.

9.2.3 *Social Location Is Epistemically Important*

Let us say that one's "social location" is determined by one's personal relationships and by one's membership, participation, and roles in a community, including a community's formal institutions. According to the present framework, one's social location is epistemically important in a number of ways. First, one's location in a community allows one to receive an important kind of testimonial evidence in the first place. Specifically, it allows one to receive testimony in its distribution function, as opposed to its acquisition function.

Second, social location affects the epistemic quality of that evidence, including whether testimonial knowledge is thereby transmitted. Specifically, one's social location will be constituted by personal, social, and institutional relations that are more or less enabling or undermining of the reliable distribution of information and hence the successful transmission of knowledge. In these ways, social location very much determines epistemic position. Put differently, one's epistemic position is partly constituted by one's social location.

9.2.4 *Moral and Practical Aspects of the Social Environment Have Epistemic Consequences*

The reliable distribution of information, and hence the effective transmission of testimonial knowledge, depends on moral and practical aspects of interpersonal relations, informal communities, and formal institutions. This is true for a number of reasons.

First, testimony in the distribution role depends on phenomena such as trust, authority, expertise, and social position, all of which clearly have practical and/or moral dimensions. Second, the very existence of personal relations, informal communities, and institutions, as well as one's participation in them, depends largely on their moral and practical value. For example, one goes to a school, or attends a church, largely because of its moral and practical benefits, real or perceived. Or from a different angle: There is pressure to leave a social environment, or not enter into it in the first place, if it fails to serve practical and/or moral purposes.

Third, the epistemic efficacy of a social environment is often parasitic on its practical/moral efficacy. For example, there is a reliable channel of communication between mother and child largely because the mother loves the child and is motivated by that (and other moral and practical considerations) to care for her. There is a reliable channel of communication between lawyer and client largely because the lawyer is paid by the client, and is motivated by that (and other moral and practical considerations) to act in her interest. All this implies that the epistemic value of our relationships is often parasitic on their moral and practical value. The epistemic efficacy of our relationships often rides on their moral and practical efficacy.

9.2.5 Obstacles to Transmission

A third implication of our model is that failures of transmission can be varied. That is, when things don't go well in a testimonial exchange, the explanation can lie in a number of places. Here we may use the case of religious belief as an example.

First, the problem might lie in the personal character of the speaker (e.g., a believer), who lacks the moral virtue, or the motivation, or the practical talent, or the intellectual competence, to cultivate trust in the hearer. Second, the problem might lie in the informal community (e.g., a family), which lacks the motivation or resources to adequately teach its children about their own religious tradition. Third, the problem might lie in the formal institution (e.g., a church), which lacks the moral integrity or practical competence to attract new members and keep old ones.

Here is a more specific example. A combination of institutional arrogance and incompetence undermined the ability of the Catholic Church to address various sexual abuse scandals.[34] This in turn undermined the moral authority of the Church for many of its members, which in turn undermined its teaching authority. This is an effective illustration of how the transmission of knowledge can be adversely affected by practical and moral considerations. To be clear, the idea is *not* that members of the Church argued from premises about practical and moral failure to conclusions about epistemic authority. Rather, effective channels of testimony were eroded or destroyed, because members of the Church became less

---

[34] As documented, for example, in Michael Rezendes, Matt Caroll, and Sacha Pfeiffer, "Clergy Sex Abuse Crisis," *The Boston Globe*, January 6, 2002. Available at www.bostonglobe.com/metro/specials/clergy.

trusting of the institution and its authorities, or simply opted out altogether.

All of these considerations further support the conclusion, already drawn above, that the "flawed atheist" response to the Problem of Divine Hiddenness is rendered unnecessary by an adequate epistemology of religious belief. On the present view, explanations of nonbelief might be found in religious believers and in the social environment, where the latter includes the nature and quality of interpersonal relations, informal communities, and formal institutions, in both their moral and practical aspects.

9.2.6 Too Rosy a Picture?

Finally, it might be asked whether the present approach to religious testimony paints too rosy a picture. Specifically, does it make reasonable religious belief and religious knowledge too easy? That depends on the answers to some further questions.

First, as already noted in Section 9.1, it depends on the existence and the extent of originating sources of religious knowledge. Knowledge (or reasonable belief) cannot be transmitted from speaker to hearer if the speaker does not have knowledge (or reasonable belief) to begin with. Accordingly, the present approach to testimony and religious belief depends on more traditional issues in the epistemology of religion – that is, on issues regarding originating sources of knowledge and reasonable belief.

But suppose we take it for granted that there are such originating sources, and that they are fairly widespread. That is, suppose we take it for granted that the *generation* of religious knowledge is fairly common. Questions still remain concerning the conditions for the successful transmission of that knowledge. What, in general, are the conditions for the successful transmission of knowledge within a testimonial tradition? And are those conditions met by religious traditions today?

These questions further divide. For we may ask: What are the conditions for successful *interpersonal* transmission? At the very least, those would seem to include personal expertise and interpersonal trust. What are the nature and conditions of these in general, and in regard to religious belief in particular? Similarly, we may ask about the social norms structuring our informal religious communities, and whether they are apt to underwrite the transmission of religious knowledge across members of those communities. And we may also ask: What are the conditions for successful *institutional* transmission? At the very least, those would seem to include institutional expertise and institutional integrity. In other words, institutional transmission requires institutional *authority*. What are the nature and conditions of these in general, and in regard to religious belief in particular? And do religious institutions today satisfy those conditions?

More generally, whether religious knowledge can be transmitted *easily* depends on whether it can be transmitted *at all*. And that, in turn, depends not only on the conditions of knowledge transmission, but on the nature and health of our religious communities. In any case, these questions about the transmission of religious knowledge frame a research program for social religious epistemology. If the arguments of the present chapter are correct, then answers to them are required to determine the full extent of reasonable religious belief and religious knowledge. Put differently, questions about knowledge generation will tell only part of the story about the epistemic standing of religious belief. Questions about knowledge transmission will be at least as central.

Appendix: The Garbage Problem

It is now commonplace in epistemology that any non-skeptical epistemology must allow that the transmission of knowledge is widespread. That is, putting aside disagreement about *the conditions* for successful transmission, the consensus among non-skeptical epistemologies is that testimony often manages to transmit knowledge *one way or another*. In this Appendix, I want to consider a problem for anyone in this non-skeptical camp.

Stated in its starkest form, the problem is that knowledge is often transmitted right alongside garbage. For example, parents often transmit groundless prejudice to their children, teachers often transmit cultural myths to their students, and doctors often transmit pseudo-science to their patients, all at the same time, we would like to think, that they are transmitting knowledge. Call this "the garbage problem." The problem, more carefully stated, is to explain how is it that knowledge can be transmitted right alongside garbage. Alternatively: How can we theorize transmission, so as to explain how knowledge can be transmitted right alongside garbage?

It is important to note that the problem is not avoided by reductionism about testimonial knowledge. In particular, we don't avoid the problem by saying that, in the good case (knowledge), the hearer has good evidence of speaker competence and sincerity, whereas in the bad case (garbage) she does not. That is because evidence of competence and sincerity, even when we have it, is often not so fine-grained – that is, not so fine-grained as to separate the knowledge from the garbage. For example, in the typical case a child will have only *general* evidence regarding the competence and sincerity of a parent – she will not have evidence that mom is sincere and competent regarding this one thing but not this other. The same for students with respect to their teachers and for patients with respect to their doctors, or at least often that will be so in cases where we want to attribute knowledge.

Here is a more extended example to make the point. Consider a culture that accepts a spirit theory of disease. Such a culture will nevertheless enjoy a fair amount of knowledge regarding the symptoms of different illnesses, which diseases are contagious, prognoses for recovery, etc. All of this knowledge can be gained by observation and induction, despite being embedded in bad explanatory theory. But now consider members of the culture who have not made the observations or done the reasoning for themselves. That is, consider those members of the culture who are relying only on the testimony of those who do know. Presumably, these laypersons can come to know (now through the testimony of experts) such things as that *this person is sick*, *this person is contagious*, and *this person's prognosis is poor*. The problem is, testimony to this effect will be right alongside testimony that *this person is possessed by a bad spirit*, *this kind of spirit easily jumps from one body to the next*, *this kind of spirit kills you*.

And now the point is this: Even if laypersons often have good evidence regarding the competence and sincerity of experts, that evidence will often not be so fine-grained as to sift knowledge from garbage. And, of course, the point generalizes: In general, hearers often do not have that kind of evidence regarding their speakers. And yet knowledge manages to get transmitted nonetheless. Somehow, parents still manage to transmit knowledge to their children, teachers to their students, doctors to their patients, etc.

The garbage problem, then, is a problem for any non-skeptical position: How can this happen? How does it work? *How is it that knowledge can be transmitted right alongside garbage?*

Section A.1 further considers the garbage problem, as well as some inadequate strategies for resolving it. Section A.2 introduces, and begins to defend, what I take to be a more promising approach. Looking ahead, the approach will be to treat the garbage problem as a kind of generality problem – the trick is to characterize transmission channels at the right level of generality. In short, we need to understand how the right kind of knowledge can be transmitted by the right kind of knower, in the right kind of circumstances. By way of developing this proposal, I will exploit resources from the information economy framework defended in this book. In short, we begin to get a handle on "the right level of generality" by considering the functional role of knowledge transmission within an epistemic community.

A.1 The Garbage Problem Again

So far, we have described a problem for any non-skeptical account of testimonial knowledge. Specifically, it looks as if knowledge is often transmitted right alongside garbage. For example, parents often transmit groundless prejudice to their children, teachers often transmit cultural myths to their students, and doctors often transmit pseudo-science to their patients. But how is that possible? We called this "the garbage problem" – the problem of *explaining how* knowledge can be transmitted alongside garbage.

To be clear, the problem is not to explain *the difference* between transmitting knowledge and transmitting garbage. On the contrary, any theory that sets down conditions for the transmission of knowledge will count some cases as transmitting knowledge and some cases as failing in that respect – as transmitting mere garbage. Rather, the problem is to explain how knowledge can be transmitted *alongside* garbage. How are we to understand knowledge transmission in such a way that knowledge and garbage can be transmitted *together*? The reason that this is a problem is because, intuitively, knowledge shouldn't be transmittable alongside garbage. Knowledge is supposed to be reliable, or safe, or sensitive, or grounded in good evidence. Yet all of these properties make it hard to see how one can come to know that p by being told that p, while at the same time believing that q because told that q, but where q is garbage. So, another way to put the problem is this: Given what knowledge is supposed to be like, what must knowledge transmission be like in order that knowledge can be transmitted alongside garbage? Of course, one possible answer is that knowledge *can't* be transmitted alongside garbage. But this answer ignores the other side of the problem – that, intuitively, it *can* be. Intuitively, there are cases where knowledge *is* transmitted right alongside garbage.

I next want to argue that some familiar approaches to testimonial knowledge are at a loss in this respect. We can begin to see this by looking at several reliabilist theories. Various versions of reliabilism are possible, but any will require some combination of speaker reliability, hearer reliability, or reliability in a process encompassing both speaker and hearer. The problem is, it is hard to see that any of these reliability conditions are met. First, consider hearer reliability.[1] As noted in

---

[1] A number of authors have defended a hearer reliability condition on testimonial knowledge. For example, see Greco, "The Nature of Ability and the Purpose of

various of our cases above, the hearer believes both the knowledge and the garbage, failing to discriminate between the two. In this sense, there is no hearer reliability. In agent-reliabilist terms, the hearer in these cases lacks the ability to reliably discriminate between good and bad testimony, or to otherwise form her testimonial beliefs reliably.

Likewise, there is no speaker reliability in our cases.[2] That is, in the situations we are considering, the experts speak both knowledge and garbage, and in this sense they are not reliable speakers. We have to be careful here. In our cases, we are assuming that the speakers do have some knowledge. And if knowledge requires reliability, then our speakers must be in some sense reliable. The problem is that they do not reliably speak from knowledge. In that sense, they are not reliable speakers, they are not reliable testifiers.

What about some broader seat of reliability, one that encompasses both the speaker and the hearer? A promising view is that testimonial knowledge requires a reliable testimonial exchange, and that this kind of reliability involves a speaker and hearer working together.[3] Even more promising is the idea that speaker and hearer need not shoulder the burden alone – that aspects of the social environment can contribute to the reliability of a testimonial exchange.[4] The problem is that, in the cases reviewed above, the social environment fosters no such reliability. On the contrary, features of the social environment (e.g., divisions of epistemic labor, institutional structures, authority relations) ensure that transmission channels carry knowledge and garbage together. Put differently, not even "diffuse epistemic dependence" underwrites reliability in our problem cases.[5]

    Knowledge" and "A (Different) Virtue Epistemology"; Riggs, "Two Problems of Easy Credit."
[2] As endorsed by, for example, Jennifer Lackey. See her *Learning from Words*. Lackey emphasizes the distinction between being a reliable speaker and being a reliable believer, and endorses a reliable speaker condition on testimonial knowledge. As Lackey points out, numerous philosophers endorse a reliable believer condition in virtue of requiring that, in cases of testimonial knowledge *that p*, the speaker knows *that p*.
[3] Cf. Goldberg, *Relying on Others*.
[4] As argued in Chapter 4. Cf. also Goldberg *Anti-Individualism* and *Relying on Others*; Graham, "Epistemic Normativity and Social Norms" and his "The reliability of Testimony and Social Norms" (manuscript).
[5] The term is Goldberg's. See his *Relying on Others* and "The Division of Epistemic Labor."

Might non-reliabilist accounts fare better? We have already seen above that evidentialist accounts do not. That is because, even if we grant that hearers typically have substantial evidence regarding the sincerity and competence of speakers, that evidence is too general to discriminate knowledge from garbage in our cases. That is, even in the cases where we want to attribute testimonial knowledge (about prognosis in the spirit culture, for example), the hearer lacks the kind of evidence necessary to discriminate the good stuff from the bad stuff.

What about modal approaches, such as safety and sensitivity theories? This is a somewhat tricky matter, owing to the problems associated with formulating plausible safety and sensitivity conditions. First, consider sensitivity. Here is a standard formulation:

S's belief that p is sensitive (in the sense required for knowledge) just in case: (1) S believes that p via method M; and (2) if p were false, S would not believe that p via M.

Alternatively: (1) S believes that p via method M; and (2) in the closest possible worlds where p is false, S does not believe that p via M.[6]

This condition plausibly gives us a good verdict in our cases. Consider the spirit culture case, and the true proposition that H's disease has a good prognosis. In that case, the relevant method (let's say) is *believing on the basis of the doctor's testimony*, and H's belief about her good prognosis is clearly sensitive relative to that method. In the case we described, the doctor is an expert on symptoms and their progress, and H believes that there is a good prognosis on the basis of the doctor's testimony. But if p were false, then the doctor would not have testified that p, and so H would not have believed that p. The sensitivity condition is satisfied and we get the right verdict. Likewise, the sensitivity condition is not satisfied for propositions about spirits. Let's suppose that there really is a bad spirit inhabiting H, and that this kind of spirit really does leave the body after a short time, although the spirit has nothing to do with H's symptoms. The doctor's testimony to the effect that there is a bad spirit in H is not sensitive to the truth – the doctor would testify that there is such a spirit even if there were none. Moreover, H would believe him. Because that is so, H's belief about the bad spirit is not sensitive. Again, we get the right verdict.

[6] Adapted from Robert Nozick, *Philosophical Explanations* (Cambridge, MA: Harvard University Press, 1981), p. 179.

The problem is that the sensitivity condition as formulated above is too weak. And when we strengthen it, we get right back into the garbage problem. That the condition is too weak is well known. Here is an example that shows that it is too weak:

Quirky Liar: Sam is a pathological liar, but due to a quirk in his pathology, he finds it impossible to tell any lie about his mother. Sam is talking with Heather and proceeds to tell her lie after lie about his family, with the exception of one true assertion about his mother, that *Sam's mom likes to wear flowery dresses*. Heather has no reason for thinking that Sam is a liar and every reason to think that he is completely sincere about his family.

Does Heather know that Sam's mom likes to wear flowery dresses? Clearly not. But her belief satisfies the sensitivity condition as formulated above – there is no close world where she forms *this* belief on the basis of Sam's testimony and where that belief is false. The problem with the sensitivity condition as formulated is clear – it focuses too narrowly on a single belief, or a single propositional content. What would fix the problem is to frame the condition in terms of classes of beliefs; for example, beliefs based on Sam's testimony. Here is what that would look like.

S's belief that p is sensitive (in the sense required for knowledge) just in case, (1) S believes that p via method M; and (2) for any belief that q formed by S via M, if q were false then S would not believe that q via M.
 Alternatively, (1) S believes that p via method M; and (2) for any belief that q formed by S via M, in the closest possible worlds where q is false, S does not believe that q via M.

This version of the sensitivity condition handles Quirky Liar – Heather's belief about Sam's mother is not sensitive because, more generally, her beliefs based on Sam's testimony do not track reality. But this version also gets us right back into the garbage problem. For example, H's belief about her good prognosis is not sensitive on the revised condition. More generally, none of the beliefs in our "good" cases are sensitive in the way laid out by the revised condition. This was predictable. The essence of the garbage problem is that, in some cases where we want to attribute testimonial knowledge, the hearer lacks the ability to discriminate knowledge from garbage *within a class* of beliefs based on testimony. As soon as we revise the sensitivity condition so as to be about classes of belief, we fall right back into this problem.

The same dialectic applies to safety conditions. Here is a standard version of the safety condition:

S's belief that p is safe (in the sense required for knowledge) just in case, (1) S believes that p via method M, and (2) if S were to believe that p via M, then p would be true.[7]

Alternatively, (1) S believes that p via method M, and (2) through a range of close worlds, in every world where S believes that p via M, p is true.

But this standard formulation is too weak, and Quirky Liar can be used to make the point – Heather's belief about Sam's mother comes out safe on this formulation. Once again, we can reformulate in terms of classes of belief, and this will fix the problem.

S's belief that p is safe (in the sense required for knowledge) just in case, (1) S believes that p via method M; and (2) for any belief that q formed by S via M, if S were to believe that q via M, then q would be true.

Alternatively, (1) S believes that p via method M; and (2) for any belief that q formed by S via M, through a range of close worlds, in every world where S believes that q via M, q is true.

But also once again, this new formulation gets us right back into the garbage problem. H's belief about her good prognosis does not satisfy this revised condition, and neither do the beliefs in our other "good" cases. And once again, this was predictable.

Before moving to a positive proposal, I want to consider a strategy for solving the garbage problem that seems initially plausible but that in fact is a dead end. The plausible idea is this: The way to understand knowledge transmission is in terms of conditional reliability rather than simple reliability. In effect, the idea is to assimilate our treatment of testimonial exchanges to a plausible treatment of inference and memory. In the case of reliable inference, we expect true conclusions from true premises. We don't expect true conclusions from false premises. Likewise in the case of memory: We think that reliable memory reliably preserves *true* belief, not that it turns stored false beliefs into remembered true beliefs. The general rule here is: garbage in, garbage out. And this does in fact mark a distinction

---

[7] Adapted from Ernest Sosa, "How to Defeat Opposition to Moore," *Philosophical Perspectives* 13 (1999): 142.

in our cases. In cases where our hearers were transmitted knowledge, it was knowledge in, knowledge out. In cases where our hearers believed garbage, it was garbage in, garbage out.

The problem with this approach to knowledge transmission is that it is far too weak, and Quirky Liar is enough to show this. Clearly, Heather's belief about Sam's mother is not knowledge, and so it is not a viable option to endorse the "knowledge in, knowledge out" principle for transmission.

Finally, it is important to note that Quirky Liar is not all that quirky. That is, it is typically the case that testifiers say some things that are true and some things that are false. And it is often the case that our evidence for sincerity and competence is only general, and too general to discriminate the difference. And yet we think that, in many cases, knowledge gets transmitted anyway. Quirky Liar, then, is just one side of the garbage problem. On the one hand, there are cases (like Quirky Liar) in which knowledge is not transmitted, and this seems due to a paucity of resources on the part of the hearer. On the other hand, there are cases where knowledge *is* transmitted, but where the hearer seems to suffer from the same paucity of resources. The garbage problem is the problem of explaining what is going on here. How is it that knowledge is not transmitted in the first set of cases, but is transmitted in the second?

A.2 A Proposal for Solving the Garbage Problem

My general strategy will be to treat the garbage problem as a generality problem.[8] The key to solving the problem, I will argue, is to properly conceive the parameters of transmission channels, including the range of content that a particular channel can transmit. To get the idea, it will be helpful to take a look at a generality problem for perception.

Plausibly, our perceptual faculties generate knowledge only if they deliver perceptual truths reliably. And it is natural to think that they often do. Thus, it is natural to think that visual perception delivers a high percentage of truths about physical objects. Here is the problem: That natural idea is right only if we are thinking about the relevant parameters in the right way. Presumably, we are thinking of good

---

[8] Earl Conee and Richard Feldman, "The Generality Problem for Reliabilism," *Philosophical Studies* 89, 1 (1998): 1–29.

lighting conditions, a direct view of the object, an object that is not too small, etc. If we play with these various parameters, we can easily arrive at the result that our visual perception is not reliable. For example, it is not reliable at identifying very small objects in poor lighting conditions. More specifically, the problem is this: How do we set the relevant parameters in the right way? That is, in a way that (a) is theoretically principled (e.g., not *ad hoc*, not question-begging), and (b) gives the right results regarding what we can and cannot know by visual perception.

We may now see an analogous problem for transmission channels. Plausibly, testimonial channels transmit knowledge only if they do so reliably. But it is natural to think that often they do not. Thus, it is natural to think that testimony often transmits garbage right alongside knowledge. That is the garbage problem. The current suggestion is that we need to conceive of transmission channels and the information they transmit more narrowly. For example, doctors *are* reliable testifiers about well-known, highly common symptoms of highly common diseases. If we think of transmission channels in that way, then they do transmit information reliably. But the problem is as before: How do we set the relevant parameters in the right way? That is, in a way that (a) is theoretically principled (e.g., not *ad hoc*, not question-begging), and (b) gives the right results regarding what we can and cannot know by transmission.

We see the general strategy. The more specific proposal follows our information economy framework by suggesting that relevant parameters are set by relevant practical concerns. More exactly, the idea is that knowledge attributions are always made from within an epistemic community, defined by some set of shared, information-dependent practical tasks. The current proposal is that these practical tasks determine the relevant parameters of transmission channels.[9]

---

[9] Does this entail a kind of contextualism regarding the semantics of knowledge attributions? It does if the same knowledge attribution can be evaluated from multiple conversational contexts defined by multiple epistemic communities, and the standards for attributing knowledge are variable across these contexts. And it does seem that this can happen. For example, suppose that a job applicant S tells a personnel director H that she worked for 10 years as an engineer in her previous job. Relative to that context, S and H are not cooperating members of the same epistemic community, and so their testimonial exchange is governed by the norms and standards of knowledge generation rather than knowledge transmission. Accordingly, if H's boss asks how H knows that

The current proposal can be developed by exploiting the idea – also from our information economy framework – that epistemic communities can be characterized as having two kinds of informational needs. The first is the need for acquiring the information that is relevant to their information-dependent practical tasks. The second is the need for distributing relevant information to those members of the community who need it. Moreover, in a well-functioning epistemic community, the flow of information will be governed by appropriate norms or standards. What is needed is *quality* information, relative to the tasks at hand, and a well-functioning community will have norms or standards to ensure appropriate quality.

A further idea to consider is that, plausibly, different epistemic communities will have different norms or standards, depending on the relevant tasks at hand. For example, different communities will have different norms or standards for determining when perceptual information is good enough for the task at hand. And this will plausibly include the parameters regarding the conditions and scope of adequate perception. For example, if our practical task is to find the restaurant, it won't matter if lighting on the street is not optimal or if a street sign is partly obscured. So long as perception is "good enough for practical purposes," it will be perfectly appropriate to make perceptual observations under such conditions. But suppose our practical task is to build a bridge, and that requires observing whether a concrete piling has cracks in its foundation. Or suppose the task is to track the progress of a disease, and that requires observing whether a rash on the patient's skin has become better or worse. Now the lighting had better be excellent, and partially obscured surfaces will not do. In these cases,

---

S has this work experience, and H answers only that S told him so, then the boss would be right to criticize H for being epistemically irresponsible, for failing to do his epistemic duty. But suppose that S and H are also friends, and that a mutual friend asks H if he knows what S did in her previous employment. Relative to this context, it does seem appropriate for H to believe what S says on trust, or at least on less evidence than would be required relative to the first context. For example, suppose H were to answer the mutual friend by saying, "Well, she told me that she worked as an engineer, but I don't really know." In that case, S would be right to take offense. This suggests that, relative to this second context, S and H are members of the same epistemic community, and their testimonial exchange is governed by the norms and standards relevant to knowledge transmission.

what counts as adequate perception will be defined by very different parameters.

Similar points can be made regarding the "scope" or "range" of perception. Suppose that Pete is looking at the bridge's concrete pilings from about 10 feet and in normal daylight. If our task is to paint the concrete pilings, and we need to know whether there are cracks that first need repairing for that purpose, Pete's visual perception is perfectly adequate to the task – if there are cracks in the piling that matter for our purposes, Pete will easily see them, and reliably so. But if we are safety engineers and our task is to determine the soundness of the concrete, then Pete's perception is not adequate to the task. There might be cracks in the piling that matter for our purposes, but that Pete will not reliably see. For example, there might be cracks that are internal to the pilings, and that Pete's vision cannot detect. Put in terms of scope: The scope of Pete's reliable perception is adequate for the first task but inadequate for the second. That is, the range of information over which Pete's visual perception is reliable is adequate for the first task but inadequate for the second.

These latest remarks are regarding the norms or standards for information *acquisition* – they concern the norms or standards for acquiring information in the first place. But now we can say the same thing about the *distribution* of information within an epistemic community: Each community will have norms or standards for judging when a testimonial exchange is good enough for the task at hand. And here again, the parameters regarding the conditions and scope of adequate testimony will be set by relevant practical concerns.

To see the point with regard to scope, we need only consider Pete in the role of informant.[10] For the purposes of painting the bridge pilings, Pete is a perfectly reliable informant. That is, over the range of information relevant to painting the bridge, Pete's testimony will be perfectly reliable. But for the purposes of safety engineering, Pete is an inadequately reliable informant. That is, over the range of information relevant to bridge safety, Pete's testimony will not be very reliable at all. The reason for this is not that Pete is insincere – it is that he does not have the perceptual competence to see all the cracks that are relevant to the bridge safety task.

---

[10] Here we assume that Pete's only source of information about the bridge pilings is visual perception under present conditions.

We can make the same point by exploiting ranges of sincerity rather than ranges of competence. For some practical tasks, a speaker will be reliable across a range of relevant information because she is sincere and competent over that range. But that same speaker might be insincere over a different range of information, and so an unreliable testifier over that range. If different tasks require reliability over these different ranges of information, she will be a reliable testifier relative to one task and an unreliable testifier relative to the other.

All of this is in support of the current proposal: that relevant practical tasks determine the relevant parameters of transmission channels. This is the proposal for setting the parameters in a way that is (a) theoretically principled, and (b) gives the right results regarding what we can and cannot know by transmission. Before considering exactly how the proposal helps to address the garbage problem, a few more points of elaboration are in order.

First, we may note that the norms or standards around information distribution will apply to speakers as well as hearers. Thus, there will be (a) norms or standards regarding how careful a speaker should be when giving testimony; and also (b) norms and standards regarding how careful a hearer should be when accepting testimony. The idea is that, when both speaker and hearer do their jobs properly, the testimonial exchange as a whole will be of a relevantly high quality.

The second point to note is that knowledge transmission, conceived in this way, allows for both an epistemic division of labor and diffuse epistemic dependence. First, and obviously, it allows for a division of labor between speaker and hearer – each is constrained by norms that enable a successful transmission of knowledge. Each must do her part for the testimonial exchange to successfully transmit knowledge. Second, the position allows for diffuse dependence on the broader social environment. For example, contributions to reliable transmission by speaker and hearer might be bolstered by licensing agencies, supervisors, fact checkers, eavesdroppers, and the like. That is, the reliability of a given transmission channel might be seated in the broader social environment, and not only the contributions of speaker and hearer.

Finally, the position allows that the burdens on speaker and hearer (and the broader social environment) might be distributed differently in different testimonial exchanges. For example, in a child–caretaker exchange, the burden for a reliable transmission of knowledge might fall predominantly on the caretaker, whether the caretaker is in the speaker position or the hearer position. In the hearer position, the caretaker will have to ask the right questions, follow up with appropriate checks, etc. In the speaker position, the caretaker will have to craft the message in a child-friendly way, and otherwise work to ensure appropriate uptake. In an exchange between two friends or colleagues, the burdens on speaker and hearer might be more equally distributed.

By this time, it should be fairly clear how these considerations can be applied to the garbage problem. Suppose you are in your doctor's office to see about how you should treat a medical condition, and suppose your doctor is perfectly knowledgeable about this kind of condition and how to treat it. That is, suppose your doctor is highly reliable within this range of information. But suppose that during your visit your doctor starts spouting off some ridiculous political views, together with various misconceptions that support those views. Clearly, your doctor is not very reliable within this second range of information – she is spouting garbage. The present idea is that this does not matter for the purposes of your visit – you came in to get information about how to treat your medical condition, and your doctor *is* highly reliable in that regard. More exactly, the combination of (a) your contributions as a hearer, (b) your doctor's contributions as a speaker, and (c) broader social conditions, all combine to create a highly reliable transmission channel between you within the range of information that matters.

Similar points can be made regarding the other cases we have considered. Thus, for practical purposes requiring information about symptoms, how different diseases progress, which diseases are contagious, etc., our doctors in the spirit culture are reliable testifiers, participating in reliable exchanges with their patients. Since this is the kind of information that matters for their patients' purposes, the doctors manage to transmit knowledge to them. For other purposes, such as *explaining the causes* of symptoms, the spirit culture doctors are unreliable. But that doesn't matter for relevant practical purposes, and so that garbage does not get in the way – the knowledge still flows.

Of course, we can imagine different practical concerns, with different ranges of relevant information. Our speakers might be unreliable in those different ranges, and if so would fail to transmit knowledge in those ranges, even when they know. This is the way we can diagnose Quirky Liar. In that case, Sam knows that *Sam's mom likes to wear flowery dresses*, but he fails to transmit that knowledge to Heather, because he is unreliable relative to the broader range of information in which Heather is interested. More exactly: Sam is unreliable, and neither Heather nor the broader social environment do anything to make up for Sam's lack, and that is why there is no effective transmission channel between them.

But can't we imagine other cases, where it is unclear what the relevant practical concerns are, or otherwise unclear what the relevant parameters of a transmission channel should be? Yes. But that is just to say that we have not given a fully specified answer to the generality problem. The question is whether this constitutes a problem for the present account. I will end by arguing that it does not.

The main idea here piggybacks on Mark Heller's approach to the generality problem for reliabilism. According to Heller, context fixes relevant parameters of generality, and does so in ways that are too complicated to be codified in useful rules or principles:

"Reliable" is a perfectly ordinary word that in perfectly ordinary situations is applied to tokens which are instances of several types, where those types have different degrees of reliability. Yet we somehow manage to use this word without difficulty in ordinary discourse. Just as our use of the term in ordinary discourse is context relative, reflecting the different concerns of different speakers on different occasions of use, "reliable" is also context dependent in epistemological discourse ... Just as I can use the everyday term "reliable" when describing my car, the epistemologist can use that same term when describing belief producing processes. And just as one can unproblematically assert that a car is worth buying only if it is reliable, an epistemologist can unproblematically assert that a belief is knowledge only if it is produced by a reliable process.[11]

The take-home point is that it is unreasonable to look for a detailed principle here – that is, a principle that could be used to determine relevant parameters in every case. For one, things are too messy for that – we just don't have the requisite grasp of the myriad contextual features that go into setting the parameters. Second, no such principle is needed – we are adept enough at recognizing when a process is or is not reliable for practical purposes.

[11] Mark Heller, "The Simple Solution to the Generality Problem," *Noûs* 29, 4 (1995): 502–503.

That is not to say that epistemologists should say *nothing at all* about the various features and mechanisms responsible for setting relevant levels of generality. On the contrary, we should try to be as informative as we can on this point, and here and elsewhere I have tried to fill in the details to some degree.[12] The point, rather, is that we should not expect that these details can be clearly and exhaustively specified, and certainly not that they can be codified into principles that will pronounce on every case.

The present suggestion, then, is that we have said enough to make substantial progress on the garbage problem. First, we have defended a general strategy – that of treating the garbage problem as a generality problem. According to this general strategy, transmission channels must be conceived, in part, in terms of relevant ranges of information. Second, we have filled in at least some of the details regarding how informational range (and other relevant parameters) of transmission channels are set. In short, knowledge attributions are always made from within some relevant epistemic community, defined in terms of some set of relevant practical tasks. These practical tasks determine relevant ranges of information. For example, the practical tasks associated with a doctor's visit (at least typically!) carry informational needs regarding medical diagnoses, medical treatments, etc., but not regarding politics, sporting events, etc. That's why a conversation with your doctor can transmit knowledge about a diagnosis, even if it comes with a lot of garbage about politics.

---

[12] See also John Greco, "What's Wrong with Contextualism?" *The Philosophical Quarterly* 58, 232 (2008): 416–436; and "A (Different) Virtue Epistemology."

Bibliography

Achinstein, Peter, *The Nature of Explanation* (New York: Oxford University Press, 1983).

Adler, Jonathan, "Transmitting Knowledge," *Noûs* 30, 1 (1996): 99–111.

Adler, Jonathan, "Epistemological Problems of Testimony," in Edward N. Zalta, ed., *The Stanford Encyclopedia of Philosophy* (Fall 2008 edition), available at: http://plato.stanford.edu/archives/fall2008/entries/testimony-episprob.

Alston, William P., "Christian Experience and Christian Belief," in Alvin Plantinga and Nicholas Wolterstorff, eds., *Faith and Rationality* (Notre Dame, IN: University of Notre Dame Press, 1983), pp. 103–134.

Alston, William P., *Perceiving God: The Epistemology of Religious Experience* (Ithaca, NY: Cornell University Press, 1991).

Alston, William P., *The Reliability of Sense Perception* (Ithaca, NY: Cornell University Press, 1993).

Anscombe, G.E.M, "What Is It to Believe Someone?" in *Faith in a Hard Ground: Essays on Religion, Philosophy and Ethics* (Charlottesville, VA: Imprint Academic Philosophy Documentation Center, 2008).

Austin, J.L., "Other Minds," in J.L. Austin, *Philosophical Papers*, 3rd edition (Oxford: Oxford University Press, 1979).

Baillargeon, Renée, and DeVos, Julie, "Object Permanence in Young Infants: Further Evidence," *Child Development* 62, 6 (1991): 1227–1246.

Bechtel, William, "Connectionism and the Philosophy of Mind: An Overview," in William Lycan, ed., *Mind and Cognition* (Oxford: Basil Blackwell, 1990).

Beer, A.L., Heckel, A.H., and Greenlee, M.W., "A Motion Illusion Reveals Mechanisms of Perceptual Stabilization," *PLoS ONE* 3, 7 (2008): e2741.

Bergmann, Michael, "Skeptical Theism and Rowe's New Evidential Argument from Evil," *Noûs* 35, 2 (2001): 278–296.

Bicchieri, Cristina, *The Grammar of Society: The Nature and Dynamics of Social Norms* (Cambridge: Cambridge University Press, 2006).

Bicchieri, Cristina, Muldoon, Ryan, and Sontuoso, Alessandro, "Social Norms," in Edward N. Zalta, ed., *The Stanford Encyclopedia of*

Philosophy (Winter 2018 edition), available at: https://plato
.stanford.edu/archives/win2018/entries/social-norms/

Bogardus, Tomas, "The Problem of Contingency for Religious Belief," *Faith and Philosophy* 30, 4 (2013): 371–392.

Bowles, Samuel, and Gintis, Herbert, "Origins of Human Cooperation," in Peter Hammerstein, ed., *Genetic and Cultural Evolution of Cooperation* (Cambridge: MIT Press, 2003), pp. 429–443.

Bowles, Samuel, and Gintis, Herbert, *A Cooperative Species: Human Reciprocity and Its Evolution* (Princeton, NJ: Princeton University Press, 2011).

Bratman, Michael E., "Shared Cooperative Activity," *Philosophical Review* 101, 2 (1992): 327–341.

Bratman, Michael E., "Shared Intention," *Ethics* 104, 1 (1993): 97–113.

Bratman, Michael E., *Faces of Intention: Selected Essays on Intention and Agency* (Cambridge: Cambridge University Press, 1999).

Bratman, Michael E., "Shared Agency," in C. Mantzavinos, ed., *Philosophy of the Social Sciences: Philosophical Theory and Scientific Practice* (New York: Cambridge University Press, 2009), pp. 41–59.

Burge, Tyler, "Content Preservation," *The Philosophical Review* 102, 4 (1993): 457–488.

Carballo, Alejandro Pérez, "On Greco on Transmission," *Episteme* 13, 4 (2016): 499–505.

Cartwright, Nancy, "From Causation to Explanation and Back," in Brian Leiter ed., *The Future for Philosophy* (New York: Oxford University Press), pp. 230–245.

Chisholm, Roderick, *Theory of Knowledge*, 2nd edition (Englewood Cliffs, NJ: Prentice-Hall, 1977).

Christensen, David, "Epistemology of Disagreement: The Good News," *Philosophical Review* 116, 2 (2007): 187–217.

Clark, Herbert H., *Using Language* (Cambridge: Cambridge University Press, 1996).

Coady, C.A.J., *Testimony: A Philosophical Study* (Oxford: Oxford University Press, 1992).

Coliva, Annalisa, *Moore and Wittgenstein: Scepticism, Certainty and Common Sense* (Basingstoke: Palgrave Macmillan, 2010).

Collins, Patricia Hill, *Black Feminist Thought: Knowledge, Consciousness, and the Politics of Empowerment* (London: Routledge, 2002).

Conee, Earl, and Feldman, Richard, "The Generality Problem for Reliabilism," *Philosophical Studies* 89, 1 (1998): 1–29.

Craig, Edward, *Knowledge and the State of Nature* (Oxford: Oxford University Press, 1990).

Elga, Adam, "Reflection and Disagreement," *Noûs*, 41, 3 (2007): 478–502.

Elgin, Catherine, *Considered Judgment* (Princeton, NJ: Princeton University Press, 1996).

Falcon, Andrea, "Aristotle on Causality," in Edward N. Zalta, ed., *The Stanford Encyclopedia of Philosophy* (2011), available at: http://plato .stanford.edu/archives/fall2011/entries/aristotle-causality.

Fantl, Jeremy, and McGrath, Matthew, "Evidence, Pragmatics, and Justification," *Philosophical Review* 111, 1 (2002): 6–94.

Fantl, Jeremy, and McGrath, Matthew, *Knowledge in an Uncertain World* (Oxford: Oxford University Press, 2009).

Faulkner, Paul, *Knowledge on Trust* (Oxford: Oxford University Press, 2011).

Frances, Bryan, "Disagreement," in Duncan Pritchard & Sven Bernecker, eds., *Routledge Companion to Epistemology* (New York: Routledge, 2010), pp. 68–74.

Fricker, Elizabeth, "The Epistemology of Testimony," *Proceedings of the Aristotelian Society* 61 (suppl.) (1987): 57–83.

Fricker, Elizabeth, "Against Gullibility," in B.K. Matilal and A. Chakrabarti, eds., *Knowing from Words* (Boston, MA: Kluwer, 1994), pp. 125–161.

Fricker, Elizabeth, "Second-Hand Knowledge," *Philosophy and Phenomenological Research* 73, 3 (2006): 592–618.

Fricker, Miranda, *Epistemic injustice: Power and the Ethics of Knowing* (Oxford: Oxford University Press, 2007).

Gelman, Susan A., *The Essential Child: Origins of Essentialism in Everyday Thought* (New York: Oxford University Press, 2003).

Gettier, Edmund, "Is Justified True Belief Knowledge?" *Analysis* 23, 6 (1963): 121–123.

Gilbert, Margaret, "Walking Together: A Paradigmatic Social Phenomenon," *Midwest Studies in Philosophy* 15, 1 (1990): 1–14.

Goldberg, Sanford, "Reductionism and the Distinctiveness of Testimonial Knowledge," in Jennifer Lackey and Ernest Sosa, eds., *The Epistemology of Testimony* (Oxford: Oxford University Press, 2006), pp. 127–144.

Goldberg, Sanford, *Anti-Individualism: Mind and Language, Knowledge and Justification* (New York: Cambridge University Press, 2007).

Goldberg, Sanford, "Testimonial Knowledge in Early Childhood, Revisited," *Philosophy and Phenomenological Research* 76, 1 (2008): 1–36.

Goldberg, Sanford, *Relying on Others: An Essay in Epistemology* (Oxford: Oxford University Press, 2010).

Goldberg, Sanford, "The Division of Epistemic Labor," *Episteme* 8, 1 (2011): 112–125.

Goldberg, Sanford, "A Proposed Research Program for Social Epistemology," in P. Reider, ed., *Social Epistemology and Epistemic Agency* (Lanham, MD: Rowman and Littlefield, 2017).

Goldberg, Sanford, "'Analytic Social Epistemology' and the Epistemic Significance of Other Minds," *Social Epistemology Review and Reply Collective* 2, 8 (2013): 26–48.

Goldberg, Sanford, and Henderson, David, "Monitoring and Anti-Reductionism in the Epistemology of Testimony," *Philosophy and Phenomenological Research* 72, 3 (2006): 576–593.

Goldman, Alvin, "What Is Justified Belief?" in George Pappas, ed., *Justification and Knowledge* (Boston, MA: D. Reidel, 1979), pp. 1–25.

Graham, Peter, "Transferring Knowledge," *Noûs* 34, 1 (2000): 131–152.

Graham, Peter, "Can Testimony Generate Knowledge?" *Philosophica* 78 (2006): 105–127.

Graham, Peter, "Liberal Fundamentalism and Its Rivals" in Jennifer Lackey and Ernest Sosa, eds., *The Epistemology of Testimony* (Oxford: Oxford University Press, 2006), pp. 93–115.

Graham, Peter, "Epistemic Normativity and Social Norms," in David Henderson and John Greco, eds., *Epistemic Evaluation: Purposeful Epistemology* (Oxford: Oxford University Press, 2015), pp. 247–273.

Graham, Peter, "The Reliability of Testimony and Social Norms" (manuscript).

Greco, John, *Putting Skeptics in Their Place: The Nature of Skeptical Arguments and Their Role in Philosophical Inquiry* (New York: Cambridge University Press, 2000).

Greco, John, "Knowledge as Credit for True Belief," in Michael DePaul and Linda Zagzebski, eds., *Intellectual Virtue: Perspectives from Ethics and Epistemology* (Oxford: Oxford University Press, 2003), pp. 111–134.

Greco, John, "The Nature of Ability and the Purpose of Knowledge," *Philosophical Issues* 17 (2007): 57–69.

Greco, John, "Friendly Theism" in James Kraft and David Basinger, eds., *Religious Tolerance through Humility* (Aldershot: Ashgate, 2008), pp. 51–58.

Greco, John, "What's Wrong with Contextualism?" *The Philosophical Quarterly* 58, 232 (2008): 416–436.

Greco, John, "Religious Knowledge in the Context of Conflicting Testimony," *Proceedings of the American Catholic Philosophical Association* 82 (2009): 61–76.

Greco, John, *Achieving Knowledge: A Virtue-Theoretic Account of Epistemic Normativity* (Cambridge: Cambridge University Press, 2010).

Greco, John, "Evidentialism and Knowledge," in Trent Dougherty, ed., *Evidentialism and Its Discontents* (Oxford: Oxford University Press, 2011), pp. 167–178.

Greco, John, "Recent Work on Testimonial Knowledge," *American Philosophical Quarterly* 49, 1 (2012): 15–28.

Greco, John, "A (Different) Virtue Epistemology," *Philosophy and Phenomenological Research* 85, 1 (2012): 1–26.

Greco, John, "Episteme: Knowledge and Understanding," in Kevin Timpe and Craig Boyd, eds., *Virtues and Their Vices* (Oxford: Oxford University Press, 2014), pp. 285–302.

Greco, John, "Testimonial Knowledge and the Flow of Information," in David Henderson and John Greco, eds. *Epistemic Evaluation* (Oxford: Oxford University Press, 2015), pp. 274–290.

Greco, John, "Intellectual Humility and Contemporary Epistemology: A Critique of Epistemic Individualism, Evidentialism, and Internalism," in Mark Alfano, Michael Lynch, and Alessandra Tanesini, eds., *The Routledge Handbook of the Philosophy of Humility* (New York: Routledge, 2020).

Greco, John, and Turri, John, "Virtue Epistemology," in Edward N. Zalta, ed., *The Stanford Encyclopedia of Philosophy* (2015), available at: http://plato.stanford.edu/archives/sum2015/entries/epistemology-virtue.

Green, Adam, "Reading the Mind of God (without Hebrew Lessons): Alston, Shared Attention, and Mystical Experience," *Religious Studies* 45, 4 (2009): 455–470.

Green, Adam, "Deficient Testimony is Deficient Teamwork," *Episteme* 11, 2 (2014): 213–227.

Green, Adam, *The Social Contexts of Intellectual Virtue: Knowledge as a Team Achievement* (New York: Routledge, 2017).

Grimm, Stephen R., "Is Understanding a Species of Knowledge?" *British Journal for the Philosophy of Science* 57, 3 (2006): 515–535.

Grimm, Stephen R., "Understanding," in Sven Bernecker and Duncan Pritchard, eds. *The Routledge Companion to Epistemology* (New York: Routledge, 2011), pp. 84–94.

Hankinson, R.J., "Philosophy of Science," in Jonathan Barnes, ed., *The Cambridge Companion to Aristotle* (Cambridge: Cambridge University Press, 1995), pp. 109–139.

Hardin, Russell, *Trust and Trustworthiness* (New York: Russell Sage Foundation, 2002).

Hardwig, John, "Epistemic Dependence," *Journal of Philosophy* 82, 7 (1985): 335–349.

Hardwig, John, "The Role of Trust in Knowledge," *Journal of Philosophy* 88, 12 (1991): 693–708.

Harris, Paul L., and Koenig, Melissa A., "The Basis of Epistemic Trust: Reliable Testimony or Reliable Sources?" *Episteme* 4, 3 (2007): 264–284.

Hawthorne, John, *Knowledge and Lotteries* (Oxford: Oxford University Press, 2004).

Heller, Mark, "The Simple Solution to the Generality Problem," *Noûs* 29, 4 (1995): 501–515.

Henderson, David, "Motivated Contextualism," *Philosophical Studies* 142, 1 (2009): 119–131.

Henderson, David, and Graham, Peter, "Epistemic Norms and the 'Epistemic Game' They Regulate: The Basic Structured Epistemic Costs and Benefits," *American Philosophical Quarterly* 54, 4 (2017): 367–382.

Henderson, David, and Horgan, Terence, "What's the Point?" in David Henderson and John Greco, eds., *Epistemic Evaluation: Purposeful Epistemology* (Oxford: Oxford University Press, 2015), pp. 87–114.

Hess, John E., *Interviewing and Interrogation for Law Enforcement*, 2nd edition (New Providence, NJ: Matthew Bender and Company, 2010).

Hick, John, *Evil and the God of Love* (Basingstoke: Macmillan, 1966).

Hinchman, Edward, "Telling as Inviting to Trust," *Philosophy and Phenomenological Research* 70, 3 (2005): 562–587.

Holton, Richard, "Deciding to Trust, Coming to Believe," *Australasian Journal of Philosophy* 72, 1 (1994): 63–76.

Horgan, Terence, and Tienson, John, "Connectionism and the Commitments of Folk Psychology," *Philosophical Perspectives* 9 (1995): 127–152.

Horgan, Terence, and Teinson, John, *Connectionism and the Philosophy of Psychology* (Cambridge, MA: MIT Press, 1996).

Howard-Snyder, Daniel, *The Evidential Argument from Evil* (Bloomington, IN: Indiana University Press, 1996).

Howard-Snyder, Daniel, and Moser, Paul K., "Introduction: The Hiddenness of God," in Daniel Howard-Snyder and Paul K. Moser, eds., *Divine Hiddenness: New Essays* (Cambridge: Cambridge University Press, 2002), pp. 1–23.

Hume, David, *Enquiries Concerning Human Understanding and Concerning the Principles of Morals*, 3rd edition, L.A. Selby-Bigge, ed. (Oxford: Clarendon Press, 1975).

Hume, David, *A Treatise of Human Nature*, 2nd edition, L.A. Selby-Bigge, ed. (Oxford: Clarendon Press, 1978).

Hyde, Krista, "A Virtue-Theoretic Account of the Epistemic Effects of Marginalization," (PhD diss., Saint Louis University, 2017).

Johnson, Scott P., Amso, Dima and Slemmer, Jonathan A., "Development of Object Concepts in Infancy: Evidence for Early Learning in an Eye-Tracking Paradigm," *Proceedings of the National Academy of Sciences of the United States of America* 100, 18 (2003): 10568–10573.

Jones, Karen, "Trust as an Affective Attitude," *Ethics* 107, 1 (1996): 4–25.

Kallestrup, Jesper and Pritchard, Duncan, "Robust Virtue Epistemology and Epistemic Anti-Individualism" *Pacific Philosophical Quarterly* 93, 1 (2012): 84–103.

Kelly, Thomas, "The Epistemic Significance of Disagreement," in John Hawthorne and Tamar Gendler, eds., *Oxford Studies in Epistemology*, vol. 1 (Oxford: Oxford University Press, 2006), pp. 166–196.

Kitcher, Philip, "Explanatory Unification and the Causal Structure of the World," in Philip Kitcher and Wesley Salmon, eds., *Scientific Explanation* (Minneapolis, MN: University of Minnesota Press, 1989), pp. 410–505.

Kornblith, Hilary, *Inductive Inference and Its Natural Ground: An Essay in Naturalistic Epistemology* (Cambridge, MA: MIT Press, 1993).

Kutz, Christopher, "Acting Together," *Philosophy and Phenomenological Research* 61, 1 (2000): 1–31.

Kvanvig, Jonathan, *The Value of Knowledge and the Pursuit of Understanding* (New York: Cambridge University Press, 2003).

Lackey, Jennifer, "Testimonial Knowledge and Transmission," *Philosophical Quarterly* 49, 197 (1999): 471–490.

Lackey, Jennifer, "Knowing from Testimony," *Philosophy Compass* 1, 5 (2006): 432–448.

Lackey, Jennifer, "Why We Don't Deserve Credit for Everything We Know," *Synthese* 158, 3 (2007): 345–361.

Lackey, Jennifer, *Learning from Words: Testimony as a Source of Knowledge* (Oxford: Oxford University Press, 2008).

Lackey, Jennifer, "Knowledge and Credit," *Philosophical Studies* 142, 1 (2009): 27–42.

Lipton, Peter, *Inference to the Best Explanation*, 2nd edition (New York: Routledge, 2004).

List, Christian, and Pettit, Philip, *Group Agency: The Possibility, Design, and Status of Corporate Agents* (New York: Oxford University Press, 2011).

Mackie, J.L., "Evil and Omnipotence," *Mind* 64, 254 (1955): 200–212.

McGinn, Marie, *Sense and Certainty: A Dissolution of Scepticism* (Oxford: Blackwell, 1989).

McLeod, Carolyn, "Trust," in Edward N. Zalta, ed., *The Stanford Encyclopedia of Philosophy* (Fall 2015 edition), available at: https://plato.stanford.edu/archives/fall2015/entries/trust.

McMyler, Benjamin, *Testimony, Trust, and Authority* (New York: Oxford University Press, 2011).

Medina, José, *The Epistemology of Resistance: Gender and Racial Oppression, Epistemic Injustice, and the Social Imagination* (New York: Oxford University Press, 2013).

Miller, Seumas, *Social Action: A Teleological Account* (Cambridge: Cambridge University Press, 2001).

Moore, G.E., "Proof of an External World," *Proceeding of the British Academy* 25 (1939): 273–300. Reprinted in G.E. Moore, *Philosophical Papers* (New York: Macmillan, 1959).

Moore, G.E. "A Defense of Common Sense," *Philosophical Papers* (New York: Macmillan, 1959).

Moran, Richard, "Getting Told and Being Believed," in Jennifer Lackey and Ernest Sosa, eds., *The Epistemology of Testimony* (Oxford: Oxford University Press, 2006), pp. 272–306.

Moran, Richard, *The Exchange of Words: Speech, Testimony, and Intersubjectivity* (New York: Oxford University Press, 2018).

Moser, Paul K., *The Elusive God: Reorienting Religious Epistemology* (Cambridge: Cambridge University Press, 2008).

Moser, Paul K., *The Evidence for God: Religious Knowledge Reexamined* (Cambridge: Cambridge University Press, 2010).

Moyal-Sharrock, Danièle, *Understanding Wittgenstein's on Certainty* (Basingstoke: Palgrave Macmillan, 2004).

Moyal-Sharrock, Danièle, "The Animal in Epistemology: Wittgenstein's Enactivist Solution to the Problem of Regress," in Annalisa Coliva and Danièle Moyal-Sharrock, eds., *Hinge Epistemology* (Leiden: Brill, 2016), pp. 24–47.

Nozick, Robert, *Philosophical Explanations* (Cambridge, MA: Harvard University Press, 1981).

Pettit, Philip, "Virtus Normativa: Rational Choice Perspectives," *Ethics* 100, 4 (1990): 725–755.

Pettit, Philip, "The Reality of Group Agents," in Chrysostomos Mantzavinos, ed., *Philosophy of the Social Sciences* (Cambridge: Cambridge University Press, 2009), pp. 67–91.

Plantinga, Alvin, *God, Freedom, and Evil* (Grand Rapids, MI: Eerdmans, 1974).

Plantinga, Alvin, "Reason and Belief in God," in Alvin Plantinga and Nicholas Wolterstorff, eds., *Faith and Rationality* (Notre Dame, IN: University of Notre Dame Press, 1983), pp. 16–93.

Plantinga, Alvin, *Warranted Christian Belief* (Oxford: Oxford University Press, 2000).

Pritchard, Duncan, *Epistemic Luck* (Oxford: Oxford University Press, 2005).

Pritchard, Duncan, "Knowledge and Understanding," in Adrian Haddock, Alan Millar, and Duncan Pritchard, *The Nature and Value of Knowledge: Three Investigations* (Oxford: Oxford University Press, 2010).

Pritchard, Duncan, *Epistemic Angst: Radical Scepticism and the Groundlessness of Our Believing* (Princeton, NJ: Princeton University Press, 2016).

Quinn, Philip L., and Meeker, Kevin, eds., *The Philosophical Challenge of Religious Diversity* (New York: Oxford University Press, 1999).

Reibsamen, Jonathan, "Social Epistemic Dependence: Trust, Testimony, and Social Intellectual Virtue," (PhD diss., Saint Louis University, 2015).

Reid, Thomas, *Philosophical Works*, H.M. Bracken, ed., 2 volumes (Hildesheim: Georg Olms, 1983).

Rezendes, Michael, Caroll, Matt, and Pfeiffer, Sacha, "Clergy Sex Abuse Crisis," *The Boston Globe* (January 6, 2002), available at www.bostonglobe.com/metro/specials/clergy.

Riggs, Wayne, "Reliability and the Value of Knowledge," *Philosophy and Phenomenological Research* 64, 1 (2002): 79–96.

Riggs, Wayne, "Understanding 'Virtue' and the Virtue of Understanding," in M. DePaul and L. Zagzebski, eds. *Intellectual Virtue: Perspectives from Ethics and Epistemology* (New York: Oxford University Press, 2003), pp. 203–226.

Riggs, Wayne, "Why Epistemologists Are so Down on Their Luck," *Synthese* 158, 3 (2007): 329–344.

Riggs, Wayne, "Two Problems of Easy Credit," *Synthese* 169, 1 (2009): 201–216.

Ross, Angus, "Why Do We Believe What We Are Told?" *Ratio* 69, 1 (1986): 69–88.

Roth, Abraham Sesshu, "Shared Agency," in Edward N. Zalta, ed., *Stanford Encyclopedia of Philosophy* (2011), available at: https://plato.stanford.edu/entries/shared-agency.

Rowe, William L., "The Problem of Evil and Some Varieties of Atheism," *American Philosophical Quarterly* 16, 4 (1979): 355–341.

Russell, Bertrand, *Problems of Philosophy* (Oxford: Oxford University Press, 1997).

Salmon, Wesley, *Scientific Explanation and the Causal Structure of the World* (Princeton, NJ: Princeton University Press, 1984).

Sankey, Howard, "Induction and Natural Kinds," *Principia: An International Journal of Epistemology* 1, 2 (1997): 239–254.

Schellenberg, J.L., *Divine Hiddenness and Human Reason* (Ithaca, NY: Cornell University Press, 1993).

Schellenberg, J.L., "The Hiddenness Problem and the Problem of Evil," *Faith and Philosophy* 27, 1 (2010): 45–60.

Schellenberg, J.L., "Divine Hiddenness and Human Philosophy," in Adam Green and Eleonore Stump, eds., *Hidden Divinity and Religious Belief: New Perspectives* (Cambridge: Cambridge University Press, 2015), pp. 13–32.

Schmid, Hans Bernhard, "Trying to Act Together: The Structure and Role of Trust in Joint Action," in B. Kobow, H.B Schmid, and M. Schmitz, eds., *The Background of Institutional Reality* (Dordrecht: Springer, 2013), pp. 37–55.

Searle, John, "Collective Intentions and Actions," in Philip R. Cohen, Jerry Morgan, and Martha Pollack, eds., *Intentions in Communication* (Cambridge, MA: MIT Press, 1990), pp. 401–415.

Simion, Mona, "No Epistemic Norm for Action," *American Philosophical Quarterly* 55, 3 (2018): 231–238.

Sosa, Ernest, "How to Defeat Opposition to Moore," *Philosophical Perspectives* 13 (1999): 141–153.

Sosa, Ernest, *A Virtue Epistemology: Apt Belief and Reflective Knowledge*, vol. 1 (Oxford: Oxford University Press, 2007).

Sosa, Ernest, *Knowing Full Well* (Princeton, NJ: Princeton University Press, 2011).

Sosa, Ernest, *Judgment and Agency* (Oxford: Oxford University Press, 2015).

Spelke, E.S., Breinlinger, K., Macomber, J., and Jacobson, K., "Origins of Knowledge," *Psychological Review* 99, 4 (1992): 605–632.

Sripada, Chandra, and Stich, Stephen, "A Framework for the Psychology of Norms," in Peter Carruthers, Stephen Laurence, and Stephen P. Stich, eds., *The Innate Mind*, vol. 2: *Culture and Cognition* (Oxford: Oxford University Press, 2006), pp. 237–256.

Stanley, Jason, *Knowledge and Practical Interests* (Oxford: Oxford University Press, 2005).

Stump, Eleonore, *Wandering in Darkness: Narrative and the Problem of Suffering* (Oxford: Oxford University Press, 2010).

Tollefsen, Deborah, *Groups as Agents* (Cambridge: Polity Press, 2015).

van Cleve, James, "Reliability, Justification, and the Problem of Induction," *Midwest Studies in Philosophy* 9, 1 (1984): 555–567.

Welbourne, Michael, "The Transmission of Knowledge," *Philosophical Quarterly* 29, 114 (1979): 1–9.

Welbourne, Michael, "The Community of Knowledge," *Philosophical Quarterly* 31, 125 (1981): 302–314.

Welbourne, Michael, *The Community of Knowledge* (Aberdeen: Aberdeen University Press, 1986).

White, Roger, "You Just Believe that Because…," *Philosophical Perspectives* 24 (2010): 573–615.

Williams, Bernard, "Deciding to Believe," in *Problems of the Self* (Cambridge: Cambridge University Press, 1973), pp. 136–151.

Williamson, Timothy, *Knowledge and its Limits* (Oxford: Oxford University Press, 2000).

Wittgenstein, Ludwig, *On Certainty*, G.E.M. Anscombe and Go Ho von Wright, eds., Denis Paul and G.E.M. Anscombe, transl. (Oxford: Blackwell, 1969).

Woodward, James, *Making Things Happen: A Theory of Causal Explanation* (Oxford: Oxford University Press, 2003).

Wright, Stephan, "In Defence of Transmission," *Episteme* 12, 1 (2015): 13–28.

Wykstra, Stephen, "Toward a Sensible Evidentialism: On the Notion of 'Needing Evidence'," in William Rowe and William Wainwright, eds., *Readings in the Philosophy of Religion*, 2nd edition (San Diego, CA: Harcourt Brace Jovanovich: 1989), pp. 426–437.

Zagzebski, Linda, *Virtues of the Mind: An Inquiry into the Nature of Virtue and the Ethical Foundations of Knowledge* (Cambridge: Cambridge University Press, 1996).

Zagzebski, Linda, "What Is Knowledge?" in John Greco and Ernest Sosa, eds., *The Blackwell Guide to Epistemology* (Oxford: Blackwell Publishers, 1999), pp. 92–116.

Zagzebski, Linda, "Recovering Understanding," in Matthias Steup, ed., *Knowledge, Truth, and Duty: Essays on Epistemic Justification, Responsibility, and Virtue* (New York: Oxford University Press, 2001), pp. 235–251.

Zagzebski, Linda, *Epistemic Authority: A Theory of Trust, Authority, and Autonomy in Belief* (New York: Oxford University Press, 2012).

Index

acquaintance knowledge, 141–142
action theory. *See* joint agency
agent reliabilism. *See* reliabilism
aim of belief, 83
Allston, William P., 161–162
Anscombe, G.E.M., 59
anti-reductionism, 2, 6, 13, 145. *See also* reductionism
  source anti-reductionism, 8–10, 13, 14–15, 26–27, 145
  transmission anti-reductionism, (*See* transmission anti-reductionism)
Aquinas, Thomas, 175
Aristotle, 126–127, 131–133
artificial intelligence, procedural knowledge and, 20, 117
Assertion Problem, 107, 111–112
awareness of reliability. *See* reliability, awareness of

Baillargeon, Reneé, 119
ball passing example, 60–61
Berkeley, George, 123
betting example, 60–61
Big Science, 21–22, 23–24, 145–146
Bratman, Michael, 55, 56

Calvin, John, 175
Catholic Church, 182–183
causation, 131–133
Chicago visitor example, 94–95
Clark, Herbert H., 57
cognitive agency, 88–89, 123
cognitive psychology, 20, 117
Comanche example, 135–137, 143–144
common knowledge, 20–21, 23–24, 103–104, 110
conditional reliability, 191–192
connectionist networks, 115–116, 117

contextualism, 193–194
Craig, Edward, 38–39
critical theory, 76

DeVos, Julie, 119
divine hiddenness problem, 163, 172
division of labor. *See* epistemic division of labor
doctor-patient example, 197

efficient cause, 131
episteme, 131, 133. *See also* understanding
epistemic communities, 17, 25–26, 137–138, 193–196
epistemic dependence
  in Big Science, 21–22, 145–150, 151, 154, 157–160
  garbage problem and, 196
  knowledge transmission and, 3
epistemic division of labor, 3, 5, 69, 70–71, 196–197
epistemic evaluation, 92–93
epistemic norms, 74–77, 92–93
Epistemic Problem, 107, 108–110, 111–112
epistemology
  religious epistemology, (*See* religious epistemology)
  traditional epistemology, (*See* traditional epistemology)
  virtue epistemology, (*See* virtue epistemology)
essentialism, 119–120
evidentialism, 6, 7, 9–10, 17, 19–20, 70–71, 77–78, 125
  garbage problem and, 189
  hinge commitments and, 104, 108
  religious epistemology and, 161–162
Evil. *See* nonbelief, problem of

For EU product safety concerns, contact us at Calle de José Abascal, 56–1°, 28003 Madrid, Spain or eugpsr@cambridge.org.

www.ingramcontent.com/pod-product-compliance
Ingram Content Group UK Ltd.
Pitfield, Milton Keynes, MK11 3LW, UK
UKHW020352140625
459647UK00020B/2428